COLLEGE WOMEN IN THE NUCLEAR AGE

COLLEGE WOMEN IN THE NUCLEAR AGE

Cultural Literacy and Female Identity,

1940–1960

BABETTE FAEHMEL

RUTGERS UNIVERSITY PRESS

New Brunswick, New Jersey, and London

Library of Congress Cataloging-in-Publication Data

Faehmel, Babette, 1970–

  College women in the nuclear age : cultural literacy and female identity, 1940–1960 /
Babette Faehmel.

    p. cm.

  Includes bibliographical references and index.

  ISBN 978-0-8135-5140-1 (hardcover : alk. paper)

  1. Women—Education (Higher)—United States—History—20th century. 2. Women
college students—United States—History—20th century. 3. Sex differences in
education—United States—History—20th century. 4. Feminism—United States—
History—20th century. I. Title.

  LC1756.F34 2012

  378.1'98220973—dc22

                          2011001100

A British Cataloging-in-Publication record for this book is available from the British Library.

Frontispiece: Mount Holyoke College women studying together. Courtesy Mount Holyoke
College Archives and Special Collections, South Hadley, Mass.

Copyright © 2012 by Babette Faehmel

Visit our Web site: http://rutgerspress.rutgers.edu

Manufactured in the United States of America

Dedicated to past, present, and future geeks and "greasy grinds"

Contents

Acknowledgments

My work on this project was made possible thanks to the help and support of a great many people and institutions. A generous Sexuality Research Dissertation Fellowship from the Social Science Research Council not only allowed me to travel to archives across the United States but also put me in touch with scholars who grappled with issues of identity and coming of age from a variety of disciplinary perspectives. The University of Massachusetts at Amherst provided additional funding, and I spent one of the best years of my life at the Five College Women's Studies Research Center at Mount Holyoke College in the company of some simply amazing female scholars and artists. I also owe a huge debt to the staff at the Smith College and the Mount Holyoke College Archives, the Center for Archival Collections at Bowling Green State University, the Schlesinger Library on the History of Women in America, the Bentley Historical Library at the University of Michigan at Ann Arbor, the Iowa Women's Archives in the University of Iowa Libraries in Iowa City, the Louis Round Wilson Special Collections Library at the University of North Carolina at Chapel Hill, and the American Jewish Archives at Hebrew Union College in Cincinnati, Ohio. I would never have noticed a number of my sources had it not been for the suggestions of a librarian or archivist, and while the staffs were great in all the repositories I visited, I want to thank especially Nanci Young at Smith College and Patricia Albright at Mount Holyoke for all their help. Margaret Whitfield, Sheila Owen Monks, Leilah Jackson Poullada, Elinor Offill, and Marjorie Hibbard Lauer shared with me their diaries and letters from student days, and I can only hope that my analysis confirms their sense that they could trust me with their private papers.

I also want to emphasize the debt I owe to the historians with whom I had the pleasure and honor of working. Norbert Finzsch at the University of Hamburg in Germany first introduced me to the study of women and gender. After I moved to the United States, Joanne Meyerowitz, Kathy Peiss, Kevin Boyle, Laura Lovett, Daniel Horowitz, and Joyce Berkmann made sure that I was on top of the literature. Rachel Devlin and John Spurlock commented on presentations of my work at an early stage of the research and Daniel Horowitz, Laura Lovett, Christine Stansell, Jessica Delgado, Constance Ostrowski, Eileen Abrahams, and Anna Biel read drafts of this book and gave helpful feedback on revisions. Thanks as well to the anonymous readers for Rutgers University Press for their insights and suggestions, and to Leslie Mitchner and Katie Keeran at the press, and to Patti Bower, for their patience and support.

Throughout the research for and the writing of this book, many of my relatives, friends, and colleagues have rooted for me. My parents, Inge and Bruno Fähmel, my brother, Sascha, and my grandmother, Hilde Purschke, followed my work from a distance but always with interest. Sadly, neither my father nor my grandmother lived to see the completion of this book. I hope, however, they knew how much I wanted them to be proud of me. When I was getting close to the finish line with this project, my department chair, Carol DeFries, offered good cheers whenever she saw me morph into a headless chicken. Colleague Reneé Adamany always found exactly the right words when she saw my anxiety level spike, and office mate Eric Carlson kindly shared his insights into adolescent psychological development and supplied me with readings. I owe the largest debt to the people who offered me their friendship while I was struggling with the completion of a project that turned out to be a lot more intricate than I thought it would be when I started it as a somewhat conceited graduate student: Elizabeth Ramey, Adam Chill, Jessica Delgado, Liane Jeschull, Bill Bergmann, Barbara Hahn, Nela Trifkovic, Heather Murray, Julia Sandy-Bailey, Sara Connolly, Bill Weye, Ed and Ineke Valerio, Nora Groves, Bob Nakosteen, and Sibylle Warnecke; thank you all so, so much for everything. And last but not least, I want to thank my students for keeping me thinking about the challenges they face when they transition to college. I hope that I am doing not too shabby a job in trying to help them along on their ways.

COLLEGE WOMEN IN
THE NUCLEAR AGE

Introduction

Betty Friedan, a graduate of the private, all-women's Smith College, in her 1963 bestseller *The Feminine Mystique* described what had struck her as common sentiments among the young women she met and interviewed when she returned for research to her alma mater. "Taught to pity the neurotic, unfeminine, unhappy women who wanted to be poets or presidents," they had surrendered to fear that too much education hurt their chances to catch a husband. Glorifying marriage and motherhood as the be-all and end-all of a woman's existence, they early on made it their goal to find husbands. On dates, they played dumb. As soon as they had made their catch, they dropped out. By the mid 1950s, wrote Friedan, 60 percent of women left college before completion of their degrees either "to marry, or because they were afraid too much education would be a marriage bar." Instead of trying to achieve in their own right, they contended themselves with a "'Ph.T.' (Putting Husband Through)" degree. "The suburban housewife" she concluded, became "the dream image of the young American women."[1]

Friedan told her readers that she herself had become a victim of the "mystique." As a young woman, she argued, she too had fallen for the message that even the most satisfying career could not possibly compare to the heights of happiness that a woman reached through marriage, motherhood, and sex with her husband. Yet while she conceded that only the benefit of hindsight had enabled her to look with critical distance at the messages with which the mass media and the mental health profession were bombarding American women, her evaluation of the marriage craze among female students was harsh nonetheless: Women who had enjoyed all the educational privileges imaginable, she argued, "adjusted" to the feminine mystique because it was "easier to build the need for love and sex into the end-all purpose of life, avoiding personal commitment to truth in a catch-all commitment to 'home' and 'family.'" In spite of their high level of educational attainment, they contented themselves to live through their husbands and children. Craving only to be loved and secure, and accepted by others, they "chose . . . not to use the door education could have opened for them" and "race[d] back home." In other words, Friedan likened the nation's most highly educated women to dupable consumers who had fallen for a sales pitch. Rather than tackling the challenge of making autonomous decisions for their futures, they had become herd animals hungering for the comfort that came with conformity to a media-packaged role. Only after years of trying to ignore the nagging sense of discontent, Friedan concluded in her influential analysis, did women realize that their suburban homes were in fact what she provocatively called "comfortable concentration camps." To give their life meaning, she urged her readers, they ought to leave the home and finally use the education that many years ago they had so readily abandoned for the sake of marital bliss.[2]

Widening the lens beyond Friedan's sample of Smith College students, in this book I take another look at the relationship between college women and the feminine mystique. Based on a close reading of diaries and letters written by female undergraduates, *College Women in the Nuclear Age: Cultural Literacy and Female Identity, 1940–1960* explores in depth the experiences of women who on first sight fit the profile of Friedan's dupable conformists. The authors of my sources often started their education with dreams of professional careers or artistic fame. Over the course of their stay in college, however, they embraced the notion that by virtue of their potential for motherhood, they had interests, views, and talents that differed significantly from those of men, and began to look at marriage and motherhood as essential prerequisites for happiness. This, however, was not because they had uncritically fallen for a "mystique" of finding fulfillment in a narrowly defined sex role. Rather, they actively participated in the definition of their gender role and forcefully promoted ideas of difference for their own complex and strategic reasons. This book thus adds new layers of complexity to Friedan's interpretation and contributes to an ongoing revisionist project of the history of women in the mid-twentieth century United States.

While *College Women in the Nuclear Age* is hardly the first new look at Friedan's "feminine mystique" thesis, it fills a gap in the revisionist literature. We now know that the cultural messages with which mid-twentieth-century women were inundated were a lot more complex than Friedan made them out to be. Parallel to images of happy homemakers and mothers, the visual media, for instance, celebrated women who successfully balanced household responsibilities with careers, and magazines targeting a college-educated female readership especially encouraged dreams of glamorous jobs and literary fame. For example, *Mademoiselle*, subtitled the "magazine for smart young women," featured regular writing contests that rewarded winners with a guest editorship, and in general portrayed the lives of women who after graduation joined the job market in appealing ways. In "Manhattan Girl with a Job," four female roommates, for example, in spite of parental offers for financial help, proudly insist on getting by on their own wages, host parties for their friends, and talk about politics and art into the wee hours.[3]

We now know that the mental health discipline produced a more multifaceted discourse than the biological determinism Friedan saw responsible for tricking women into believing that they needed a husband and a child to be fulfilled. Moreover, while certainly there existed women who wholeheartedly embraced their roles as wives and mothers, the experiences of others challenge Friedan's portrayal of suburban domesticity as a normative experience for women in general. Throughout the Cold War era, women from various class and race backgrounds, including middle-class, college-educated ones, were active in labor unions, the civil rights movement, and civic and religious institutions. Betty Friedan herself confirms this contention. As Daniel Horowitz has recently demonstrated, contrary to the way Friedan presented her past, marriage and motherhood had put no sudden automatic end to her public activities as a writer and labor activist.[4]

Even in popular culture we nowadays find diverse and complex images of mid-twentieth-century middle-class women. The 1980s and 1990s especially, as Stephanie Coontz has shown, were a high time for nostalgic musings about the traditional family and its stay-at-home moms coupled with dependable breadwinner husbands.[5] The television series *Mad Men*, set in the early 1960s and, by the time I am writing, in its fourth season on AMC, by contrast, thrives on the disconnect between media-created images of family harmony and the actual lives of the main characters. In this series, husbands are unfaithful, outwardly flawless suburban wives at least fantasize about affairs if they are not actually having them, mothers get divorced, and single working girls give their children up for adoption. The character of Margaret "Peggy" Olson nicely illustrates that the wish of *having it all* is not a recent phenomenon among young women. By virtue of spunk and talent, Peggy Olson works her way up from secretary in an advertising agency to copywriter. At the first season's beginning, she is a somewhat dowdy-looking girl from Brooklyn. Soon, however, she acquires poise and sex appeal and takes a lover, and this assertion of her right to fulfill herself professionally *and* sexually reminds the viewer that a woman should not have to choose between having a career and finding love.

Yet, while *Mad Men* is a far cry from nostalgic images of an age of family togetherness, parts of the storyline are still wedded to a conventional interpretation of Cold War America. By the time the Kennedys move into the White House and the civil rights movement resurges in the South, a new era is clearly on the horizon. But what is still left open is the possibility that there once was a time of simpler family and gender relations: a time when couples waited to have sex until they were married, when spouses were faithful, and when a girl's dreams centered on a diamond on her ring finger. The very image, in other words, that we have long associated with the fifties. Moreover, the inspiration for the character of Betty Draper, wife of leading man and creative advertising genius Don, could easily have come from *The Feminine Mystique*. In spite of holding a degree from a prestigious private women's college, Betty never used her education. Portrayed as a protected, somewhat pampered offspring of an upper-middle-class family, she worked as a model for a few years after graduation. As soon as she met Don Draper, however, Betty settled for the "dream" of suburban wife and motherhood. The show's creators add complexity to the character of Betty by portraying her psychological struggles as a result of her lack of nondomestic outlets. Yet this, too, still follows rather closely the narrative we know from *The Feminine Mystique*.

In its portrayal of an upper-middle-class college woman as an epitome of gender conservatism, *Mad Men* is far from alone. Even though revisionist historians have left us with an increasingly multifaceted picture of women's experiences in the mid-twentieth century, female undergraduates, especially those who studied in costly private women's colleges and liberal arts programs, still seem to have been, as Elaine Tyler May put it, "homeward bound." By the mid 1950s, 60 percent left college before completion of their degrees. Conclusive data about their motivation does not exist, but their actions seem to speak for themselves.[6] In a departure from historical trends, college-educated women of the 1950s married younger and had more children than any group since the 1890s. During the period famous for its baby boom, marriage and birth rates increased among all social demographics, but the steepest rise occurred among the nation's highest educated women. Through their own choices, college women of this period thus still seem to confirm feminist historian Eileen Kendall's 1976 argument that as "chief casualties of the feminine mystique," they followed "with appalling docility" the period's most conservative prescriptions.[7]

Indeed, from the 1940s through the 1950s, college women's very own words, as I found them in diaries, scrapbooks, and letters to friends and family, on first glance affirm this observation. Even women who started their studies with ambitious dreams of careers experienced a conversion in college. "I have so much potential love, tenderness + giving pent inside me + no object," deplored a Smith College student. A peer at Stanford University in 1956 confessed to her diary: "I do want a man." She wanted to be needed and worshipped and held close. Meanwhile at the University of California at Los Angeles, another young woman wrote that she was "sad and alone and discouraged" and wanted to "have someone to make happy, someone [she could] please." Having once dreamed about accomplished futures as professionals or artists, these talented undergraduates now mused about their potential for love, care, and nurture. Not only that, they also increasingly dwelled on the idea that by virtue of their sex, they differed in essential and profound aspects from men. "Women are not men," declared a Bryn Mawr student. "They never see as men do; they aren't made to fight their battles as men do; they don't understand as men do."[8] In this and in other similar entries, college women seem to echo the antifeminism and essentialism that also characterized the conservative advice literature of their times. But what did women actually mean when they wrote these words? Yes, they dreamed of finding true love, but did that necessarily mean that they were ready to embrace exclusive domesticity and had no other goals but to be a wife and mother? Yes, they longed for acceptance by their peers, but did this longing mean that they just wanted to fit in with the crowd? Did their infatuation with gender difference preclude the goal of achievement in their own right? Moreover, what caused women who at one point had sincerely considered preparing for postgraduate careers to shift course? Was it really the easy road they were taking? How did their situational context influence their decision making? And how was their identity impacted by the academic and political debates of their time?

In the attempt to offer answers to these questions, *College Women in the Nuclear Age* builds on recent works in the history of gender in the mid-twentieth century. In *To Have and To Hold* (2000), for instance, Jessica Weiss uses data from two longitudinal studies conducted by the Berkeley-based Institute of Human Development to illustrate that even women who married young and became mothers right away have participated in a gradual revamping of middle-class gender and family roles, and in the process, together with their mates, have laid the groundwork for the sweeping cultural changes of the 1960s.[9] My study of introspective writings complements Weiss's analysis with an interpretation of why highly educated women especially privileged the choice of young marriage in the first place. While Weiss focuses on change over time, my use of diaries makes possible a reconstruction of how women—at the time they went to college—actively constructed their identity and what exactly they saw in the decisions they made within the larger context of their culture.

Gender historians have long recognized the usefulness of young women's autobiographical writings to gain insights into the complexity of their experiences. For the nineteenth century, Jane Hunter in *How Young Ladies Became Girls* (2002) illustrates how, influenced by their experiences in mixed-sex high school classrooms and their ventures into the hetero-social world of the peer culture, late Victorian girls already broke with expectations of proper ladylike behavior.[10] John Spurlock and Cynthia Magistro, in *New and Improved* (1998), offer intriguing insights into how women in the early twentieth century engaged with the cultural materials at their disposal to give meaning to their lives.[11] For the post–World War II period, Wini Breines, in *Young, White, and Miserable* (1992), culls from an array of autobiographical writings by women how even outward conformists in the late 1950s chafed under the gender conservative restrictions imposed on them—a discontent that eventually drove them, like Breines herself, into the women's liberation movement.[12]

While my own work is especially influenced by Breines's engaging analysis of the 1950s, I bring a different perspective to the topic. Breines's focus is on the second half of the decade and on the factors that caused the consensus on middle-class gender and family roles to crumble. I, however, am interested in the process through which, after the upheaval of world war and depression, educated young women came to adopt particular definitions of their role and nature to begin with. Moreover, Breines uses writings by authors who later became feminists and who then looked back at their youth in an attempt to explain their choices. Yet, as sociologist Maurice Halbwachs has argued, the memory of the past is inextricably linked to the social context existing within a particular group at the time in which the act of remembering takes place.[13] As Breines writes, the women's liberation movement changed the lens through which women evaluated themselves and the decisions they made. *Young, White, and Miserable* thus provides a view of the 1950s that is refracted through the perspective of the late 1960s. My use of diaries that women wrote while still in college and before they had settled for a particular definition of their role, by contrast, allows me to explore the question of the range of constructions of female identity that were possible on the basis of the cultural raw material available to college women in the years between 1940 and the early 1960s. I am not proposing that the way in which feminist writers have presented their youth is inaccurate. Critical distance certainly gave women very valuable insights. In their reconstruction of the past, however, writers privileged certain aspects while downplaying or neglecting others. As a result, some of the complexity of young women's experiences in the 1950s got lost.

I propose a reevaluation of why and how a group of culturally literate young women became infatuated with ideas of gender difference. Most of the women whose papers I studied indeed married early, had children right away, and put professional plans on the back burner. Nonetheless, they actively shaped and promoted ideology by drawing selectively on the discourses at their disposal. The ideas about their needs and desires echo aspects of the conservative literature of advice, but while the latter had an antifeminist bent, this does not hold true for what I found in women's own writings. Female students shied away from labeling themselves feminists. They also believed that by virtue of their reproductive role, they had interests, talents, and instincts that set them apart from men. But they did not think that these traits ought to limit them—or women in general—in their pursuits. Rather, they conceived of difference as a special strength. Moreover, the fact that college women highlighted the centrality of their reproductive role in the makeup of their identity needs to be seen as part of a struggle for leverage and authority in a setting in which stereotypically male interests and traits were granted superiority and male needs were treated as entitlements, but in which the voices, interests, and special needs of women counted very little. In this masculinist environment, insistence on feminine distinctiveness was a remarkable assertion of agency, the product of experience, and the result of a realistic weighing of options.

This said, the fact remains that 1950s college women not only opted in unusual numbers—at least temporarily—for motherhood and domesticity, but their personal writings also show evidence that their decisions were often preceded by a personal crisis. While I acknowledge the role of gender conservatism in this development, I highlight further the influence of a different kind of "mystique" than the "feminine" one: the myth of individualism. In the social scene that academically ambitious liberal arts students frequented, there circulated a particular idea about the characteristics of a truly self-realized person. A genuine individual, the thesis went, stood aloof from peer pressure, was in possession of complete self-awareness, and refused to allow competing desires to conflict with a goal. This ideal of the rugged, self-sufficient individualist was deeply embedded in American culture and the nation's political iconography. Its importance grew exponentially after World War II, however, because the experience of fascism, closely followed by escalating concerns about national security in the Cold War, ushered in a heightened concern with the question of how an individual functioned in groups. In the student culture, this discourse encouraged the spread of an exaggerated individualist ideal that made it exceedingly hard for young women to arrive at a stable and comfortable sense of identity.

Although the ideology of individualism resounded in the personal writings of both male and female students, it affected the identity of women in particular ways. In a setting that upheld radical independence from the opinion of others as the highest developmental accomplishment, any adolescent would have been susceptible to self-doubt. The coming-of-age of college women, however, was especially difficult because it coincided with a dramatic sexualization of the student dating culture, to which higher education officials responded by stepping up their attempts to contain change. Female students were caught between the clashing expectations of, on the one hand, their dating partners and, on the other, the arbiters of official morality. What ensued was profound personal conflict. Because of the way they experienced themselves as sexual actors, women earlier than men became aware of the high costs of nonconformity to traditional middle-class gender and sexual norms for themselves. As one result, they drew attention to the exaggerated and unrealistic nature of the ideal of the radical individualist. Yet, while women came to reject the applicability of this ideal for themselves, they could not quite shake the belief that there were people who actually approached it. Increasingly, however, they associated the ability to do so with being a man. College women's immersion in student culture, combined with their familiarity with cutting-edge academic debates, ultimately encouraged the nation's most highly educated women to glorify the idea of fulfillment in a marriage with a man whose potential for genius would justify the sacrifice—or at least a postponement—of their own professional and academic goals and ego needs.

My evidence in this book is often, but by no means exclusively, anecdotal. Considering that I am interested in the private experiences of women from the relatively recent past, it will not come as a surprise that collecting sources for this book posed somewhat of a challenge. A nationwide search resulted in the find of seventeen unpublished journals written between 1940 and 1960. Not all of these sources, however, were useful for the purpose of this book. Because I wanted to learn about the intersection of private experiences, public events, and intellectual debates, I needed diaries by women who were not only introspective but who also addressed the books they read and theories they encountered. This narrowed the number of useful sources down to ten. The authors of all of them were enrolled in a liberal arts college or course of study and all but one majored in the humanities, most often in English literature. My close reading of all these diaries influenced my analysis. The focus in this book, however, is on those diaries that enabled me to gain a good understanding of the writers' surroundings and circumstances. Moreover, the use of some of the diaries was restricted, and the author of one diary preferred to conceal her identity. In addition to the unpublished diaries, I have also read three published journals, including that of poet and writer Sylvia Plath, who graduated summa cum laude from Smith College in 1955.[14] I found many parallels between Plath's experiences and those of other college women, but because I want to focus on the stories of lesser-known historical actors, the reader will not find quotations from Plath's writings in the chapters that follow.

Aside from diaries, I read about twenty letters exchanged between college women and their parents, friends, and romantic partners. Some of these are from college archives, others I have solicited through calls in alumnae magazines. Like the personal journals, they offer intriguing insights into the world of ideas in which college women of the immediate post–World War II period moved. To complement my findings from introspective writings, I have also consulted student newspapers, yearbooks, scrapbooks, class notes, and term papers left by the women whose private writings I analyzed. Moreover, I have followed the trail of intellectual influences left by diarists and correspondents by reading the works of literature, philosophy, and the social sciences they found worthy of mentioning.

Although I have made an effort to address in this book the experiences of women from a variety of backgrounds, it needs to be said that the students who will appear in the pages that follow are a select lot, set apart from other members of their generation by class, race, and heterosexual privilege. To some extent, however, this was required by the nature of my research questions. Because I was interested in why they made the decisions they made and what they saw in them, I needed to focus on women who had the luxury of choice to begin with. Only women who identified, at least for the time covered in this book, as heterosexual had the option to choose marriage and motherhood over wage work. The writers are also almost all white. Black women have historically had to shoulder greater responsibility for the economic survival of their families than white ones. Even if they had felt torn between conflicting prescriptions of their role, they could less often look at marriage as an alternative to wage labor. The black middle class also already had a strong tradition of support for female education and wage labor. For these reasons, black college women transitioned into the labor force with less conflict and less fanfare than their white peers. Moreover, black college women were also less likely to leave personal journals that documented private and social events. The experience of blatant discrimination that African American students endured as a group because of their race politicized them more strongly and faster than white students. As a consequence, a black college woman whose personal journal dealt mainly with day-to-day social events of campus life was less likely than her white counterpart to regard it as something that ought to be preserved in an archive than her white counterparts would be. The one diary I found that was written by a black woman only made it into an archive as part of a larger collection documenting the civil rights and church activism of the author. Unfortunately, I can therefore not draw on the experiences of African American college women to the extent that I would have liked.[15]

Neither will I address the potentially different experiences of women in two-year and teacher's colleges, and of women who majored in the hard sciences. Junior and teacher's colleges tend to prepare students in a directed fashion for a postgraduate vocation or job. Students also tend to opt for these institutions because they are significantly less costly than other alternatives, so I assume that financial circumstances deprived graduates of the option to decide on full-time domesticity, even had they wanted to. In addition, libraries at public two-year institutions tend to lack the archives and special collections found in most universities and four-year colleges, where alumni could donate mementos from their days as students. I was also largely unsuccessful in locating diaries of female science majors. On the one hand, this was certainly because a student of the humanities might have been more inclined to cultivate the habit of journal writing than, say, a physics major. But the underrepresentation of the latter also reflects the lack of support young women received for majoring in these male-dominated fields. World War II constituted a notable exception to this trend, and not surprisingly, the one diary from a science major that I managed to find was from this period. My research and findings are therefore somewhat skewed to the experiences of literary-minded women whose financial circumstances allowed them to pursue a broad comprehensive liberal arts education instead of preparing directly for a specific vocation, such as high school teaching. I do not believe that this limits the usefulness of my findings for our understanding of the experiences of educated young women in more general terms, though.

Their positions as relatively privileged social actors aside, the women who appear in the pages that follow are representative members of a new post–World War II middle class. Government subsidies for housing, job training, and education provided by the Serviceman Readjustment Act of 1944 made possible a long-contested transition from elite to mass higher education and added new and diverse members to the white middle class. Many of the women who, thanks to the spread of prosperity, gained access to college or university during this time were the first in their families to do so. Many also came from families who, after their encounter with financial hardships during the Depression, were willing to reconsider the traditional middle-class hostility to the wage labor of married women. As a cohort, however, newcomers to higher education faced the special challenge of having to negotiate their goals and identity in a setting that was in a state of rapid but contested transformation. Diarists and letter writers therefore offer insights into the experiences of a transitional generation of female undergraduates who gained access to higher education when this was no longer a privilege of an elite but before their contemporaries had fully come to terms with this development. The journal and letter writers who left a record of this experience might therefore have been unusually articulate members of their generation of students. Because their situation was typical, though, the conflicts they faced and the coping strategies they adopted were likely shared by many others.

The introspective accounts of young women that follow are of course also representative of a common psychological dynamic and as such not particular to the mid-twentieth century. In Western societies for the last two hundred years at least, individuals struggling to come to terms with their sense of self have turned to diary writing to construct narratives about their past, their present, and their anticipated futures. Moreover, the developmental phase that coincides with the years when young adults typically start college is also the period when they are particularly prone to toy with different personas as part of their exploration of identity.[16] A diary here is a safe way to experiment and an ideal medium to justify one's actions and put a positive spin on events. The ideas about the self that a person articulates in a personal journal are thus not necessarily stable or consistent. The identity a diarist expresses on the page might also not always conform to the way others perceive the writer.[17] The question of what constitutes women's true self or their genuine desires, however, does not really concern me. Rather, I want to investigate what kinds of constructions of female identity were possible in the context of mid-twentieth-century culture and how the experience of college life influenced which of the available models students found most appealing. The discussion of private thoughts against the background of cultural frames of reference will show that women who went to college between 1940 and the early 1960s had the bad fortune of experiencing a common process of adolescent identity development at a time when historically specific factors were making it exceedingly difficult for them to arrive at a stable and realistic sense of self.

1   Campus Life in Times of Crisis

"GREASY GRINDS," "COEDS," AND
THE LIMITS OF DIVERSITY

In the summer of 1940, shortly before she started her freshman year at the Philadelphia Museum School of Industrial Art, Helene Harmon, a seventeen-year-old, white, middle-class Catholic turned to her diary to ponder her future. From the time she was a child, Helene reflected, she had imagined herself with a "house, . . . garden, [and] children." A husband, she mused, would be a necessary and desirable part of this picture, and she certainly expected to fall in love one day. Yet these conventional dreams aside, Helene's diary also reflects her avid interest in nondomestic pursuits. She wrote in her journal: "This I know: if I should ever settle down to be just a housewife . . . it will be an acknowledgement that I have failed in what I have set out to make of my life. Love and marriage of this sort is all very well . . . but I know so many housewives who . . . married in fear of a solitary life or because they could not be self sufficient (financially or friendshiply).—From this I pray to be saved."[1] Before she would "settle down" to a homemaker routine, Helene continued, she would rather stay single. "I think . . . being an old maid is much preferable to this." Many of her contemporaries thought that such women ought to be pitied, but not she: "A few old maids' lives might be soured by solitude but most of the old maids I know have had wonderful experiences . . . and can talk to hold me spellbound."

Yet, although she emphasized that the fate of spinsters held no horrors for her, it also becomes quite clear from Helene's journal that she would prefer to get married. After all, "since [she] was very young," she had pictured herself with a "house," a "garden," and "children." The man she wanted to start a family with, however, would have to share her interests and values and accept her just the way she was. He would, as she put it, be in "complete agreement" with her: "not about trivialities . . . but in great things," and this would need to include respect for her desire to pursue her passion for art and the theater.

Helene did not believe that nondomestic interests on her part would strain her marriage in any way. On the contrary, she wrote, women who lacked interests other than those traditionally associated with the domestic and reproductive realm posed the gravest danger to the stability of the family. Full-time homemakers and mothers, Helene believed, turned homes into claustrophobic prisons. Bored and frustrated because of their lack of satisfying outlets, they turned into domestic shrews who "yell at their children, pester their husbands about money, and when they get together with others of their kind gossip viciously about the lady next door." Yes, she could see herself getting interested in "cooking and children." But clearly, Helene felt that these pursuits should not be the be-all and end-all of a woman's existence. Married or not, she wanted to be able to pull her own weight financially, and along the same lines, she wanted to be an intellectual partner for her husband. In Helene's mind, marriage thus ought to be a union of two self-fulfilled individuals. She expected her stay in college would give her the training that would actually enable her to become the kind of modern woman she considered ideal: a personally fulfilled, economically independent one who had a happy marriage but who also found an outlet in a nondomestic vocation, if not a career. In other words, Helene wanted to be a woman who would have it all.[2]

With her criticism of full-time homemakers, the young Philadelphian was not advancing a completely new concept. The "clinging vine" type of wife, as she was often called, had been a target in the social scientific and advice literature since the teen decades of the twentieth century and the critique gained ground against the background of rising divorce rates in the 1920s and growing familial problems in the Depression decade. Experts came from a variety of academic and ideological backgrounds, but they tended to share a theory of how modernity had affected the position of women and the family. Women's traditional responsibilities for children and the household, the argument went, no longer had an essential economic value and no longer filled her day. Positing the living conditions of relatively affluent, urban, middle-class women as the national norm, writers argued that laborsaving devices had turned housework into an almost leisurely pursuit that could be completed within a few hours' time. Teachers and other trained professionals, meanwhile, had taken over the once highly demanding task of bringing up and educating children. In its most drastic form, this theory held that modern women had essentially become parasites. Financially dependent, emotionally needy, and notoriously dissatisfied, they vented their anger against their loved ones.[3]

As a remedy to the crisis of modern marriage, social science experts proposed a revamping of the institution as a more egalitarian, less patriarchal, "companionate" union. Building on ideas first promoted by bohemian radicals and feminists in the 1910s, marriage modernizers urged wives to discover and develop interests and vocations not related to their reproductive role and to become fully realized individuals. Husbands, meanwhile ought to grant their spouses more of a say in decision making. Even though this model broke with the traditional emphasis on duty and obligation as tenets of the marital union, by the 1920s supporters had largely abandoned attempts to radically transform gender roles. Supporters of modern marriage applauded women who had found nondomestic outlets in the form of a hobby, job, or in volunteer work and lauded husbands who took an interest in their wives' daily activities. Although the partners ought to grant to each other that each one's role was equal in value, modern social science experts held on to the notion that for marriages to function, the roles of husbands and wives ought to complement each other but not overlap. Even modern social scientists continued to see childrearing and housework as primarily the responsibility of wives, and support for the career aspiration of a married woman remained low. In fact, public commentators increasingly equated "feminist" with "careerist" and saw both as women who repressed the feminine aspects of their personality, who suffered from a pathological hatred of men, envied them their stature in society, and as a result competed ferociously for social status and slots in the professions.[4]

Helene's journal entries, however, do contain the seeds of something new. By the 1920s, the model of "companionate" marriage as promoted by social scientists and advice writers no longer included proposals for a radical redefinition of gendered power relations. This notwithstanding, historian Rebecca Davis has recently shown that large parts of the middle class, and especially devout religious such as the Catholic Harmon family, opposed even the limited modernization of gender roles as proposed by marriage modernizers.[5] Once the Depression struck, historians have demonstrated, hostility and resistance toward the wage labor of married women increased even more. Yet, as the diary of the young Philadelphian suggests, the financial hardships that families experienced as a result of the Depression opened up new support for the view that women should receive economically viable training.[6]

That the Great Depression affected how the Harmons thought about their daughter's future is readily apparent from Helene's journal. Helene's childhood had been a sheltered one. While her parents, Marian Grace and Harry Murphy Harmon, had an Irish immigrant background, they had clearly made the jump into the middle class by the time their only daughter reached her teenage years. With that they would also have come to adopt a particular concept of family roles. The ability of a male provider to earn an income sufficiently high so that his wife could stay home had long been a status marker through which middle-class families distinguished themselves from working-class and minority counterparts.

As a result, daughters were not normally expected to combine marriage and a career. Indeed, judging from Helene's diary, her high school education had focused on her cultural and moral training, not on preparation for a vocation, career, or job. On Sundays, Helene taught Bible school. During the week, she attended the single-sex Holman School for Girls, where her education centered on literature and poetry, on art and drama classes.[7]

Helene's sheltered adolescence, during which she had developed an avid interest in "art and beauty," was challenged by the Depression. The economic emergency had hurt the Harmons financially, and by 1940 money was still tight.[8] Helene's stay in college would probably not have been possible without the partial scholarship the Philadelphia Museum School of Industrial Art had granted her, but as was typical of the financial aid that was available in this period, the award was insufficient to cover the costs of Helene's education. Their daughter's stay in college thus caused the Harmons financial strains. That they nonetheless were willing to make the investment reflects their hope that her course of study would improve Helene's employment opportunities and lighten her family's burden.

Diary entries in which Helene commented on discussions with her mother about what course of study she should pursue indicate that the Harmons wanted their only daughter to receive economically viable job training. "Mother still wants me to take costume design," Helene recorded; she added that this preference was shaped by her parent's concern about "making a . . . living." That Marian Grace and Harry Murphy Harmon wanted Helene's schooling to translate into a remunerative job also demonstrated that they expected her to use her earnings to help bring a younger brother through college.[9] For her part, Helene felt at times that her parents were asking her to give up her artistic interests. However, she agreed that she needed to receive practical preparation for her adult life. Musing about her passion for "art and poetry," she wrote: "I don't want to choose my vocation with nothing but making a good living in view." Yet she conceded that her parents had a point: "neither do I want to be disregardless [*sic*] of this. . . . After all, a certain amount of security is necessary."[10]

What Helene expressed in this short journal entry was more than just a quirk peculiar to her particular household. Rather, because of the way in which the economic collapse affected the workforce, the spread of the notion that middle-class women needed to shoulder a larger share of the financial burden in their families was a broader phenomenon. While the male-dominated production sector was hardest hit, the semiprofessional and white-collar fields that employed a large number of women proved to be less susceptible to the vagaries of the market.[11] Families adjusted to this reality, and the wages a wife or daughter brought home helped put bread on the table. Even though professional careers for married women remained controversial, economic need therefore at least fueled the idea that daughters and wives could serve as an economic reserve army.

These developments affected the realm of female higher education as well. Although middle-class families had already warmed to the idea that their daughters benefited from a stay in college or university, equipping them with actual career or job skills had not necessarily been the main motivation. In the course of the first two decades of the twentieth century, growing affluence of the white middle class and the spread of new ideas about the female gender role had led to a steady increase in the number of women in institutions of higher education. When this option was no longer chosen only by a tiny minority, however, ideas about the purpose of a higher education for women became more conservative. Already in the early twentieth century, women's colleges in particular faced charges that they were contributing to a "race suicide" by dissuading white, native-born women from marriage and motherhood. In response, educators of women downplayed the academic and economic opportunities that a stay in college might yield and stressed instead their role in creating better-educated wives and fitter mothers. Even in schools that added classes in children's psychology and scientific housekeeping, the curriculum continued to offer academically rigorous training and real economic opportunities, but by that time the image of college life for women had undergone significant changes. As portrayed in popular novels and movies, the modern "coed," as she was now often called, was a fun-loving young thing who did not have to work for a living and who enjoyed the extracurricular and social offerings of campus life alongside college men.[12]

The spread of the coed image in popular culture is significant for at least two reasons. First, we can see the term as a reflection of a lack of acceptance of the presence of women in institutions that increasingly served as gatekeepers to lucrative and high-status positions. The image highlights youth and femininity while it downplays academic interests or economic motivations. Modern and fun-loving, a college woman was first and foremost an agreeable consort to a college man. She was not a competitor for a professional job or an antagonist out to challenge conventional gender divisions of power. Moreover, the growing visibility of the coed as an icon in popular culture set trends in campus life. While there were always female students who studied hard and aspired to professional careers, either because of interest or real economic need, the women who captivated the public imagination and who ranked highest on the scale of prestige and popularity in the student culture were those who matched the image of a fun-loving, all-around girl. When in the 1920s the spread of prosperity in the white urban middle class brought to college more and more young women from affluent families, their styles and expectations increasingly shaped the conventions and norms on campus.

The women whom Depression-era developments pushed and pulled into higher education brought with them the potential to change the common perception of the shape and purpose of an undergraduate education for women. During times of prosperity, being able to send a daughter to college to provide her with the background, poise, and experience that would ultimately make her a more polished wife and a better-educated mother, and who then also had a little fun outside class, had certainly been a marker of status for many middle-class families.[13] The economic collapse, however, dealt a blow to this model of collegiate life. Moreover, because the student body continued to diversify in terms of its goals, family background, and experiences, this challenge persisted even after prosperity returned in the course of national mobilization for war. On campuses nationwide, daughters of privilege increasingly met female peers who knew that their studies were first an opportunity for academic and economically viable training that ought not to be squandered. How this diversification of the female undergraduate student body affected the experiences of newcomers to campus is the subject of this chapter.

The spread of socioeconomic diversity on American campuses was a new and significant feature. In spite of political rhetoric that emphasized equality of opportunity, American higher education was still highly stratified when the Depression struck. Land-grant institutions and junior colleges offered affordable access to the offspring of farmers and the lower-middle class. The men expected to become the leaders of business and politics and the shapers of culture; the women who would become their wives, however, were educated in a small number of private institutions largely located in the Northeast. Faced with competition from newer institutions, schools such as Dartmouth, Harvard, and Yale already by the late nineteenth century emphasized the exclusive and culturally homogenous profile of their student body as a main asset and remained adamantly resistant to the idea of broadening access to new groups by offering financial aid or scholarships.

A first federal work-study and financial aid program passed Congress in response to skyrocketing attrition rates of students following the stock market crash.[14] Even in the face of the economic emergency, however, prestigious institutions tried to maintain their exclusive character. As Dixon Fox, president of Union College, argued in a 1934 article in the *New York Times*, for instance, "not everyone can go to college." Only "first-rate minds" should have the opportunity. These "first-rate minds" were apparently only found in the traditional elite, and rather than accepting federal monies, Ivy League schools and those striving to approach their status competed, in historian of higher education Lawrence Levine's words, "fiercely" for undergraduates from a small group of wealthy, native-born, Anglo-Saxon, Protestant families, also referred to as WASP.[15]

While the male Ivy League schools continued to emphasize exclusivity and cultural homogeneity as their main asset, the Depression put their female equivalents on a different trajectory. Although the most prestigious private women's colleges on the East Coast had in the 1920s begun to refer to themselves as the "Seven Sisters" of the male Ivy League, they lagged behind in terms of their financial resources. Private collegiate institutions for men were able to afford exclusivity thanks mainly to endowment monies from wealthy alumni who had become captains of industry and business. Women's colleges, by contrast, were less able to draw on comparable amounts of support from affluent patrons. When the financial crisis threatened to lead to a mass exodus of students, they increasingly offered measures that allowed financially embattled families to keep their daughters in college. While the Ivy League thus remained distinctly elite, even in the most prestigious ones of their sister institutions, socioeconomic diversity was growing.

Letters and diaries of women who went to college in the late 1930s and 1940s reflect the diversification of the student body. At private institutions such as Smith and Mount Holyoke Colleges, even a casual reading in their archives shows the considerable number of young women who were not able to take their education for granted and who were conscious of the financial burden their stay in college caused their families.[16] Daughters from affluent households increasingly rubbed elbows with peers from financially struggling homes who were more likely than their privileged contemporaries to expect from college preparation for careers instead of the cultural accoutrement and social poise associated with middle-class ladyhood. In addition to this, wartime developments further led to a diversification of the undergraduate population in its religious, ethnic, and national composition.

For Jewish and Catholic students from first- or second-generation American families in particular, the 1940s were a decade of substantial change. In the past, religious minorities had tended to avoid nonsectarian institutions of higher education because the liberal secularism widespread among faculty and officials struck them as a threat to their own group's religious and ethnic cohesiveness. In addition, anti-Catholic and anti-Jewish nativism in the prestigious colleges and universities especially had made it difficult even for assimilated and liberal Jews and Catholics to get an education side by side the traditional Protestant elite. These patterns of separatism and exclusion, however, began to unravel in the middle of the twentieth century.[17] During World War II, in an attempt to build citizens' morale and commitment to the defense of American democracy, the government engaged in a large-scale public relations effort in the course of which tolerance for diversity and the inclusion of minorities assumed center stage as alleged core national values. Civil rights activists after the war continued to use this rhetoric in their struggle against discrimination. In the case of African Americans, this quest soon fell victim to a Cold War backlash. Jewish organizations, however, were a lot more successful in dismantling the admissions quotas through which the traditional Protestant elite had in the interwar period tried to protect itself from competition from an increasingly successful minority.[18] Catholic liberals, meanwhile, began attacking the "siege mentality" that in their view had kept Catholics entrapped in a self-imposed "ghetto" and prevented their full acceptance as part of the American mainstream. By the middle of the 1950s, the success of these campaigns for assimilation showed when Will Herberg, in his influential *Protestant-Catholic-Jew* (1955), described Judaism, Protestantism, and Catholicism as the "three great faiths of democracy."[19]

Ideological challenges did not put a sudden end to discriminatory practices in the student culture. Because most administrators at elite institutions were unwilling to interfere with prejudicial practices in campus social organizations and athletics, a greater inclusion of minorities never became mandatory. The federal government also did not alter its restrictive quotas that prevented immigrants, especially Jews from Eastern Europe, from entering the United States. This notwithstanding, the war increased the likelihood of interpersonal encounters between members of different religions and ethnicities. When looking for diaries and letters of college women, I found that a considerable number came from Jewish and Catholic families and some even featured a refugee past. Reflecting the fact that discrimination against African Americans in northern institutions took far longer to soften than that against Jews and Catholics, I also found diaries and letters from no more than just a few token black students for the entire period under study.[20]

As limited as the trend toward diversity may have been, it affected student life. In particular, it challenged the prominence of the coed ideal. Extracurricular activities, dances, mixers, and athletic events had long been a prominent feature of undergraduate culture. Yet in order to participate in the hustle and bustle of campus life, college women needed to keep up with fashion, hairstyles, and other aspects of youth culture. Membership in sororities was costly. As a result of Depression and war, however, even the most prestigious institutions now witnessed growing numbers of women whose experiences put them at odds with collegiate culture. Students on financial aid had to maintain certain grade point averages and thus by necessity needed to concentrate on their coursework. If their studies left them time for socializing and extracurricular activities, a scarcity of funds limited their opportunities. Youngsters from financially struggling families would also be aware of the vagaries of the market and the need for women, too, to shoulder financial responsibilities. Minority students, meanwhile, were still likely to encounter obstacles to their participation in social life. While Jewish and Catholic students could join separate clubs and organizations, encounters with prejudice would certainly have had a tendency to politicize newcomers and make them critical of the established patterns of collegiate life.[21] With family histories that had early on alerted them to the importance of planning for their future, we can reasonably assume that wartime students approached college with an interest in and dedication to its academic aspects. Such attitudes were even more likely to grow in the context of the cultural atmosphere of crisis in which commentators called for more studious attitudes and somber outlooks among the educated young.

The politically charged atmosphere on wartime campuses needs to be understood against the background of the failure of appeasement. Between the wars, college students in the Western democracies had earned themselves a reputation for pacifism. Up to the mid 1930s, the student peace movement united under its umbrella a broad coalition of Marxists, socialists, liberals, and Christian pacifists who joined with communist students in the Popular Front and although, even at its height, only a small proportion of students were actively involved, it was a highly visible minority.[22] Inspired by overseas peers who introduced the Oxford Pledge on British campuses in 1933, the American Student Union the same year launched a petition drive. Signers of the American pledge vowed never to take up arms on behalf of their country "except in cases of the invasion of the mainland of the United States" and to work instead "actively for the organization of the world on a peace basis." The campaign for the pledge was covered by mainstream middle-class publications; the strength of anti-interventionist sentiment also showed when mass magazines published the results of peace polls on campuses such as Columbia, Brown, and the elite women's colleges.[23] Among their less activist-oriented peers, meanwhile, commentators detected an equally alarming spread of "social irresponsibility." With growing probability of a U.S. entry into war, the voices of those urging youth to adjust their attitudes picked up momentum.

Supporters of an American intervention in the war from the onset included women in their appeals. Public intellectuals saw especially the failure of the United States to join the League of Nations as a reason for the breakdown of the international system and strove to prevent another withdrawal of the country into isolationism. To secure the support of the educated young, they appealed to their responsibility in highly idealistic language. Here, the loyalties of college men were certainly the most coveted goal. Yet because male students were expected to ultimately serve their country in the military, it was also clear that they would not be available for long as an audience. This left their female peers as a target population for appeals that highlighted the principles the United States allegedly stood for: liberty, democracy, equality. Female students repeatedly heard the message that, for democracy to survive, they needed to commit themselves to active political work and use their expertise for the building of the postwar order. Public speakers, of whom the liberal Christian theologian and writer Reinhold Niebuhr, the anthropologist Margaret Mead, and First Lady Eleanor Roosevelt were but the most prominent, encouraged college women to educate themselves in politics, foreign languages, and their own nation's as well as other cultures' histories.[24] Adding to such appeals to women's international and national responsibility to train and educate themselves was that the war also produced what Margaret Rossiter described as a virtual "torrent" of promotional literature urging female students to major in the sciences to meet the demand for trained professionals expected as a result of the war.[25]

As historians have amply demonstrated, most politicians and academics would support the government's "womanpower" campaign only for the duration and never with a lot of commitment.[26] Yet, while women in the labor force received frequent reminders of the temporary nature of their new roles, the same cannot be said for their female contemporaries in higher education. In line with the traditional notion that women served as transmitters of values and culture to their families, wartime commentators turned to female students as the brokers of the ideals of democracy. More importantly, there was no time limit attached to this role.[27]

The wartime rhetoric that women had a special responsibility in the current crisis was an additional challenge to the mores in a student culture already affected by the diversification of the student body. Reminders of new and urgent responsibilities were all pervasive. Public intellectuals addressed young women as guest speakers in chapel or at commencement. A student who missed a personal encounter could read about campus guests' activities and publications in her alma mater's newspaper, where she would find enthusiastic support for women's new responsibilities in the present crisis and beyond. How this boosted the assertiveness of the most politically active and studious especially shows in official college publications. The student editors of the *Smith College*

Associated News in 1943, for instance, approvingly quoted an address by their school's president, Herbert Davis, who had argued, "college life" had to change in response to the new challenges of the times. The honors student rather than the social butterfly deserved to be upheld as a model to be emulated by all. Students should develop expertise in a specialized area, rather than approaching their stay on campus as "a process of growing up, in the course of which it may be possible to pick up a little miscellaneous information as painlessly as possible, and gather a little worldly wisdom." Instead of the students who flocked to "committees, . . . house dances, Rally Day, soccer games" it should be those in the "honors system" who were lauded as exemplary figures on campus.[28] This appeal to their peers to change their attitudes was also the tone adopted by a group of women at Michigan State University. In one of their pamphlets, these coeds, who organized as the "Women's War Council," explicitly singled out the type of fellow student who came from an upper-class neighborhood and chose a cultural course of study. "It is also your war, Suzy Smith, Lit major, from Cleveland Heights, Ohio," sounded one of their flyers: it was "time to awaken" and "to put away . . . bridge games and all night bull sessions."[29]

There is evidence that appeals to female students' sense of patriotism were successful. In letters and diary entries written in the direct aftermath of Pearl Harbor, discussions of political affairs and global events dominated. Young women reported that they were "glued to the radio" to follow presidential speeches and political debates.[30] Many had friends and relatives who were drafted or enlisted into military service, and their letters and diary entries show their concern for the well-being and safety of those directly exposed to the fighting. Letters often echoed the rhetoric that college youth needed to accept their responsibility for the shaping of the postwar world. It was time for "partygoers," Ruth Honamann, a student at Smith College put it, to turn into "men and women" concerned about "the future" and what it "*must* hold" (her emphasis).[31] Because of age restrictions, it was not possible for many students to enlist in the military. Many women who remained in school, however, used their leisure time to help in agriculture or to fill vacancies in other jobs. They donated blood, bought war bonds, and attended or organized events to entertain servicemen and servicewomen.[32] Clearly, many young women responded with fervor and commitment to idealistic wartime appeals. And yet, in spite of an upsurge in patriotism, there is also plenty of evidence for continuity in terms of values and styles in the student culture.

Students affected by wartime idealism often lamented that, in spite of international crises, the values, styles, and mores in the student culture had not changed. Politically active students and concerned commentators shared a sense that the majority of their peers did not show the needed level of commitment. Newspapers and campus speakers did not tire in appealing to college women's responsibilities. Contemporary sociological articles reflect this sentiment. Female students were portrayed as "lethargic" and politically uninformed. Despite the war, they concentrated on social pursuits.[33]

An analysis of student letters and diaries from the war years indeed suggests that even women who arrived on campus with career and vocational goals and somber political outlooks quickly adjusted their attitudes to conform to campus life conventions. Helene Harmon's experiences at the Philadelphia Museum School of Industrial Art provide a case in point. Once immersed in the student culture, the young woman's views and interests underwent a significant transformation. At first, the academic aspects of her life were predominant in her journal. Striking a balance between her interests in art and the theater and the practical considerations of her parents, she had chosen stage craft as a major, and the prospect of embarking on this course of study excited her. Soon, however, the focus of Helene's entries shifted. She became "better acquainted" with "upper class men" and befriended a young woman from a much more financially secure background than her own. Curricula aspects of her education largely disappeared as a topic in her journal. Instead, Helene now adopted as her goal becoming more popular and gaining access to a mixed-sex crowd of students she referred to as the "gang." As Helene admitted herself, collegiate living "changed" her. "I care so much more for clothes [and] jive" now, she admitted, and not even the outbreak of war sufficed to take her mind off campus life. "It continually surprises me," she wrote the day after the Japanese attack on Pearl Harbor, "that my personal concerns still mean more to me than the fate of humanity."[34]

Helene's transformation mirrors that of a contemporary, the Jewish refuge Judith Lauterbach, whose personal background and experiences introduced her to hardships at a tender age. Judith was born and raised in Britain where her father was a secretary of the Zionist Executive in London. In this capacity, Leo Lauterbach already in the late 1930s had become aware of the extreme danger Nazi anti-Semitism posed to European Jewry. When the blitzkrieg of the German Luftwaffe began, Judith and her mother were evacuated from the British Isles and Leo Lauterbach went to Palestine to work for the cause he had long supported: an independent Israel. After a short stay in Montreal, Judith and her mother arrived in New York City in 1941 where Judith attended Dalton, a prestigious preparatory school, as well as the experimental Walden School, which focused on education in the visual and performing arts. Meanwhile, she maintained an active correspondence with her father. Although Leo Lauterbach's letters have not survived, it is clear from Judith's responses that he encouraged his daughter's interest in politics. In addition to this personal influence, Judith's political consciousness was also raised by the fact that she could consider herself lucky; most European Jews had not managed to enter the United States and escape European anti-Semitism.[35]

In 1943 the politicized and academically talented Judith entered the private liberal arts Smith College with the help of a scholarship of four hundred dollars. As becomes clear from her letters to her father, her expectations for the intellectual atmosphere on campus were high: Her "idea of college [was] contact with serious thinkers." As she wrote to her father shortly after arriving at Smith: "I am working very busily now, and find it interesting. I am taking what I consider, and know you do, too, a useful course in Public Speaking. I feel that I'm getting a lot out of college."[36] Yet, Judith, too, like Helene, was soon immersed in social activities. She was a frequent guest at Hillel, the Jewish student organization to which, in Judith's own words, "all the Jewish girls automatically belong," and to which most went mainly because of its "social functions."[37] To her father, this seemed frivolous. In her response, however, Judith defended herself: she could not see how even "useless company can be harmful," because at the very least, making friends would serve to "further [her] experience." A short time later, she listed what she now regarded as the main benefits of her education. First of all, she wrote, college would offer her "a very good time," secondly, "a feeling of unity," and lastly "a little learning." When, shortly after the war, her father criticized her younger sister for also privileging social over academic and political activities, Judith came out in her defense: "There is nothing shallow or aimless in the urge . . . to enjoy one's self in social ways. To learn such things when one is young is as valuable and probably more lasting than other things one learns at school."[38]

To a reader familiar with the social life of campus students at the beginning of the twenty-first century, it might not come as a surprise that two young women removed from the direct supervision of their parents wanted to enjoy themselves in the student culture. We do, however, need to keep in mind the historically specific circumstances of their adolescence. As highlighted earlier, neither Judith nor Helene could take the opportunity to gain a higher education for granted. Their families had made financial sacrifices to send them to college and reminded them of the need to take their studies seriously. The political context of the time greatly raised the stakes for taking an interest in the fate of humanity. Moreover, while still in their respective high schools, each woman had managed to hold on to her view and attitude even though already then she had been at odds with the styles, behavioral expectations, and attitudes in the peer culture. Neither Judith at Walden or Dalton nor Helene at the Holman School had been active participants in the peer culture. What was it, then, about college that caused their transformation?

That contacts with a one-generational peer culture did not inevitably cause a homogenization of attitudes becomes apparent if one looks at the high school experiences of Judith and Helene. When both were in their teens, they would have already encountered normative pressures to model their behavior and styles after those of their peers. On the eve of Pearl Harbor, participation in high school youth culture unified the experiences of more and more American teenagers. Compulsory schooling laws caused the rate of high school attendance to climb throughout the first half of the twentieth century. One could argue that, with the exception of the South, a stay in high school was a common feature of the childhood and adolescence for the majority of Americans by the late 1930s. Along with this, Beth Bailey has argued, came a homogenization of attitudes and styles.[39] Exposed to their peers for long stretches of the day, high school youths increasingly took their clues about values and norms from each other rather than from traditional authority figures such as parents, teachers, or religious or community leaders. The world these high school–age youths created was one in which dating couples and their friends went, often in groups, to soda parlors, skating rinks, or movie houses. Depression-era scarcity put a damper on the spread of this commercial leisure culture. However, even the economic emergency ultimately did not stop its expansion.

Observers greeted the expanding youth culture with ambivalence. Social scientists welcomed the rejection of Victorian mores as evidence of their own growing influence over traditional sources of authority. Already in the 1920s, however, many were worrying about the effects of new attitudes on the nation. As a rise in divorce rates suggested, couples were increasingly discontented with marriage and no longer willing to stay in relationships that were unfulfilling. When family breakdowns and marital strains reached new proportions in visibility and scope in the course of the 1930s, experts took an increasingly proactive stance toward preparing young Americans for their future responsibilities in the family. Here the literature highlights two developments in particular as root causes of family crisis: the spread of popular culture and the changing expectations of women.

Depression-era social scientists were of two minds regarding the changing behavioral patterns among the young. Autocratic parent–child relationships had lost legitimacy by the 1930s. Rather, theories of psychological development held that youth needed to collect experiences independent of parental control in order to shed repression and fear of the opposite sex. The desired result of development was that of mature heterosexuality expressed within marriage. Yet because dating was seen as an important intermediary stage on this path, parents who prohibited their children from associating with peers essentially prevented them from reaching maturity. Once the adult children entered marriage, they then experienced adjustment problems that easily ended in divorce. Modern, mature heterosexual outlooks free of old-fashioned repression needed to be cultivated. In the words of influential and prolific writer of marriage advice Paul Popenoe, for example, the "fears brought along from childhood and adolescence" spent in families with old-fashioned parents, needed to be "eradicated" for marriages "to run . . . successfully." For this purpose, "young people [needed to] get acquainted" with each other and "build up a normal social life with their equals."[40] Modern experts thus supported the spread of a one-generational youth and dating culture. Yet, while family experts wanted youth to cut the umbilical cord to the home, they also wanted to keep them committed to the institution of marriage. However, social scientists did not take for granted the young generation's commitment to this institution, which all but a radical minority of social scientists regarded as essential for social stability. Movies, novels, and magazines, they feared, actually held greater sway over the views of modern youth than scholarly articles and books. While these products of popular mass culture were of course consumed by members of both sexes, public commentators increasingly saw women as a group that had the cultural influence to shape the content of popular mass culture. Older women who organized as members of consumer protection leagues or reform groups were often portrayed as a lobby powerful enough to influence what the producers of mass culture offered their audience. Young women, meanwhile, were seen as particularly susceptible to fall for the unrealistic portrayal of modern relationships in the mass media.[41]

From the late 1930s through the 1940s, a variety of social scientists concerned about marriage and the family feared that, inspired by the plots of movies and magazine stories, women entered relationships with unrealistic expectations. Enticing adventure stories and sentimental romances encouraged them to expect from their adult relationships an endless succession of thrilling and exciting adventures. Moreover, the relative independence that girls had enjoyed in the youth culture would lead them to believe that as adult women, too, they would continue to be treated as a pal. This might have been the ideal central to the model of the companionate marriage, which social scientists supported. Yet social scientists were also aware of studies arguing that outside the ranks of an educated minority, national attitudes toward masculinity and femininity were changing only gradually. Culture lag was a catchphrase appearing frequently in the literature. A lack of exposure to level-headed advice, experts feared, would lead young wives to expect far more egalitarianism in their marriages than was likely to lay in their future. For the sake of preserving the stability of the American family, experts thus felt that they needed to counter the influence of modern media and high school peer culture through the promotion of a rational, social scientific, and allegedly objective approach toward relationships and marriage.[42] Here, maturity and adjustment became the most common slogans of social scientists.

In advice literature published at the eve of Pearl Harbor, readers again learned about a particular theory of successful personality development. A mature individual, the message went, grasped what kinds of actions yielded the greatest social benefits and subsequently adjusted his or her attitudes. Considering that mature men were still "attracted by womanliness," and repelled by women who acted as if they were one of the boys, Paul Popenoe explained, any woman who still acted like a high school student "pal" should not be surprised if she was "still single at 40."[43] For happiness and success in life, it was ultimately best not to stray too far from well-established social expectations but to play according to the rules. This emphasis on adjustment and conformity entered middle-class homes through the growing body of advice literature. The place where the young generation encountered it most directly, however, was high school.

Although it is difficult to generalize about the high school experiences of American youth, late 1930s and early 1940s classrooms tended to expose youth to an ambivalent but ultimately quite conservative message. Lesson contents varied depending on region and school district, and teachers' inclinations and personalities played a role as well. Increasingly, however, educators were influenced by the same trends in the social sciences, mental hygiene, and psychology. These modern disciplines caused them on the one hand to encourage adolescent boys and girls to separate from parents and to collect experiences of their own in the one-generational world of their peers. On the other hand, teachers reminded their pupils often and early of the need to adjust their behavior to commonly held behavioral expectations. Courses like "Basic Living," "Common Learning," or "Life Problems," were products of an earlier wave of progressive reform designed to make the classroom more youth-centered and democratic. Ultimately, however, these classes tended to reproduce typical middle-class values and expectations. Pupils were encouraged to develop outgoing personalities but not to stray too far from conventions. Teachers highlighted the ability to fit into groups as a sign of good social adjustment. Personal idiosyncrasies and unusual displays of behavior, by contrast, came under suspicion as signs of psychological problems or the influences of a bad environment.[44]

For American teenagers, the spread of the high school youth culture, combined with intellectual trends in secondary education and the social sciences, produced a mixed message with a very conservative undercurrent. On the one hand, youth found encouragement to separate from parents and to collect experiences of their own. On the other, they were constantly reminded of the need to adjust their own behavior to commonly held behavioral expectations. Well-adjusted adolescents, the thesis went, would find it easy to fit into a group. Their outgoing personalities allowed them to be a good sport and to have fun. Personal idiosyncrasies and unusual displays of behavior, meanwhile, came under suspicion as signs of psychological problems or the influences of a bad environment.

Facilitated by the expansion of formal education and the mass media, social scientific and psychological theories of development spread into the middle class where they boosted the acceptance of youth culture and dating. This development did not lead to a homogenization of styles right away, however. In fact, the journal of Helene Harmon shows quite clearly that, at the eve of World War II, the extent to which Americans accepted the youth culture and social science–informed notions of personality still depended a lot on their regional, ethnic, and religious backgrounds.

The journal entries Helene Harmon made the summer before college reveal that as a high school student she had merely been a spectator of, rather than a participant in, the world of her peers. Even though many of her friends in the Holman School for Girls had already started dating, she spent her hours after class socializing with a small group of female friends or recording her thoughts about life, books, and poetry in her journal. Her Sundays, meanwhile, she devoted to teaching a Bible studies class. The fact that she deviated from increasingly pervasive patterns among her peers at times made Helene suspect that there might be something wrong with her. "Surely I cannot be normal," she wrote, for instance, the summer before she began college. As a "girl of 17" she should by now "to all rights and purposes [be] boy-crazy over anything in trousers."[45] Yet she also insisted on the legitimacy, if not superiority, of her own views over those of her peers. While the latter spent hours watching movies, listening to jazz, and "spooning" with the opposite sex, Helene argued, she was holding out for "true love." What would make her happy, she wrote, "would not be 'Hollywood Love'—that is a lot of petting and mouthing, nor would it be storybook love—they married and lived happily ever after." Instead, she was waiting for a partner who would share her outlook on "things such as music, art, humor, humanity, [and] ideals."[46]

The vocabulary with which Helene justified her deviation from common behavior patterns among high school youths shows the degree to which the debate about popular culture's dangerous influences had entered the middle class. Yet although this debate crossed denominational, ethnic, and class lines, Helene's justification of her outlook also reflects the fact that attitudes toward youth and popular culture differed considerably depending on a family's background. Especially when it came to the question of daughters' participation in the dating culture, Catholic households remained steeped in conservative values longer than urban Protestants.[47] Her journal entries clearly reflect that, despite her insights into high school youth culture, Helene, too, held on to the values held in her community of origin. She did not believe, for instance, that dating was really an adequate preparation for marriage. On the contrary, to go out with a number of different partners before settling for a spouse struck her as dangerous. It seemed to her "a kind of mental adultery," which although it might not be as "immoral in the world's eyes" as actual, physical unfaithfulness, "might become as dangerous spiritually." All in all, she contended, she could not "reconcile" the spreading patterns around her "with [her] religion." In her opinion, a likelihood of "adultery or at least . . . a couple of divorces" lay in wait for many of her peers.[48]

Helene's was not an isolated case. In fact, women from Catholic, Jewish, and rural families, who had only recently entered the American middle class, had not been active participants in the youth culture. In contrast to Protestant peers from more affluent families, they were less likely to have the permission of their parents to spend their leisure hours unsupervised by adults. Families of immigrant, working-class, and rural backgrounds also tended to still expect daughters to help with household chores. For families severely affected by economic hardships, participation in commercial leisure was often not an option for financial reasons. By the 1940s, class, religion, location, and ethnicity thus still influenced the extent to which American adolescents participated in the urban youth culture.

The experience of growing up in isolation from the high school youth culture had a complex effect on the identity of daughters. As Helene Harmon's diary shows, such isolation could lead young women to hold on to rather traditional notions. Her musings about "mental adultery" indicate that she still conceived of marriage as a spiritual union that ought to be formed for life. In this she echoed the resistance to divorce that unified urban Catholic Americans far longer than their Protestant contemporaries. Helene was also of the opinion that present-day youth were exposed to the realities of adult life at a much too early age. "I think the youngsters ought to be kept in ignorance," she wrote, about "anything . . . unpleasant and complex."[49] Yet while she was out of step with some modern attitudes, Helene did embrace a progressive notion about the need for women to plan for economically self-sufficient futures. The effect of her upbringing was thus a quite broad conception of her gender role and of the purpose of her education. Yet, although the late 1930s and early 1940s brought to college a number of women with expectations and outlooks similar to that of Helene, their exposure to campus life undermined their beliefs in the legitimacy of their views.

To understand why normative pressures were more powerful in college than in high school, it helps to look at exactly how newcomers were introduced to new expectations. On the midcentury campus, young women from diverse backgrounds whose social position was precarious met peers upon whom class privilege had bestowed an air of worldliness and sophistication. These students' evaluation of the legitimacy of different styles, interests, and goals reflected longstanding prejudices against Jews, Catholics, immigrants, and the working class. Because a seemingly objective language of personality development concealed class- and ethnicity-based evaluations, however, they acquired an aura of scientific objectivity that made them hard to contest.

An article published in the *Journal of Abnormal and Social Psychology* in 1941 serves as an illustration of the extent to which the language of social science naturalized behaviors and values rooted in class privilege and ethnic bias. For the study "Fad and Fashion Leadership among Undergraduate Women," researcher J. E. Janney relied on student informants to observe their peers at an unnamed private women's college. From their reports, the writer then proposed an explanation of what kind of women enjoyed the greatest influence in setting conventions on campus and for what reasons. Here, Janney argues, neither "academic standing, intelligence, athletic participation, financial income," nor "health" accounted for the hierarchy among college women. Rather, women became trendsetters based on their personalities. In this interpretation, students naturally gravitated to peers who navigated the student culture with ease and grasped even the "subtle aspects" of the right social "etiquette." The ability to grasp these subtle cues, however, is attributed to personal maturity, not to class privilege. As Janney contends, one could find students on scholarship alongside students from elite families in the upper echelons of the campus hierarchy.[50]

While Janney and her informants argue that personality serves as the most important factor in elevating a student's social standing, they also point to it as the cause that kept some women at the bottom. In the view of Janney's informants, the least popular women on campus had—despite encouragement and prodding by their peers—either refused to join them in social events, or had tried too hard to join the popular crowds. These women fell into two basic categories: They were spoilsports who spent their "free time in self-imposed solitary confinement in their rooms," and who refused to "appear at teas [and] receptions." Or they tried to join the ranks of the trendsetting crowd but, because their lack of comprehension of social mores, failed to fit in.[51] Either way, the women's inability to comprehend and then to adjust to the conventions of campus life, according to this study, earned them their marginalized position on campus.

Janney's study reflects the stigmatization of scholarship students and ethnic minorities that had shaped admissions policies of colleges since the 1920s. Women on scholarship who needed to maintain grade-point averages would have to spend their free time studying in their rooms. Similarly, women from non-East Coast, white, Protestant families were ignorant of the subtleties of cultural styles by which the WASP elite defined itself. Janney's study also shows, however, how successful the discourse on personality concealed prejudices against newcomers to college culture. From the perspective of the student informants and the researcher, the women who refused to appear at a social event did so either because of a misguided choice or because of a developmental flaw that they had not yet overcome. They were unpopular not because of their backgrounds but because they were either too "obstinate" to conform to convention or too shy. For those women who tried to join the ranks of the most popular girls but who failed to succeed, their rejection, according to Janney's study, was because of their annoying personalities, not because they were feared as social climbers threatening to gain access to the traditional elite.

Based on a small sample of students at only one private women's college, Janney's study is of course hardly a comprehensive look at student culture. However, the personal writings of women in colleges and liberal arts programs reveal that the article described a very common view. Female students from a broad variety of backgrounds shared an overwhelmingly negative opinion of studious peers who concentrated on their class work, who turned down opportunities to socialize, or who became active in campus life in ways deemed inappropriate. Women whose extracurricular activities centered on political causes, for instance, easily acquired negative reputations among their less active peers. On the Smith College campus, students found the writer for the student newspaper Bettye Goldstein (later Betty Friedan) "strident," and the young woman was painfully aware of this image. On the Mount Holyoke campus, similar attitudes existed. As one student wrote about a peer who perhaps not coincidentally happened to be Jewish: "We discussed Census Points and R. *Agitator* H. was all for abolishing them. I think that's a dumb idea" (emphasis added).[52] A common epithet to describe studious women, meanwhile, was the "grind." As one student at Mount Holyoke

College described "the type" in a 1943 letter to her parents, a grind-like woman did not know how to dress. She wore "a drolly skirt and a V-neck cardigan with no blouse underneath—you know the type" and combined this with "knee-socks of drab colors and 'sensible shoes.'" Not only did she have a bad fashion sense, she also by virtue of her conduct appeared developmentally challenged: she "kept her hands in her pockets all the time and managed the most moronic expression!"[53]

Although the student's description of the "type" of a "moronic" grind came from a play performance and did not describe an actual peer, it reflects a widespread attitude. Her "average" was only a B-, wrote another Mount Holyoke College student in a letter home at the end of her freshman year in 1942. She was "really quite happy with this, she assured her family, however, because she would "hate to be" like one of the "three girls in [her] dorm who got all A's and such." They, she contended, were "sadly enough . . . the sort of drips that will be Phi Bets." Students were likely to make similar evaluations in response to women they encountered as professors or in other positions of authority. In those evaluations, however, students focused on the extent to which these women conformed to a narrow norm of acceptable feminine styles and well-rounded personalities, not the extent to which they were good teachers or made intellectual contributions.[54]

Students thus evaluated their female peers and older women based on the extent to which they matched conventional expectations of middle-class femininity. Alternative styles and interests, meanwhile, were heavily stigmatized. In the psychological literature, uneasiness with, if not hostility toward, female intellectualism showed in the extreme when women professionals or artists were painted as lesbians.[55] In none of the letters and diaries I consulted did students actually go so far as to insinuate that a peer or a professor might be a sexual deviant. What they clearly did see in bookish women, however, were pitiable wallflowers who were not only socially awkward but physically unattractive to boot. When referring to a woman as a studious "grind," for instance, "greasy" often was the adjective that accompanied the label. Whether they were aware of the class- and ethnicity-based assumptions underneath the label or not, by applying it the speaker did deny that a woman's studiousness could be grounded in agency and choice, or could be based on legitimate needs or interests.[56] "Grinds" according to the common view, acted the way they did because they did not know any better. Because of a psychological flaw, they never acquired the interests that would make them pleasant company for their peers. For the same reason, they had miserably failed to develop their femininity. Lacking feminine appeal and social poise, they acquired notoriety as "types" deserving pity but certainly not emulation.

The fact that class- and ethnicity-based value judgments appeared to be an impartial evaluation of personality created a campus social environment in which the interests and goals of many newcomers were denied legitimacy from the onset. For students from diverse backgrounds, campus life thus meant that they would find it difficult to see in a positive light the outlooks they had brought with them to campus. This is demonstrated by the way encounters between women of different backgrounds played out.

The uneven playing field newcomers faced in the collegiate setting is poignantly illustrated by the friendship that developed between Helene Harmon and a fellow coed, "Dena," who played a major role in introducing the young Catholic to the dos and don'ts of student life. Helene's journal is short on information about Dena's family. It is clear, though, that she came from a different socioeconomic background than the scholarship student Helene. A comment Helene made at a later stage of the relationship reveals that Dena's adolescence was shaped by her parents' ability to "feed" their daughter with "tennis and financeering [*sic*]."[57] In contrast to Helene, Dena came from a fairly affluent home, and the material circumstances of her upbringing affected her ability to navigate the collegiate environment successfully. Allowed and able to enjoy costly leisure activities, she had collected experiences in the youth culture that had not been available to Helene. These experiences rooted in class privilege put Dena in a position of a conveyor of norms.

In Helene's reaction to Dena, we can clearly see how newcomers came to accept women from affluent backgrounds as brokers of cultural conventions on campus. From entries in which Helene described Dena as given to "screaming ecstasies," it becomes clear that the relationship between the two young women was not free of tensions. However, the features that set Dena apart from herself, including her extroverted persona and her familiarity with dating and social conventions, also impressed Helene. Even though Dena often annoyed her, she accepted her as an authority on questions of social etiquette. As students of drama and related subjects, Dena and Helene probably moved in a world in which a larger tolerance existed for idiosyncratic styles and behavior than elsewhere. In fact, students in both women's inner circle seemed to have been intrigued by examples of bohemian artists who led unusual lives. Helene, for instance, described conversations she had with fellow students about "a Gaugin-like [*sic*] existence." From Dena, however, Helene had learned that while flaunting some elements of "bohemian existence" might be all right, if a woman "acted too bohemian," it would lead to her well-deserved marginalization in the peer culture. Helene not only cited Dena's opinion on other women's personality and style but also learned from her which of the male students were considered desirable as dating partners. For instance, after a young man walked Helene home one day, Dena approached her and "confided" that he was a man who ranked high on the student scale of popularity. Helene subsequently recorded in her diary that she considered him a "very nice boy" and that she was "flattered that he had paid [her] attention."[58] Thus, Helene learned through Dena what kind of behavior enhanced her prestige and what actions her peers considered inappropriate. And it was also this woman on whom Helene soon began to model herself. It was after befriending Dena that Helene recorded that she now cared "so much more for clothes [and] jive." The extent to which she accepted these interests as a desirable norm shows in the way she evaluated the change in her outlook as compared to her high school past. "A great many extraordinary things have happened to me, I do not feel that I am so much of an introvert. . . . I do not pretend so much and I do not feel uneasy at growing up."[59]

We can see from Helene's vocabulary that after exposure to campus life, she no longer granted legitimacy to the values and outlooks that had shaped her high school past. Instead, her former distance from the peer culture and her interests in books now struck her as a pretense, a rationalization for what was at heart simply her fear of "growing up." In this she was far from alone. Like her, other students from backgrounds that put them at odds with the conventional patterns of campus life quickly grew self-conscious about their former values, styles, and interests and tried to mold themselves after a new behavioral norm. Young Catholic Patricia Beck had not been exposed to youth culture before beginning her studies at Bennington College in Vermont. Patricia had an unusual childhood. She lost her father in 1928. Five years later her mother, Margaret Beck, married Paul Swiderski, a heavyweight champion from the Bronx. With her prizefighter husband and her three children, Margaret Beck traveled for years through Europe and only returned to the United States when the outbreak of the Spanish Civil War foreshadowed the escalation of tensions on the continent. Despite her idiosyncratic lifestyle, however, Margaret Beck clearly wanted her daughter to grow up in accordance with the values of her religion. Patricia attended a convent school for a year and was brought up very strictly. As an adolescent, she was allowed very little autonomy. Because of this and her family's itinerant past, Patricia missed the opportunity to participate in the high school peer culture that increasingly shaped the experiences of American middle-class teens. Patricia had also witnessed a lot of poverty while staying abroad, and her journal entries show that she was highly conscious and critical of the social inequality she had observed as a child. It was probably because of these encounters with a harsh reality that she developed rather sincere and earnest interests. At Bennington, however, Patricia learned to become critical of those aspects of her background and interests that set her apart from her peers.[60]

Patricia revealed her acute self-consciousness about her own and her family's idiosyncrasies in a questionnaire she was asked to fill out as part of a class assignment at Bennington. Asked how she would assess her "general social adjustment," she self-critically recorded that she had never been the well-rounded type. Instead of joining her peers in the fun-filled world of youth, she had spent her childhood in a "world of adults." Consequently, she now found it difficult to "relax and have fun," and did not always "get along . . . with others." At a number of occasions, she castigated herself for her inability to loosen up and enjoy life, and until she dropped out of college she never quite managed to shake a sense of personal inadequacy.[61]

Personal conflicts because of her failure to enjoy and participate in campus life also continued to haunt Patricia's contemporary at Smith College, the Jewish refugee Judith Lauterbach. In contrast to Patricia, Judith did complete her course of study. Even as an advanced student, however, she still castigated herself for not having taken full advantage of the social opportunities of campus life. When the war was over and Judith was about to graduate from Smith, her view on what she thought she had missed is apparent once again in a letter to her father. She was a late-bloomer, she explained. She had not joined her peers in the youth culture "until [she] was about 16," and added that this was "rather too late." She "regret[ted] . . . very much" that her stay at Smith had not given her access to more socially oriented peers. Her "friends," she explained, were "a peculiar bunch" and not the kind of people who would "form a social group who go out . . . together." This was not the first time the topic of Judith's social life came up in their correspondence. In a prior letter Judith's father must have argued that it was far more important to commit oneself to Zionism rather than well-roundedness. Judith still disagreed, however. She envied women who had more opportunities for social activities than she did and found that this was ultimately "more important than joining a Zionist Club."[62]

Considering their unusual childhoods and the context of national and international crisis, it is remarkable that the women quoted here did not bring up the circumstances of their youth to explain why their personality had developed along different lines than that of a sheltered debutante. Jewish students did not mention the possibility that anti-Semitism might account for curtailed social opportunities. Lower-middle-class or ethnic students also did not suspect nativism as a factor. Rather, students like Patricia and Judith blamed themselves for their inability to relax, have fun, and mold themselves into a model coed. This fear of not fitting in, or of being somewhat lacking in comparison to seemingly more self-confident peers, is of course a common experience among adolescents in modern times. Yet in the case of the women who began their education on the eve of Pearl Harbor, we witness not just their adolescent angst but also a cultural clash. From the onset, female students whose recent past had introduced them to concepts of women's roles and responsibilities at odds with the upper-class femininity that reigned on campus faced an uphill battle. Daily encounters between students reproduced the psychological discourse that portrayed the styles, interests, and behavior of upper-class debutantes as evidence of mature adjustment. Because this discourse naturalized a class- and ethnicity-based bias, it rendered alternative styles and interests illegitimate. For nontraditional students, the onset of their studies thus easily became the start of a personal identity crisis.

Of course, the wartime situation also offered nontraditional students support. As we glean from articles in student newspapers or pamphlets such as the one of the Michigan Women's War Council, the climate of crisis encouraged many women to contest the influence of the debutante as a setter of norms. Despite the fact that many wartime commentators encouraged female students to concentrate on academics and prepare for a postgraduate career, from the onset these calls coexisted with messages of a different kind.

In spite of positive portrayals of women who majored in the sciences, prepared for professional careers, or were active in student politics, most discussions about female contributions to the war effort reflected widespread uneasiness with the prospect of changing gender roles. A number of public commentators and educators called for a long-term adjustment of women to the challenges of new political and economic realities, but their arguments coexisted with the warnings of those who feared adverse social consequences, should women continue to expand their influence and gain more independence. Especially against the backdrop of the recent Depression-era debate about a crisis of the American family, these voices were powerful.

Commentators' concerns were a response to visible changes in women's public roles. As workers and professionals, women made important gains during the war. Many lower-middle- and working-class women gained access to jobs in the defense industry that paid better than the ones they had held before. In the union movement, demands for pay equity of the sexes for the first time gained support of policy makers and labor leaders. In institutions of higher education, meanwhile, female scholars gained access to instructor positions vacated by men. Observers noted that such advances seemed to translate into a new assertiveness among women, not only in the many women who confidently assumed new roles in public but also in the popular media lauding the courage and competence of women as nurses, as members of the military, and on the home front. This very visibility, however, also boosted efforts to keep changes in family roles limited to the period of national emergency. Reflecting widespread fears of gender and family instability, for instance, policy makers opposed the expansion of child-care facilities for women workers. Attempts to keep the definition of women's roles anchored on their family responsibilities also sped up the defeat of a short-lived proposal, introduced to Congress by James W. Wadsworth and Warren Austin, to draft women to defense-related labor.[63]

In higher education, these concerns about gender-role stability are demonstrated in the hesitance, if not actual hostility, with which administrators and faculty approached the prospect of changing their treatment of women. Policy makers concerned about labor shortages in areas such as science and medicine actually urged for a more concerted utilization of female expertise.[64] Laws introduced during the Depression to prevent women in double-earner households from continuing in their jobs were relaxed. In many academic disciplines, however, scholars feared that an influx of women would negatively affect their professional prestige. Consequently, resistance to the recruitment of women remained high. The field of medicine, the youngest of the professional disciplines, held out especially long before it admitted women and did so only after the shortage of doctors had become acute. In colleges and universities, few women advanced beyond the low status of lecturer.[65] The marginalization of women as scholars and professionals is reflected in the mass media. Although a number of female scholars made essential contributions to their fields, they received at best a casual mention in magazines, and even their own research institutions often neglected to point to them in their official publications.[66] Thus, the effect of the widespread resistance to changing gender roles was a lack of positive images of accomplished women professionals that could potentially have countered the stigmatized image of the female intellectual as a developmentally arrested grind or spinster.

Practical concerns of administrators in colleges and universities further added to the mixed nature of messages directed toward female students. Women's colleges had suffered financially during the Depression. When family budgets recovered, colleges' endowments did, too, but the prospect of losing large numbers of tuition payers to the defense industry was not something educators of women could easily stomach. In coeducational institutions, meanwhile, the military draft once again created a situation in which the financial contributions of women were needed to keep doors open. Concerns about institutional survival translated into a lack of direction for female students. For college men, institutions changed term lengths and course offerings as concessions to the war. In the case of women, however, there were no uniform policies. At some colleges, such as Mount Holyoke in South Hadley, Massachusetts, the college week was adjusted to allow students to take up voluntary labor in defense-related industry. Here as elsewhere, however, school officials emphasized that "the decision" of how and whether to contribute to the national crisis ultimately "depends upon the individual."[67] While the patriotic responsibilities of college men were clearly defined, female students lacked direct encouragement for making choices at odds with traditional ideas of their roles.

In addition to the hesitancy with which educators reacted to the wartime situation, gendered definitions of patriotism also made it possible for women to simply continue social activities in a new patriotic garb. This once again grew out of the period's concern about gender role convergence that is nicely illustrated by the drawing that accompanied a *New York Times* article by Columbia English professor John Erskine about the future roles of women. The viewer sees a group of women dressed in garb traditionally worn by male workers, marching in almost military-like formation, and shouldering agricultural and industrial tools. Although their faces and hairdos are feminine, the picture is reminiscent of New Deal murals of male production workers. Contemporary observers, used to seeing growing numbers of women en route to work in slacks and coveralls, would not have missed the implication that women were becoming more like men.[68]

The inconsistent official response to the wartime contributions of women illustrates the extent of unease with the specter of gender convergence. The government's womanpower campaign actively solicited female contributions to the defense industry. At the same time, however, news coverage also emphasized that new roles ought not to come at the expense of women's femininity. Although today we tend to associate the image of the female defense worker with Norman Rockwell's drawing of a masculine-looking Rosie the Riveter, this picture was actually an exception to the general look of World War II propaganda. Here an emphasis that even employment in heavy industry would not challenge the femininity of American women dominated.[69]

In the case of college women, the discourse that portrayed the cultivation of femininity as a wartime responsibility was particularly strong. Women's magazines featured fiction and nonfiction stories applauding young women who served as hostesses in the newly created United

Service Organizations (USO) for their patriotic service. A 1942 *Woman's Home Companion* article, for example, commended a California woman's organization for hosting parties for service members. To show the service members a good time, the organization enlisted the help of college women: "Sorority girls from near-by colleges have been enrolled as dates and pay six dollars yearly dues."[70] Advertisements in the same magazines, meanwhile, cast the cultivation of sex appeal as another way in which young women ought to contribute to the war effort. Alluding to the inter-war movie star Clara Bow as the "It" girl who had a natural sex appeal that no man could resist, an ad for Evening in Paris makeup featured the slogan "Spell 'It' to the Marine." Another ad for Jergens Face Powder showed a platinum-blond young woman made up, dressed, and coiffured like a 1940s movie star looking seductively at the viewer. Between her fingers, she twirls an Air Force wings insignia like a trophy. She apparently had done her duty to the troops. To those who have not done their duty yet, the ad says: "Be his Pin-Up Girl! Wear your man-captivating shade of New Jergens Face Powder." Even the left wing American Labor Party published ads calling on young women to act as hostesses and entertain the service members.[71] As Marilyn Hegarty has argued, this portrayal of young women in the wartime news media "suggested a patriotic home-front exchange of female (hetero)sexuality for military defense."[72] By being feminine, glamorous, and a good sport, the media implied, a coed could serve her nation.

The appeal of the role of social companion as a patriotic contribution is readily apparent. Students from different backgrounds in a variety of institutions devoted time and energy to serve as hostesses. At events sponsored by the Young Women's Christian Association (YWCA), they danced with and entertained service members on leave. Some students even took matters into their own hands. At Bowling Green University, the YWCA was the official supporter of the "Campus Teen Service Club," but coeds served on the board of directors. According to its official rules, the club was a "social center for service men and civilians." Hostesses had to "attend dances or other functions . . . and help entertain or perform any other patriotic duty."[73] At Mount Holyoke, too, events designed to entertain G.I.s regularly interrupted the academic routine. Even though the college was located in an isolated rural part of western Massachusetts, the nearby Westover air base offered students a ready supply of social opportunities. "Today is the Victory Ball," wrote Grace Gray, a wartime student, and added: "All the kids are going." Alice Rigby, another Mount Holyoke student, also repeatedly went to USO dances. She and a friend, she wrote to her parents, "got all slicked up" and jitterbugged with servicemen. She had "a perfect time," she assured her parents and "found

out more about the Army" than ever.[74] Many other women enthusiasti-
cally and frequently flocked to dances and reported with pride about it in
their letters. Although the military draft, curfews, and gas rationing certainly put a damper on the social whirl on many campuses, parallel efforts
to portray social-hostess duties as a way for young women to express
patriotism supported the social interests of the part of the student population who already enjoyed a privileged position as setters of norms.

Even under favorable wartime conditions, this chapter has shown, the
cards were stacked against women who deviated too far from the coed
ideal. While we need to acknowledge that we are faced with a dominant
norm, in a different respect, the efforts of women from diverse backgrounds to mold themselves after it reflect the considerable social fluidity
of the period. Despite the fact that the hierarchy of desirable traits and
styles in the student culture had a basis in prejudices, the seemingly
neutral language of personality combined with the idealism of the war
years to bring access to elite status within reach of new groups. Wartime
propaganda might not have undermined campus conventions. It did,
however, stress the idea that in the United States of America, a person's
social position depended on individual effort alone. Intersecting with the
language of personality, this discourse thus loosened the definition of
class. This, too, influenced college women who encountered peers in
dormitories, at social mixers, or during extracurricular activities. When
women such as Helene Harmon or Judith Lauterbach confronted fellow
students from the traditional elite, they did not assume that class,
religion, or ethnicity might put them in a different league. Rather, they
believed that social prestige depended on cultivating the right kind of
style. While the threat of being labeled a wallflower or grind was the stick
that pushed women into conformity to peer conventions, the promise of
an elevated social status that went with it was the carrot.

Considering that newcomers to college saw in the successful mastery
of campus conventions a path toward membership in an elite, we might
wonder if their infatuation with campus life did necessarily harm them.
Historians who have examined encounters between different groups
have emphasized in recent years that assimilation is not a one-way street.[75]
Even populations faced with groups that own considerable power advan-
tages often manage to leave at least a partial imprint on the dominant
culture with which they interact. It seems useful, therefore, to look
beyond the emphasis women put on living up to the outward markers of
coed femininity and sophistication. Nowadays, theorists of education
actually suggest a link between immersion in social activities and the
achievement of "educational excellence."[76] To investigate the extent to
which midcentury college women genuinely internalized conservative

gender ideals, we need to look in more depth and over a longer term at the way in which they responded to their environment. As the next chapter shows, although the conservative elements of student culture not only survived the war but were actually strengthened by postwar gender conservatism, exposure to college life affected young women from diverse backgrounds in very complex ways. The clash between student culture and mores and conventions in their families of origin forced nontraditional ones especially to define new values and defend them publicly. In the process, they developed critical skills. Combined with political and intellectual factors, the social environment of college thus helped turn young women into critical thinkers and public speakers who would learn to question the sentiments held in their communities of origin and even in the nation at large.

2   "But Dad!"

CAMPUS LIFE AND
CRITICAL THINKING

In 1946 sixteen-year-old Janet Brown from the Hudson River Valley small town of Newburgh entered the private, residential, all-women's Mount Holyoke College in rural Massachusetts with the help of a scholarship. Janet was the first in her extended family to have the opportunity to get a formal degree. Her father was a sales manager for DuPont and her mother had been trained as a classical pianist. Both, however, came from an impoverished background. In addition, the Depression had hurt the Browns, and they were still struggling financially when their only child left for college. Like many students away from home in an age before it became cheap and easy to make a long-distance call, Janet regularly wrote letters to her family and in them described in a gushing tone her experiences at mixers and dances. Over time a topic of a different kind began to appear in letters between Janet and her father: politics. Janet was by no means an aggressively argumentative correspondent. One might even argue that she mapped her political allegiances onto her parents. It would certainly have pleased her father, a staunch Republican, that in October 1946 his little girl attended a rally with Senator Henry Cabot Lodge Jr. But by the second semester of her first year, Janet's views and those of her father were diverging.

The development of Janet's political views shows in the correspondence she had with her father about the political situation in Great Britain, where, since 1945, the Labour Party was in power. Under Prime Minister Clement Attlee, the United States' wartime ally had nationalized major industries and passed a comprehensive health care bill.[1] Although her father's letters did not survive, it is clear from the correspondence that he held a strongly negative view of these developments. In the eyes of Mr. Brown, the British policies were even worse than the Roosevelt administration's New Deal. Should the United States ever embark on a similar course, it would spell the ruin of a middle-class family man like himself. Janet, however, saw the matter differently. "And Dad," she wrote, "perhaps you wouldn't have the money to pay the bills in Socialist England, but I would be going to college on scholarship and have all expenses paid! Seriously, I am against Socialism from what I have been reading in the British newspapers, The Economist, etc., [but] the health bill may work out all right."[2]

Considering the passion and acrimony with which a later generation of student radicals would argue with their elders over, for instance, the Vietnam War, this quote is certainly rather tame. But although she wrote in a light tone and highlighted her anticommunist credentials, Janet still left us with a remarkable source. At home, her Republican father was the opinion leader in the family when it came to politics, and Janet was familiar with his criticism of government expansion and economic regulations under the New Deal. While away from home, however, she had not only begun to formulate political views of her own; her letter suggests that she had started to see herself as a person with insights that her father should very well consider. As she informed him, she had reviewed the topic thoroughly by studying British newspapers. Following this examination of the sources, she concluded that some of the policies of a left-wing administration might actually be quite reasonable. Janet thus cordially informed her father that she was no longer simply taking for granted the truth and value of the political views held at home. She had learned a methodology and was now able to present alternative views in an articulate fashion. Her lighthearted remark might even entail a hint of criticism. If her dad could just for a moment forget his preconceived notions that the policies of the Labour government spelled the end of free enterprise, her words imply, and if he instead examined the situation in an unbiased fashion, he, too, might see the benefits of certain proposals instead of rejecting everything a socialist party proposed out of hand.

Granted, this letter includes but a very faint rebuke of political partisanship. This notwithstanding, however, we need to see it as a challenge to patriarchal authority. As Mr. Brown would not have missed, his daughter no longer accepted his view without question. She instead had come to see herself as a person who was perfectly capable of making her own judgments. This chapter will demonstrate that many more members of Janet Brown's generation of college women underwent a similar transformation. Through a number of case studies, it illustrates the factors and the dynamics that turned a cohort of outwardly unrebellious and conforming college women into critical and, even more importantly, outspoken thinkers. These findings confirm in part a general dynamic that historians of female higher education have found by looking at a variety of time periods. By highlighting factors specific to the middle of the twentieth century, however, this chapter deepens insights into the way in which demographic, intellectual, and political trends of the Cold War affected educated young women's identity.

Barbara Solomon, one of the first historians to write a comprehensive study of women in higher education, has already found that there is a difference between official pronouncements about the purpose of a college education for women and the actual experience of it. In spite of ambivalent messages about why a woman should need an advanced education at all—should it prepare her better to be an educated wife and mother, or for a professional career?—the actual experience of studying subjects in depth, of interacting with professors, and of debating with peers often had a very concrete impact on the identity of women. Young women experienced themselves as academically gifted; developed thinking, organizing, and even leadership skills; and were thus encouraged to fashion conceptions of their roles and responsibilities that could be a lot broader than their society or home community granted them. These insights have been elaborated primarily, however, for those time periods in which only a very small number of women sought access to advanced degrees at all. When it comes to the era of mass higher education and the immediate post–World War II period in particular, writers tend to highlight the ways in which student cultures reproduce heteronormativity and exercise conformist pressures on women.[3] The following pages will illustrate, by contrast, that the relationship between the social and academic realm in institutions of higher education was a lot more complex than a look at the way college women presented themselves outwardly and in social settings suggests.

Women who went to college in the middle of the twentieth century did so in a context that was shaped by demographic and ideological factors specific to this period. The students who began their education during World War II and the early Cold War belonged to the first cohort that benefited from an unprecedented broadening of access to higher education. After years of Depression, the prospering economy led not only to an expansion of the middle class in numbers but also added new ethnic groups to this demographic. Middle-class lifestyles were increasingly possible for families that a generation earlier would still have been working class and could not have dreamt of sending an offspring to college. Many of these newly affluent Americans had a Catholic or Jewish background and came from neighborhoods and regions outside the urban Northeast where the traditional members of the WASP elite tended to be concentrated. The young women left their newly middle-class families, whether for the day or the semester, for a college setting in which attitudes and values were often significantly different than in their home communities. In this new environment even under relatively favorable wartime conditions, as the previous chapter has highlighted, the ability of career- and academically oriented students to change the conventional patterns of campus life was limited. At the same time, however, the academic set-ting, even at the height of the Cold War, remained a place where students learned to question authority.

Post–World War II campuses were staging grounds for the domestic Cold War. By the early 1950s, state and federal investigative committees had turned their attention to colleges and universities to ferret out those who might harbor sympathies for left-wing ideas. As Ellen Schrecker has successfully shown, many individuals in the "Ivory Tower" were ultimately complicit in the persecution of unpopular thinkers.[4] Yet many intellectuals and scholars struggled intensely with the question of how to establish a balance between national security interests and First Amendment rights. More heavily invested in the idea of freedom of inquiry than nonscholars, many academics spoke out against the state's curtailment of their liberties. Trying to protect themselves and their institutions, they compared the practices of government investigators to those of totalitarian regimes and argued that for democracy to survive there needed to remain spaces shielded from encroachment by the organs of the state. Higher education, the thesis went, ought to remain such a protected environment.[5] Because this discourse was quite strong in colleges and universities, it actually remained possible, in spite of the spread of censorship and the persecution of subversives, to discuss a broader range of viewpoints in this environment than elsewhere. Consequently, students from diverse backgrounds tended to find that beliefs taken for granted or considered common sense in their families and home towns were at least scrutinized if not openly questioned on campus. Moreover, because of the authorita-tive and elite aura with which higher education was imbued, newcomers to this environment tended to grant more legitimacy to the values and conventions they encountered here, than to those in their families. Exposure to higher education could therefore encourage students to consider themselves as part of an intellectual vanguard that stood above the average American. When students from diverse backgrounds started college, they learned more than to conform. They also learned to engage with views and practices they had long taken for granted, and gained practice defending their arguments in front of skeptics. In the process, they became critical thinkers.

To understand the complex impact of college on the budding identi-ties of young women, one needs to look beyond their preoccupation with social life. Although social and dating experiences often dominate correspondence and private reflections, many students followed public debates. During the war, they were particularly attentive to speakers who addressed their responsibility as educated women in the current crisis. Liberal Christian theologian Reinhold Niebuhr, for instance, was a popular lecturer. "Gosh, he's got such a brilliant mind," gushed Janet Kedney, a woman who attended Smith College on a scholarship, in a letter home in 1943.[6] A year later, Grace Gray, a science major at Mount Holyoke, echoed her sentiment after a meeting with the prominent intellectual: "He was absolutely marvelous. I've never heard anyone like him."[7] Another Mount Holyoke student who usually filled her correspondence with details about USO events and loved to "jitterbug" with servicemen also attended lectures on the political situation overseas. And from Iowa State College, farmer's daughter Beverly George assured her parents in a letter that she was "furiously reading [war correspondent] Ernie Pyle's 'Here is Your War.'"[8]

Although the subjects shifted, students continued to write about political events once peace returned. As their writings suggest, postwar students frequently encountered discussions of civil rights, economic issues, and international politics. One of the first political talks Janet Brown mentioned in the letters to her Republican parents was a "most disturbing talk" by the African American civil rights activist Bayard Rustin about "the negro situation."[9] Another one of her contemporaries, Smith College student Judith Raskin, assured her parents that she was following the news: "Yes—I've read about the [National Labor Relations Board]— and I am sick over it as you must be!"[10] Judith Lauterbach, too, did not just worry about the extent of her popularity. In letters to her father, she also informed him about what she was reading for her classes and about her thoughts about current political events.[11]

When the 1940s turned into the 1950s, political anticommunism and the spread of prosperity fueled conformity in the nation at large. The greater availability of money, transportation, and men, meanwhile, led to a renaissance of the merely social components of campus life. Still, students grappled with intellectual and political questions. Not only did I continue to find references to intellectual subjects mixed in with student accounts of social life, college women also displayed a willingness to consider the value of ideas that were already dismissed as subversive in many other environments. The stay of Alice Gorton at Smith College, for instance, coincided with the rise of McCarthyism in the early 1950s. The young woman from an affluent Ohio suburb heard the senator speak when he came to her alma mater. This notwithstanding, in 1953 the English major picked up the work of British literary critic Christopher St. John Sprigg, who was publishing under the pseudonym Caudwell. She knew that he had been a member of the Communist party in the 1930s and had died in the Spanish Civil War. Yet while these biographical details would have discredited the author in the eyes of many of Alice's contemporaries, she recorded in her diary that she was "having a great time . . . have found a new person: Christopher Caudwell (alias Sprigg) a Communist critic . . . who died in Spain in 29. Wrote a book called Studies in a Dying Culture . . . Mmmm, how I relish new ideas!" The same year, when she heard that Socialist leader Norman Thomas would speak at the New School in New York City, she planned to attend.[12] A few years later on the West Coast, in letters to her parents, Susan Sperry Borman described lectures on philosophy, and in 1958 was no less excited about hearing civil rights activist Bayard Rustin speak than her East Coast peer at Mount Holyoke had been in the late 1940s. In her letters to her parents, she also reported that, as the chair of a panel composed of "a Jew, a Catholic, a Protestant, a Negro, and a first generation American" she was preparing to moderate a discussion on the origins of religious and racial stereotypes.[13]

One can see in the evidence that the academic setting encouraged students to explore a broad range of political ideas and get involved in social issues. Yet the question of how this shaped the identity of students cannot be answered as easily. The women quoted here in many respects tried to fit into the peer culture and aspired to be popular. None of them saw herself as a political radical. They all participated in conventional campus life. In fact, in letters and personal writings, accounts of dances, parties, football games, and dates dominate. If their interest in politics and academics was merely fleeting, however, it might not have affected women's identity in a significant manner, nor left an imprint on the student culture. In addition, the fact that many of these young women attended college with the help of a scholarship or, in the case of Jews and Catholics, represented a religious minority on campus complicates the question of how to evaluate their statements. In fact, it is entirely possible that the discussions of academic or political topics in the papers of nontraditional students were of a defensive nature. After all, their families had made financial sacrifices or were aware of the precarious social position of their particular ethnic or religious group. In the eyes of parents, a daughter's immersion in campus life could easily look like a waste of opportunity or a danger to respectability. In many of the homes of these young women, a concern with popularity and social opportunities would have been treated as a problem. In this context, emphasizing academic or political interests in letters to parents might simply have served to assuage familial worries or to defend against accusations of frivolously wasting family resources. Diarists, meanwhile, might have expressed an intellectual curiosity and idiosyncratic interests that they would not publicly admit. As will become clear from the case studies in this chapter, the cultural and political developments of the midcentury left an imprint on the environments in which college women operated and on their identity.

The end of World War II brought with it a widening gender gap in higher education. In the case of men, international and economic developments encouraged increased specialization and research orientation in academic programs and departments. Women, by contrast, were increasingly channeled into liberal arts programs where they received a broad cultural education and training in moral and character development. These separate educational paths prepared the sexes very unevenly for the challenge of competing in a society in which Americans increasingly needed formal degrees for careers that paid well and were personally satisfying.

The most significant factor in the growing gender gap in higher education was the Serviceman's Readjustment Act of 1944, which brought formal degrees within reach of millions of returning veterans. At the height of its impact in 1947, 69 percent of the male student body received benefits under the "G.I. Bill of Rights." Men went to a range of educational institutions, from vocational schools and junior colleges to liberal arts colleges, but with the help of government tuition, many opted for the nation's most prestigious schools. The presence of veterans in the Ivy League was particularly consequential because the Ivy League established standards of what counted as prestigious and desirable, especially in the realm of social and extracurricular activities. As many lesser-known colleges and universities modeled their cultures after the standards set by the Ivies, the developments in these prestigious institutions affected more students than just those who actually attended them.[14]

Veterans changed the student culture in various ways. Despite the popular perception that the G.I. Bill democratized higher education, recent historical studies have shown that most veterans who went to college with the help of government subsidies would have been able to do so with or without it.[15] However, because of their nontraditional age and experience, veterans transformed the environments they entered. These were men who had served in a war allegedly fought in defense of American ideals of equality, and they considered access to opportunities an entitlement. They had spent time in the tightly controlled setting of the military and saw deployment as the beginning of a less regimented life.[16] When these men, upon starting their college education, found their access to fraternities, athletic teams, or other prestigious clubs and organizations barred by younger students, who might have the right family name but who lacked a military record, they were not likely to accept the status quo. As traditional male students soon learned, former service members were not likely to conform uncritically to campus rules and conventions. Older and more experienced than their nonveteran peers, they were not intimidated by the hierarchy of popularity based on access to exclusive clubs and fraternities.

Veterans also brought with them an unusually heightened interest in intellectual pursuits. For men who had just left the armed forces, conventional campus life, with its focus on social clubs and athletics, looked not only childish but also out of step with the demands of the nuclear age. In the World War II military, training and skill influenced rank. Scholars from a range of disciplines had lent their expertise to the war effort. Moreover, veterans had witnessed human suffering and atrocities that many of these young men found hard to comprehend. All of these experiences influenced what former G.I.s expected to gain from their education. Aware that economic success in the future would depend more on specialized knowledge than on character and a broad cultural background, veterans demanded career-directed courses. Eager to comprehend the sources of human hatred and prejudice, they expected real-life relevancy from the curriculum. The G.I. Bill thus brought to college a population of students who expected college to turn them into skilled professionals with expertise in solving complex problems.[17]

Achievement-oriented veterans benefited not only from the fact that they had strength in numbers but also from the fact that they started their education in what Ellen Herman labeled the "age of experts." Postwar Americans had a distinctly ambivalent attitude toward scientific expertise. On the one hand, many looked with confidence into a future that promised greater comforts and security with the help of science and technology. Others, on the other hand, worried about the destructive potential of nuclear technology. The possibility that new laborsaving devices and the growth of the entertainment industry would cause the strength of the nation to deteriorate was an additional specter. The question of the relative danger or promise inherent in technological developments aside, however, the recent war had demonstrated that to remain a successful global player, a modern nation needed to utilize scientific knowledge. In the post–World War II period, the prestige of the academically trained expert that had begun to grow after World War I thus came into its-own and would only increase with government investment into research universities in the course of the 1950s.[18]

A number of additional factors would make it socially more acceptable for postwar male students to display studious and career-oriented attitudes. For one, ideological challenges to the dominance of the WASP elite made the label of the "grind" less threatening for men. Once the full extent of the Holocaust became clear, the practices of prestigious student organizations to exclude Jewish and Catholic newcomers to college appeared in an increasingly negative light. Ordered by the Truman administration, the 1947 Report of the President's Commission on Higher Education for Democracy, for instance, criticized discriminatory practices against racial and religious minorities. Civil rights activists, meanwhile, drew on the idealist wartime rhetoric and on recent scholarly publications to challenge discrimination. Benefiting from the growing influence of disciplines such as culture-personality study or psychoanalysis, they presented group prejudices as signs of a pathological or backward, uneducated, mindset. With this much attention devoted to the uneven treatment of minorities, it was becoming a lot more controversial to air nativist, anti-Jewish, or racist attitudes in public.[19]

Challenges to racial and ethnic biases also impacted admissions practices. As a way to handle the swelling number of applications, most colleges after the war adopted the Scholastic Aptitude Test (SAT). Standardized tests, first administered during World War I, had initially been strongly biased in favor of "Nordic" races and students from north-eastern prep schools. Especially in the Ivy League colleges, they had been used to weed out applicants with the wrong family background. The crafters of the postwar SAT, however, made an effort to eliminate past biases and instead tried to find ways to test for "pure intelligence." By the late 1940s, the SAT was firmly on its way of becoming the universal entrance test for all college applicants nationwide.[20]

The cumulative impact of these ideological and cultural factors would affect the college experience of men as a group. When campus life lost some of its exclusive aura, the link between status and conformity to upper-middle-class culture unraveled. In addition, after SAT scores rather than family backgrounds opened doors to prestigious schools to students with diverse backgrounds and a variety of goals, the range of acceptable behavior broadened. The athlete who excelled on the football field was certainly still one of the big men on campus, but the academic achiever had gained a lot in prestige.

To say that the American system of higher education was now a meritocracy, however, would be an exaggeration. Race and gender limited the extent to which young Americans benefited from the transformation of academia. Although European ethnics were increasingly accepted as a part of "white" America and questions of racial justice were becoming more and more central to the postwar liberal progressive agenda, discrimination against African Americans and Hispanics remained high. White women also did not initially benefit from the democratization of higher education to the same degree as white men. While issues of racial discrimination were moving to the top of the liberal progressive reform agenda, the same cannot be said for sexism. Because women were presumed to have achieved equality after they got the vote, the limitations on the opportunities for female students received very little attention from academics and politicians.

The trends that changed higher education for men did not leave their female peers entirely unaffected. When the postwar economic boom broadened the ranks of the middle class, for the first time, many families were able to send a daughter to college. As a result of challenges to discriminatory admission practices, the female student body also continued to diversify in its ethnic and religious composition—a trend that especially benefited Jewish and Catholic women. Yet in spite of these trends, the effects of the G.I. Bill sharply limited the degree of diversification of the female student population.

Although the G.I. Bill essentially amounted to a federal student aid program, women were disadvantaged by the reality that subsidies were made available only to veterans (mostly male), could not be transferred to family members, and were not offered to defense industry workers.[21] In the midst of the flood of male newcomers to higher education, it was easy to overlook that the number of female students had also reached an all-time high.[22] Many women who were interested in formal degrees, however, would find it difficult to finance their education. Because few scholarship opportunities existed, aside from the subsidies under the G.I. Bill, women who lacked access to private funds faced an uphill battle. Veterans did not have to foot the bill for tuition, books, supplies, or even housing, but in the case of their female peers, either the student herself or her parents had to shoulder the costs. As suggested by statistics from the early 1950s, the lack of access to government subsidies kept at a high the proportion of women from the kind of affluent families that had traditionally made up the cultural elite. At a time when only 6 percent of all Americans had a college degree, by 1953 44 percent of women graduates came from families in which at least one parent was a college alumnus. In almost half (45 percent) of these cases, women's families had financed their daughters' education in entirety (compared to 17 percent of their male peers) and only 29 percent of female graduates had contributed more than half of the costs of college (compared to 58 percent of men).[23] Just when the female student body was diversifying in its regional, religious, and ethnic background, the needs and interests of this new population were marginalized not only due to the heavy presence of men but also on account of the strong representation of the daughters of the old WASP elite.

With women's percentage as a proportion of the student body at an all-time low, men's demand for, and interest in, higher degrees also dominated discussions in the popular media and government. Traditionally, resistance to federal aid for education had been very high, and the G.I. Bill passed mainly because fear of social upheaval caused by the return of veterans softened opposition in Congress. Even the supporters of the educational provisions in the bill believed initially that the subsidies for housing and job training would be most attractive to veterans. Once ex-G.I.s' large interest in college became apparent, however, the media turned the march of these men into a realm that had once been reserved for a tiny elite into a prime piece of evidence for the superiority of the American style of government. In this narrative, women were merely sidekicks. Academic accomplishments and scholarly expertise remained marked as distinctly male in the public image, and in none of the period's important official reports on the status of higher education did issues of gender discrimination in academia receive more than a fleeting mention.[24] All through the early Cold War, organizations urged stronger support for women who wanted careers in academia or the professions.[25] Lacking sufficient clout, however, they did not manage to turn this into a topic that received national attention. Up to the point when G.I. Bill benefits expired in 1954, young women would find it hard to enter coeducational universities and professional programs. Facing quotas and caps on freshman enrollment, many female applicants found themselves rejected or on waiting lists.[26] For the affluent, women's colleges remained a possibility. For their less privileged peers, however, teacher training programs and a small number of community colleges were often the only option.

As an unfortunate side effect, the success of the G.I. Bill drew attention away from the way in which their gender handicapped women interested in advanced degrees. Writers of official reports and members of legislative commissions were not ignorant of the postwar patterns in female higher education. They took note of the dwindling number of women in fields in which they had been well represented during the war. They also noticed that female students tended to cluster either in the liberal arts or in teacher training programs. Most observers, however, did not dwell long on the question of push and pull factors at work.[27] In the eyes of most, the patterns in female higher education stemmed from women's lack of interest in professional or academic careers. Although after World War II women flocked to college in numbers larger than ever, educators and policy makers interpreted the baby and marriage boom as evidence that the main motivation to go to college for female undergraduates was to catch a husband. Just at the moment when it was growing more and more difficult to gain entry into a professional position without an advanced degree, female students' own actions seemed to confirm that they were not really interested in competing with men.

The seeming lack of interest in careers and advanced studies put supporters of a comprehensive liberal arts education for women on the defense. Because a majority of college women seemed to choose conventional life paths, it was easy to argue that institutions of higher education should concentrate on preparing them for their domestic and reproductive role. Higher education would help these women best, the argument went, if it helped them become skilled in child psychology and housekeeping and to aid their adjustment to adult sex-role expectations.[28] A number of institutions created anew or strengthened their fields of home economics. They also instituted lecturers, classes, and invited guest speakers to help prepare young women for their conjugal futures. At the State University of Iowa, an interested student could listen to lectures about "Emotional Maturity in Marriage." For "brides of the future," there was even a noncredit course called "Major in Marriage." As the school promoted it: "If you're interested in marriage—and what girl isn't?—here is a group for you." To facilitate relationships between college men and women, the administration also sponsored large-scale mixers in the college gym.[29] In this Iowa was an early example for a trend that soon unfolded all over the nation. As Kristin Celello has shown, marriage courses and classes in "family life education" became increasingly common in the course of the 1950s. While she found it impossible to determine how many students actually took a course like this, her own anecdotal evidence supports the claim that heteronormative pressures on the Cold War campus increased dramatically.[30]

In this already difficult situation, cultural anxieties put caps on the extent to which even institutions with a good record of fostering female leadership and academic potential were able to serve the interests of talented and academically high-achieving students. All through the postwar period, there were a number of organizations that warned of the negative consequences women's choices would have over the long run. Marriage and motherhood seemed small yields for the costly investment into higher education. For the individual woman, a failure to use what she had learned might bring personal dissatisfaction and frustration. For the nation, it meant a loss of intellectual resources. Some of the flagship colleges of the Seven Sisters resisted the trend toward a feminized curriculum. Smith, Wellesley, and Mount Holyoke colleges all made mainly minor adjustments to their class catalogue. Here as elsewhere, many educators promoted honors courses and extracurricular activities that would equip female students with in-depth knowledge needed for graduate studies. The branches of the YWCA also never ceased to provide female students with training in leadership. From the start, however, support for a comprehensive education for women competed with a narrative of a different kind.

Widespread anxieties over family stability, on which—according to the great majority of social science experts—the stability of the nation depended as well, fueled the expansion not only of the marriage counseling movement but also of pro-natal efforts to encourage the white middle-class in particular to have more children.[31] Although the postwar period is famous for its statistics of escalating birth rates, which approached those of India, and a plummeting average age at first marriage, contemporary observers focused more on the fact that the United States featured the highest divorce rate in the Western world, and that the college-educated were still lagging behind in the rate at which they were reproducing. Against this backdrop, the YWCA and the women's colleges struck many observers as especially problematic. Homosocial spaces, they seemed breeding grounds for gender deviancy, depriving the young of wholesome opportunities for contacts with the opposite sex and thereby keeping them in a state of prolonged immaturity. And, in the Freudian lingo of the day, the term "immaturity" connoted nothing less than the specter of lesbianism.

A look at the Seven Sister women's colleges shows their effort to ward off charges of fostering deviancy. In attempts to soften their image as homosocial environments, a number of these institutions added male faculty members. Mount Holyoke College already in 1937 had selected in Roswell G. Ham its first male president ever. Right after the war, the proportion of female professors at Wellesley fell from 90 to 75 percent. At Smith College, the proportion of men on the faculty reached 51 percent by the late 1950s.[32] In 1947 Mount Holyoke College's President Ham assured the parents of prospective and current students that his institution would do its best to turn their daughters into "excellent wives" and to help them in the "acquisition of excellent husbands."[33] Other colleges downplayed the academic facets of the liberal arts education in their promotional brochures and emphasized instead those aspects of their curriculum that could be seen as preparing women to be better mothers and wives.[34] In addition, they increasingly promoted the (hetero-)social components of campus life by packing their brochures with images of fun-loving young women in male company. "There is always a prom" featured in the "picture books regularly published by the public relations departments of the colleges" wrote Vassar professor emeritus of economics Mabel Newcomer in 1959, "as well as informal gatherings that include plenty of well-set-up young men."[35] This claim that they educated women to be better wives and mothers was of course not an entirely new feature, but what heightened its prominence after World War II was an unusually pressing need for single-sex colleges to remake their image. Not only were they vulnerable against the background of resurgent pronatalism and antifeminism, they were also deprived of the government subsidies available to the Ivy League and coeducational institutions as a result of the G.I. Bill. In urgent need of sponsors, women's colleges thus used techniques developed in the burgeoning professions of public relations and advertising to carefully craft and promote a new image. As a result, they helped spread the message that college was first and foremost a place where the foundation for happy marital lives was created.

Antifeminism, however, was by far not the only factor that influenced the situation of women who started their studies after the war. In fact, educators and policy makers also came to believe that only by educating women differently from men would it be possible to accomplish a smooth transition to mass higher education. In spite of the mass media's romance with the story of ex G.I.s-turned-college-men as embodiments of the American dream, veterans' larger than expected interest in higher education constituted a dilemma. Professional, academic, and research positions had always been just a small segment of the U.S. economy. Not only were colleges and universities unprepared to accommodate a large number of students, most higher education officials and policy makers also did not expect the economy to be able to absorb them once they graduated. Investment into research and development in the course of expansion of the military-industrial complex would eventually open new academic jobs. From the vantage point of the immediate postwar period, however, this was not yet clear. For the G.I. Bill to meet its aim of reintegrating veterans into society, it was therefore necessary that women should not compete with men for the same scarce jobs.

A gender-specific curriculum served far more than just the practical economic purpose of neutralizing competition. The appeal of the idea that the sexes ought to be educated in complementary ways also grew because of the substantial cultural anxieties that accompanied the abandonment of the collegiate model of higher education for men. Many academics and public intellectuals felt distinctly ambivalent about the development. On the one hand, it was clear that the nation could no longer rely on well-rounded gentlemen to conduct its affairs in the nuclear age. It was time, growing numbers of public commentators agreed, to adjust the system of higher education so that it could produce the specialized experts the nation needed. This transition, however, also triggered concerns. For one, the new outlook opened access to positions of influence to new groups. University-trained individuals from backgrounds that had so far been underrepresented as part of the political and cultural establishment might now enter the upper echelons of society alongside the scions of the traditional elite. But even if the new experts had the right family background, the trend toward increased specialization worried many educators and public intellectuals. In two studies launched by President Truman's Commission on Higher Education, educators warned that "overspecialization" in liberal arts education was eroding the traditional and important goal of transmitting "a common cultural heritage towards a common citizenship." In the same vein, the Harvard Committee on General Education in a Free Society asserted that "Education must be concerned not only with imparting knowledge and skills but also with producing the 'good man' and the 'good citizen'" through schooling in "values" and "cultural tradition" and by fostering "the capacity for emotional and gregarious life."[36] Educators were not only alarmed by impending changes because they feared a threat to cultural homogeneity. The specter of narrowly specialized technocrats was also frightening against the background of the recent experience with fascist states in which scientists and bureaucrats had followed their interest in advancing science without any concern for ethics and morality. In the nuclear age, the vision of professionals who felt no higher allegiance than to efficiency and technological progress was no less frightening.[37] A complementary education of the sexes, however, seemed to hold the promise of solving the dilemma because it would make it possible to educate the specialists the nation needed while keeping them loyal to a "common cultural heritage."

It is against this backdrop that one of the most frequently cited examples for gender conservatism in higher education needs to be understood. In an address that reached a much broader audience as an essay published in *Women's Home Companion*, the Democratic governor of the state of Illinois, Adlai E. Stevenson, addressed the graduating class of 1955 at the prestigious all-women's Smith College. Acknowledging that, as women who had just successfully completed a comprehensive course of studies in the liberal arts, they might be keen to utilize their skills, he nevertheless encouraged the assembled graduates to embrace the "humble role of housewife." This would not mean, he assured his listeners, to simply swap "Baudelaire" for "the Consumer's Guide." "The peoples of the West," he explained his vision of the "purpose" of an educated modern woman, were at present "in dire trouble." Because the "typical Western man" had "sacrificed wholeness of mind and breadth of outlook to the demands of their specialties," the nation was about to lose its way. But the women who were "hitched to one of these creatures," he proposed, would be able to "rescue us wretched slaves of specialization . . . from further shrinkage and contraction of mind and spirit." Women, Stevenson proposed, should use their education in art, philosophy, and religion to keep their husbands committed to a society in which "the rational values of freedom, tolerance, charity and free inquiry" held supreme and thereby do their part in defeating "totalitarian, authoritarian ideas."[38]

As Stevenson's speech shows, supporters of a gender-specific curriculum did not necessarily want to relegate women to a socially insignificant role. The way they understood it, men would be trained to become technological and scientific specialists while the women they married would serve the important purpose as a reservoir of culture and character. Yet this idea about their role entailed that female students received little prodding to acquire the professional skills needed for economic success in the increasingly specialized economy.

A gendered curriculum did not mean that achievement-oriented students no longer found support for their interests at all, of course. Educators continued, for instance, to encourage their most talented students to take honors classes. Yet by the 1950s the dominant message had clearly become that in order to turn their education into actual opportunities for professional jobs or graduate school, women would need to be exceptionally dedicated. For the majority, combining the tasks of "making homes and whole human beings" might be the more realistic and the more satisfying option.

The rhetoric of women's socially important role as culture brokers aside, the lack of support for female achievement strengthened heteronormative elements of campus life. In line with the idea that their stay in college ought to help young women adjust to adult sex-role expectations, student-run organizations dedicated themselves to giving fashion and dating advice. Female students who conformed to conventional expectations of femininity, meanwhile, were singled out as particularly praiseworthy. "Bee Gee's" women looked "more beautiful than ever" in the season's sported fashions, a writer for Bowling Green State University's student paper, the *Bee Gee News*, rejoiced in 1952.[39] The same institution's Women's Self-Government Association pitched a similar line. It sponsored, for instance, a "style show" for the female members of the incoming class to challenge the saying: "You can always spot a freshman." Years later, its publications still offered a college woman behavioral advice to ensure that she always looked like "the lady" she was.[40] At the State University of Iowa, advanced students also allowed no time to go to waste to educate newly arriving coeds about what mattered most in the student culture. The Cosmopolitan Club recommended: "Circulate . . . radiate. . . . Being popular is easy!" The student-edited "Code for Coeds" confirmed the importance of popularity: "The more friends you have, the more college will mean to you."[41] Freshmen orientation on campuses nationwide all through the 1950s promoted the idea that what mattered most was "sports, dating, and romance," thereby creating an image of college life that one commentator and teacher compared to a "Hollywood musicale" because it had "the same emphasis."[42] Student publications also fed the image of college as a place where young marriages are put on their way. In social pages modeled on those in the *New York Times*, student newspapers reported on couples who had decided to get pinned, engaged, or married. The growing number of college students who made a permanent commitment thus became part of the public record, a trend that could only have increased the pressure on their peers to follow in their footsteps.

Women in single-sex colleges, meanwhile, did not escape the trend toward heightened heteronormative pressures either. Weekends saw a virtual exodus of college women who had received invitations to parties, proms, or athletic games. Alice Silverman, a Smith College freshman in 1948, filled her scrapbook of college life with mementos of social events at various Ivy League institutions. "Smith girls," she quipped, contributed an "impressive sum seasonally to the support of the Boston and Maine and N.Y., N.H. & Hartford R.R., as well as the local cab companies." Quoting a common adage among her peers, she recorded: "As the saying goes, 'you haven't lived' until you've experienced one of these weekend wonders. I often think it would be more appropriate to say 'It's a wonder that you lived through one of them!'" In many other women's writings, too, invitations to parties and football games at Dartmouth, Harvard, Yale, or West Point were among the subjects they considered most noteworthy.[43]

The promotion of heteronormativity took a toll. Statistics suggests that most female students contented themselves with the "humble role of housewife." As historian Eugenia Kaledin cites, graduation rates of female undergraduates fell to 37 percent in the 1950s. These figures do not tell whether it was marriage, financial difficulties, or dissatisfaction with their course of studies that caused women to drop out. The average age of first marriage for educated women plummeted, however, in the immediate postwar period.[44] By the end of the decade, the longstanding concern that education contributed to low birth rates in the upper-middle-class was put to rest. "Today the college students marry so young and have so many children so fast that the problem is how to get them educated first," noted Mabel Newcomer in 1959.[45]

Considering these developments, it will not come as a surprise that even women who had excelled academically in high school were still forcefully pulled into campus life. Alice Gorton, a young woman from the Cleveland suburb of Lakewood, for instance, had won a "News Scholastic Writing Award" in high school. Like Helene Harmon before her, she was self-conscious of her deviation from common behavior patterns among high school youth, yet she, too, tried to assure herself that she was not missing anything important. In an echo of existentialist philosophy that, at the time the young woman was writing, was only just beginning to receive a favorable reception by publishers and the media, Alice described "the instinct of people to pair off" as simply "a futile attempt to ward off the inevitable loneliness" of life.[46] But at Smith College, her outlook changed. Soon, she was immersed in a vibrant social life: "It was glorious," she rejoiced after a party. Having once described herself as socially awkward, she now relished her sense of being "successful" and in reference to her growing popularity recorded "everything else is secondary now."[47] Following her own conversion to campus life, Alice now also became an active reproducer of conventions. In reference to a studious peer, she wrote, "this afternoon" she and some other students had "straightened [her] out": "We told her off good + plenty about the selfishness and the evils of introspection."[48] Other women suggested to peers that it was "crazy" to choose studying over social life, and many women feared that they would earn the stigma of the "greasy grind with B.O." if they privileged their class work or quiet time over the hustle and bustle of campus life.[49]

Quotes by postwar students demonstrate strong elements of continuity in the normative pressures acting on them as well as continuity in the factors that pulled these women into campus life. As diaries and letters suggest, it was not always simply fear of not fitting in that caused behavioral changes but also hope of rising to an elevated social position. This link emerges particularly clearly in quotes of young women who met peers from back home after the onset of college. Class valedictorian June Calender, for instance, had felt "like an outcast" in high school in her native Versailles, a small town in Indiana. This feeling grew as a result of her academic success as well as her family background. The daughter of small-scale farmers, June had contributed to the family economy since childhood. Although the family had expanded and modernized their farm enterprise by the time she reached adolescence, June still had more labor responsibilities than many others of her age group. Her material circumstances thus account for why she found little time for dating in high school. By the mid 1950s, however, the expansion of mass media meant that the language of personality and adjustment had spread. As a result, even June's rural high school classmates saw a personality flaw instead of a different lifestyle. As they opined, June was "stuck-up."[50]

Considering her adolescent experiences, June's response to the collegiate setting will not come as a surprise. At Indiana University in Bloomington, she made a concerted effort to turn herself into "a lady." She soon rejoiced that she was now often "the first girl chosen" at dances at which she "got to dance with the best looking fellows."[51] She was most pleased, however, whenever she got a chance to demonstrate her new popularity to former high school peers. When on a date with a college man, for instance, she met a former classmate from her small town home of Versailles. "We met Linda O. and I was very glad," she wrote. When "the kids from Versailles get together and pool their information" about how the "stuck-up June who didn't date in high school" was doing in college, they would have to admit that she was not doing "too bad." An even greater triumph occurred on a different day when one of her small-town peers spotted her driving with a young man in a car with license plates from out-of-town. "A car full of men pulled up beside us at the drive-in + one of them was Gus M.—I love every chance I have to show off in front of people from Versailles—I felt such an outcast in that environment."[52]

Although June Calender's journal reflects the normative pull of campus life, it also suggests a more complex effect on newcomers to this setting. In conventions, outlooks, and mores, high school students already shared a lot with their slightly older college peers. But women raised in culturally conservative families in small towns, suburbs, or on farms attributed to well-rounded students on campus an air of superiority they had not granted to the adolescents they grew up with. Because of this link between collegiate life and high status, the conventions that students encountered in their new environment were hard to contest. Yet because of this association, newcomers were also encouraged to question beliefs and conventions previously taken for granted.

Because the values in their families and home communities deviated from those that nontraditional students found in college, this new environment confronted these women with a particular intellectual and personal challenge. They would have to find a way to bridge their two often very distinct worlds. Adopting some of the mores and conventions of the student culture would entail having to defend developing new beliefs to parents and relatives. As such, social life could become a first training ground for skills that are also valued in higher education: critical thinking and the ability to present an argument in an authoritative language. As a result, young women became potential challengers to the power structure in their families.

Although written during the war, the journal of Helene Harmon offers important insights into how a daughter's education affected power relations in the family. Before starting her course of studies, Helene did not seem to have been a particularly argumentative adolescent. When the matter of picking a major came up the summer before her first semester, Helene recorded that she wished she could "defy" her parents and follow her own inclination in her journal. But Helene seemed largely to have adhered to moral values and behavioral expectations similar to those of her Catholic parents. On campus, however, Helene learned that to become the kind of modern, sophisticated woman who held status on campus, she would have to collect her own experiences independently of her parents. The effect of this showed in the fact that the young Catholic soon chafed under what she was beginning to see as too tight a rein of parental control.[53]

Helene's growing desire for autonomy shows poignantly in a diary entry she made following a shopping spree. The encounter she described here is in many ways a product of Helene's individual situation as an arts student in a wartime urban locale, but it also illustrates a more general experience of women in higher education in the mid-twentieth century. Visiting the Wanamaker's department store with her mother and her younger brother in December of 1940, Helene ran into a male photographer she had met a little earlier at the Philadelphia School of Industrial Art. Taking Helene's pictures, "Ernest" struck up a flirtatious relationship with the young woman, who was immensely flattered. Ernest, in stark contrast to any young man Helene had ever met before, had an air of worldly sophistication. He was older than she and was an émigré from Austria. Ernest subsequently joined the Harmons for a meal. The encounter seemed to have gone quite well. As Helene wrote, they "had a good time" and Mrs. Harmon talked to the young man about "war and politics." Helene, however, was severely irritated by the fact that her mother did not allow her to be alone with Ernest. In her diary, she vented her anger: "I was rather put out," she wrote about her feelings. Because of the presence of her guardian, she missed a chance to collect mature, independent experiences with a potential beau she would have found more exciting than a discussion of current events. "Why couldn't [mother] have met him . . . and then gracefully retired?" she complained. She "had wished to talk to [Ernest] of quite different things" than "war and politics," and this "would have been the first time [she] had ever gone out to dinner with a man." Her mother, she wrote as she closed the entry, would probably never understand "how disappointed [she] was."[54]

Helene's experiences illustrate a dynamic that many women from nontraditional college backgrounds also experienced. For instance, after the war, Jewish American Merle Judith Marcus also had to bridge the different behavioral expectations in her family of origin and in the collegiate setting. In the process, she, too, came to chafe against patriarchal restrictions of her autonomy.[55] Merle Judith Marcus was accepted at Barnard College in New York City in 1948. Her mother, Antoinette Brody Marcus, was an accomplished musician; her father, Jacob Rader Marcus, a professor of history at Hebrew Union College in Cincinnati. A scholar of Jewish history and prominent reform rabbi, Merle's father would have been very conscious of the way in which ethnicity and religion limited choice. Although its Manhattan location accounts for the fact that, of all the Seven Sisters, Barnard College was the most accessible for Jewish students, Jacob Marcus would have known that the opening of educational opportunities for Jews at prestigious college was relatively recent. Mr. and Mrs. Marcus apparently found it more important for their daughter to benefit from a liberal arts education at a renowned college than to keep her close by and under direct control. This did not mean, however, that they allowed Merle to make autonomous decisions about her life. On the contrary, the influence of Merle's father in particular can be seen all over her personal records. It was her father who suggested to Merle how to best fill out a college questionnaire, and it was also he who offered his opinion on how the young woman ought to conduct herself socially once on her own in New York City. In his opinion, she should be careful not to act in ways that made her stand out in a negative fashion, and he clearly wanted her to concentrate on the academic aspects of her education. "I am," he wrote, "in touch with people who tell me there is a lot of social life in Barnard but I don't want you to go into that too heavily till you know the ropes and have decided what your responsibilities are." Merle's mother backed this line of argument and urged her daughter to heed her father's advice: "Darling," she wrote, "I had a scholarly father who never bothered about my schoolwork which is a handicap you fortunately do not have." Merle, she argued, had "an unusual opportunity," and she should abide by and treasure "any help or suggestions" from her father.[56]

Prior to her departure to Barnard, Merle seems to have acted as a dutiful daughter and followed her father's advice on how to fill out the Barnard questionnaire: "My father, a professor, has stressed the importance of an academic training + the necessity of having a profession," she recorded on a draft that survived in her personal records. Yet while the shadow of her parents' expectations followed her to New York City, other influences soon competed with those of her family of origin. As a letter to a friend Merle wrote during her second year at Barnard reveals, the Marcuses were disappointed by their daughter's academic performance. Merle sought out the help of a tutor in subjects in which she lagged behind. She mockingly informed her friend that her parents did not understand why she had not yet revealed herself to be a "genius," despite such extra counseling. Only a few lines later, however, she shifted the topic of conversation to a vivacious account of her enjoyment of football games and dates with college men.[57]

Merle's personal correspondence illustrates the gap in perspective that easily opened between Jewish American parents who sent their daughters to college after World War II, and their offspring. For the cohort of the older Marcuses, memories of anti-Semitic discrimination, especially in the realm of higher education, were still vivid. As individuals prominently involved in their Jewish community, they would also have grappled intensely with the Holocaust. Their recent memory would have been shaped by the knowledge that, even after the onset of deportations of European Jews to concentration camps in Eastern Europe, the United States had not raised immigration quotas. For them, anti-Semitism remained a force to be reckoned with. Like many assimilated members of the Jewish middle class, the Marcuses countered prejudice by trying to distance themselves from stereotypes about the character and intelligence of Jews. Here they would have had in mind in particular the working-class immigrants from Eastern Europe who entered the country in rising numbers in the late nineteenth century. Embracing a similar strategy adopted by African American middle-class households, they tried to instill in Merle a sense of the importance of proving herself the epitome of respectability. They warned her about risking her reputation by joining campus life before she had learned the "ropes." They reminded her to always watch her English and her spelling. In short, by no means should she resemble in behavior or appearance a member of the Jewish immigrant groups that had in the past received a hostile reception from Protestant Americans. To prove herself the best of her "race," she ought to conform to the standards of respectability and decorum that were also upheld in the WASP circles of polite society.[58]

For Merle, by contrast, her parents' emphasis on respectability no longer made the same sense. By the time she entered Barnard College, older prejudices had not suddenly disappeared. In fact, "day students" who hailed from inner-city New York neighborhoods and who were often from a Jewish working-class background remained marginalized in campus life after World War II.[59] Yet Judith did begin her education at a time when Jews made up an unprecedented proportion of the student body. Moreover, her young adulthood coincided with a time when anti-Semitism was deemed a thing of the past in liberal rhetoric and in popular culture.[60] In reflection on this generational gap, Merle's Jewish peers at Barnard likewise found it more important to establish their right to collect experiences than to prove that they were beyond moral reproof. In the process, these young women assimilated into a dominant culture shaped by Protestant, white, middle-class, and heteronormative values. But they also became challengers of the mores, conventions, and power relations in their family of origin.

The complex effect of exposure to higher education on the identity of young women is particularly clear in the letter of "Tasha," a woman from Merle's circle of college friends. Although there is not a lot of information about this woman's personal circumstances in the Marcus papers, Tasha seemed to have completed her course of study by the time she was writing. Her letter came from Germany where she had gone in the company of her fiancé. Abroad, the relationship dissolved. Subsequently, Tasha's parents expected her to return home and resume living with them. But their child had different plans. She considered herself "old enough to make [her] own decisions." Her parents, the friend informed Merle, were "convinced that [she was] on the road straight to hell." Rather than being devastated by her broken engagement, Tasha wanted to take advantage of the opportunity to collect social and romantic experiences while traveling and working abroad. This behavior was morally unacceptable in the eyes of her parents. Tasha contested their arguments in a highly articulate fashion, substantiating her argument by drawing from the political rhetoric of the time. "They accuse me of libertinism rather than being concerned with my liberty," she vented in her letter and proceeded to describe her interactions with her parents. "Their argument is that for all their sacrificing, the only thing they want is for me to continue living as they taught me and be a 'good daughter.' . . . They claim to love me. And yet as far as I can see, love is evident in the amount of trust one has for the person one loves, and they trust me as far as they can throw me. If I do not take advantage of the situation . . . before me now, I shall . . . probably be tied to my parents indefinitely—which is not desirable."[61]

As Tasha's letter illustrates, she had developed ideas about her rights and her opportunities that were quite at odds with the postwar promotion of stable gender and family roles. What is even more important, she had developed a language that allowed her to justify individualistic goals. Whether in her case we can credit her college experience with having produced such an effect is not clear. A person living through the early Cold War years certainly did not have to pursue an advanced degree to read about the lofty ideal of "liberty," or to learn about the importance of maturity.

The link between college experience and the ability of young women to challenge power relations in their families shows also quite clearly in the journal of Helene Harmon. After the disappointment that followed her meeting with Ernest at Wanamaker's wore off, Helene made sure that she got her chance for a tête-à-tête with the émigré photographer. While the summer before she started college she had still agreed with her elders about the need for youth to grow up shielded and protected, her views began to diverge from those of her parents. This shows, for instance, in a talk between Helene and her mother about a young couple that had eloped together. Marian Grace Harmon thoroughly disapproved. Not so her daughter. "I always wanted to run off myself," wrote Helene. "To my mind all that big church weddings are, is a show for friends and relatives."[62] She found far more appealing the image of a young couple who defied their elders and eloped.

Helene's change of view soon began to influence her behavior. In the process, family dynamics in the Harmon household changed. Helene increasingly sought out the opportunities she had missed. Not only did she meet with Ernest on her own, she also went "to dinner, to the movies" with other young men at her college and joined a mixed-sex crowd of peers from her college for social fun and excursions. She frequently came home late at night. These activities led to tensions with her mother. Yet Marian Grace Harmon was no longer willing to deny her daughter the opportunities she so eagerly sought. Although Helene described her mother in her journal as concerned about her behavior, Marian did not want to "forbid" her daughter to meet with young men all on her own because Helene would then only "deceive her" and meet them "on the sly."[63] Mrs. Harmon had thus grown unwilling to exercise her parental authority. Rather, she tried to foster a relationship with her daughter in which Helence felt she could talk to her and turn to her for help in case she needed it.

That the relationship between the two Harmon women developed in this fashion is a remarkable feat and far from predetermined. Since the 1920s, progressive writers of marital advice books had promoted more democratic relations in the family as a means to modernize the institution. Catholic families, however, had remained more resistant to changing power relations in the family and were more protective of daughters than their contemporaries in the urban Protestant middle class. Only in the 1960s would behavioral patterns in Catholic families catch up with nationwide general trends.[64] Moreover, when the numbers of young Americans who married young and often after only a short engagement period skyrocketed during the mobilization and war, advice writers responded with alarm. Even though Mrs. Harmon might have been exposed to a critique of authoritarian parent–child relations, it is unlikely that she saw challenges to the traditional division of power in a positive light. When the Harmons sent their daughter to college, however, they were put on a separate trajectory from their Catholic contemporaries.

Helene Harmon's diary suggests that she had indeed begun to function as a broker of culture. Rather than keeping a "Western husband" committed to civic virtues, however, she introduced new family-role expectations into her parental household. Her education had introduced Helene to a language with which she could defend her interests. Moreover, her status as a student gave her an air of authority. Thus equipped, she succeeded in gaining permission to join the dating culture of her peers. Despite occasional tensions with her mother, her behavior did not seem to have caused major rifts. The way in which Helene defended the legitimacy of her views does therefore seem to have been successful. Exposure to student life, Helene's example indicates, thus had a complex impact. It did not simply reinforce heteronormativity. It also led young women to chart paths of their own.

An urban young woman who associated with theater majors and dated an émigré photographer, Helene Harmon might not be a typical mid-century adolescent. But important commonalities exist between her and other students from diverse backgrounds. When behavioral expectations in families of origin clashed with those in the collegiate setting, women tended to give more legitimacy to the mores in their new environment than their old. Because the college setting was imbued with an air of authority that non-college-educated family members lacked, female adolescents came to believe that they and their peers had superior insights over traditional authorities. Arguments frequently centered on questions of dating and participation in the commercial youth culture. But more than just young women's attitudes toward social pursuits were affected. Especially after the Cold War heated up, college women would also find that their political views and those in their families of origin were drifting apart.

Although the apolitical inclinations of college men and women were a recurring theme in media coverage of student life, the actual political climate on wartime and Cold War campuses was actually quite complex. Already during the war, speakers such as Reinhold Niebuhr or First Lady Eleanor Roosevelt had appealed to students' idealism and urged them to dedicate themselves to the defense of American democracy beyond the duration of the war. This momentum in favor of political activities, as historians of the Cold War have amply demonstrated, suffered with the return of prosperity and the escalation of the domestic hunt for subversives. Politicians trying to discredit New Deal Democrats were often especially suspicious of college and university faculty because they saw academia as a stronghold of liberalism. Whether this was true or not, many academics and administrators collaborated with investigative committees, marginalized controversial colleagues, and engaged in self-censorship.[65] Especially because of this embattled position of a faculty body tainted by association with liberalism, however, the political and intellectual climate in the "Ivory Tower" remained in important ways distinct from the Cold War consensus spreading in the nation at large.

By the late 1940s, domestic anticommunism was sweeping up faculty, administrators, and scholars in a web of investigations. Scrutinized for past or current subversive leanings, many college and university professors would retreat from publicly voicing controversial viewpoints. A study for the Bureau of Applied Social Research reveals, however, that there was a difference between the public responses of academics and the discussion of political issues on campus and in the classroom.[66] Because their professional status ultimately depended on the quality of their scholarship, academics had good reason to fear the longer-term and international consequences of infringement of the freedom of speech. Their "alertness to academic freedom" translated in a far greater tolerance for "free discussion" in the semipublic sphere of classroom and lecture halls than it existed in the nation at large. Scholars justified their relative "permissiveness" regarding the airing of controversial opinions in a number of forms. Most commonly, faculty argued that due to the "intellectual role of the college" they ought to be granted freedoms that were not necessarily appropriate for the majority of Americans. In the elite realm of higher education, the thesis went, intelligent individuals could be trusted to engage in "constructive public discussion." The uneducated and the maladjusted might run the danger of falling for the manipulations of a demagogue or radical party. In academia, by contrast, participants in "free discussion" would not be likely to agree with political philosophies that limited their freedom to trade, speak, or vote. In addition, a small group based their defense of free speech on theories first developed in response to fascism, but now reformulated under the heading of "totalitarianism."[67] Government investigators who questioned individuals about their beliefs instead of actions, the argument went, acted no differently from communist commissars in Stalinist Russia who tried to extend the reach of the party into all spheres of human life. Moreover, the spread of psychoanalytically informed theories about the origins of prejudice made it possible to cast the fervent anticommunism of a Senator McCarthy as no less anti-American than Marxism or racism. Just like the latter, the former could be presented as a belief system that appealed only to people who suffered from mental pathologies or lacked intelligence or education.[68]

The construct of academia as a gathering place for elite intellectuals did not prevent anticommunist crusaders from summoning faculty in front of investigative committees. On the contrary, because of a common association between communism and atheism, academics' investment into scientific rationalism made them appear "godless" and un-American in the eyes of conservatives. This notwithstanding, however, a number of college women clearly identified with the idea that their education was enabling them to adjudicate the current political situation in more level-headed and rationalistic ways than a majority of Americans were able to. This shows poignantly in the letters in which Mount Holyoke College's Janet Brown described to her father her view of a particularly controversial event of the early Cold War, the "Cultural and Scientific Conference for World Peace," also known as the "Waldorf Conference" in reference to the New York City hotel in which most of the meetings and panels took place.

A meeting of international scientists and public intellectuals, the Waldorf Conference in 1949 became a lightning rod for conservatives and liberals alike. Its chairperson, the Harvard astronomer Harlow Shapley, was a controversial figure. Shapley was a world-renowned astronomer but also an outspoken former Popular Front liberal. One of the first scientists called to testify in front of the postwar House Un-American Activities Committee, he would appear in 1950 on Joseph McCarthy's notorious list of alleged communists in high places. He was a firm believer in internationalism and, after relations with the Soviet Union chilled, one of the few public critics of U.S. foreign policy. Like the controversial former vice president Henry Wallace, Shapley called for dialogue with the Soviet Union. Shapley was already perceived as insufficiently anti-Stalinist, so the fact that he invited citizens of communist-led nations to the Waldorf Conference only further affirmed to Shapley's detractors that he was an unrepentant fellow traveler. In an effort to distance themselves from this man whose loyalty to the nation was in question, veterans' organizations, labor unions and many religious organizations publicly condemned the Waldorf conference.[69]

The national media coverage surrounding the event makes clear that Harlow Shapley's position was a marginal one.[70] Janet's comments illustrate, however, that college campuses were somewhat of a space apart. "What do you think of [Harlow] Shapley?" she opened the conversation. Explaining that he was organizing a "gathering of artists, scientists, etc. to try to find practical ways of obtaining peace," she expressed her approval of the event. Unfortunately, she continued, her view was not shared by the majority of the American people: "The attitude of newspapers, the state dept. etc. is certainly far from helpful in stirring up the public to picketing on unproved charges. Evidently, those who try for peace are being altogether too easily classed as Communists and we are getting a much more totalitarian and militaristic government than most people realize."[71]

As Janet's application of the label "totalitarian and militaristic" suggests, she was familiar with a debate about the contemporary political context that was considerably more complex than the analysis offered in the mass media. In her view, the Cold War was not simply a contest between the forces of liberty versus Stalinism. Liberal democracies such as the United States also ran the danger of violating civil rights and adopting elements of autocratic regimes. As her letter implies, she drew a line between the college-educated young and "most people." With that, she was beginning to embrace a version of liberal politics at odds with major parts of the Cold War, anti-Stalinist consensus. Moreover, the fact that the correspondence she kept up with her parents often sounded like a textbook lecture indicates that Janet felt a responsibility to educate others.

I found in the journal of a young African American that exposure to college encouraged some women to identify as members of an intelligent elite with responsibilities to use their insights. Martha Ann Furgerson grew up in Iowa as the oldest daughter of five children of a Catholic physician and a schoolteacher. She went to Alabama for her college education, where she pursued a major in history at the historically black Talladega College. After graduating from "'Dega" in 1947, she returned to live temporarily with her family in the Midwest. Martha Ann kept her diary, which is the only personal journal kept by an African American woman that I managed to locate during my nationwide search, for only a short time after graduation. Eventually, it became part of the collection of the Iowa Woman's Archives, to which she donated her personal papers.[72]

That I did not find more introspective accounts by black women about their social experiences in college is a consequence of the way in which race made their situation distinctive. Martha Ann's diary is a rare find. Black women have been subject to racialized assumptions impugning their sexuality and morality since slavery, labeled as more primitive and hence more carnal than whites. They were highly vulnerable to rape. The African American middle class in response to pernicious stereotypes adopted a strict emphasis on respectability that is reflected in chaperonage requirements and moral regulations in historically black colleges and universities that were much harsher than in the North.[73] The social conduct of female students was supposed to be flawless not just to appear in the best possible light in front of whites but also as a means of protecting them. Because of this emphasis on respectability, a black college woman who kept a journal might have been less likely than her white contemporaries to expose such a document to public scrutiny. Moreover, the experience of racial discrimination that African American students as a group had to endure politicized them more strongly and faster than white northerners. Few female black college graduates appear to have regarded personal papers merely describing ordinary, day-to-day, social events of campus life as in need of preservation for posterity. Martha Ann Furgerson's diary only made it into an archive as part of a larger collection documenting her civil rights and church activism in later life.[74]

The specifics of her background notwithstanding, however, Martha Ann's story, just like Janet Brown's, reflects tensions between assimilation to and contestation of norms caused by the opening up of educational opportunities to new population groups. Like many of her northern counterparts, Martha Ann highlighted in her diary conventional elements of campus life such as "parties" and "glamorous adventure."[75] However, she also felt that her education at Talladega College had turned her into an expert on social and political issues; here the parallels between her analysis of the postwar situation and her role as an educated woman and that of Janet Brown are striking. Like Janet Brown, in college Martha Ann came to consider herself by virtue of her education as set apart from the members of her community of origin. In Martha Ann's case, this meant that she felt she had more in common with educated youth of either race than with the non-college-educated elders of her own community.

That Martha Ann felt she ought to use the insights a higher education had equipped her with shows clearly in the activities she took up after graduation. In November of 1947 she spoke at a "Christian . . . Ladies Aid Group," and afterward recorded: "I hope my little effort brought the women a knowledge of what Negroes (some, anyway) are thinking." In Martha Ann's mind, these thoughts of "some" African Americans included faith in education as a tool for social reconstruction. Pondering the root causes for growing political hysteria in her diary, Martha Ann wrote in November of 1947: "Americans haven't been taught to see things the way they are. We haven't been shown how to examine a situation + really look under to find what is what. If we can all wake up to the implications + causes of the conflict + disturbances in the world today—eventually, war as a means of getting what the other fellow has will not be the politician's method."[76]

Martha Ann's belief in the power of education, and her embrace of her own responsibility to work for social progress, does of course put her into a longer tradition within her own community. Described by W.E.B. Du Bois as the "talented tenth" in reference to their proportion of the black population as a whole, college-educated African Americans have long been active in social reform. Yet even though Martha Ann's parents were educated professionals, the Cold War created a rift between the young woman and her family. While Martha Ann's views had been shaped in a college environment in which controversial ideas could at least be discussed, her home community endorsed a far more rigid set of beliefs. Upon her return home, Martha Ann thus found that she could no longer relate to her parents' way of thinking.

The widening gap between her own political views and those in her family became especially apparent to Martha Ann one day in the fall of 1947 after the family's Catholic priest had come by for a visit. The situation in China had made national headlines at the time, and Martha Ann's father and the priest talked about the confrontation between the nationalist Kuomintang and the communists. Both espoused the hard-line anti-communism that was also becoming the official foreign policy consensus. Martha Ann, however, was skeptical. At Talladega she "read books . . . which showed the Nationalists no better" than the communists in China.

Her teachers had also introduced her to a more balanced view of the virtues of the American, as opposed to the Soviet, political system. "I had a teacher once who always used to ask: 'what is more important, freedom or security?'" Clearly, Martha Ann had pondered this question. As she wrote in her journal: "The Russians have security, but no freedom. . . . We have freedom (at least we think we do, but right now that is in danger), but no security."[77] Compared to the style in which she had learned to think about international affairs in college, however, the way in which Cold War events were presented in her parents' house disappointed Martha Ann. The young woman portrayed her priest's comments as the opinion of an uneducated man who was also biased because of his religion: "Naturally," she wrote in her journal, her priest held "the Catholic viewpoint about the Communists." Mocking the man's dialect, she recorded "He's 'agin 'em'" and then turned to also express her disappointment with her father's analysis of the situation. "The way father talked, the Nationalists were good, the Communists + Japs about equally bad." She, by contrast, felt she had transcended her rural upbringing and learned a more sophisticated view of the world.[78]

Martha Ann's diary poignantly shows that she felt her education had equipped her with insights that were intellectually superior to those of anyone who had not had the advantage of attending "'Dega." In fact, she felt that the differences between a college-schooled woman such as herself and the members of her home community amounted to a generational divide. "The world is in a period of great change," she wrote right after the priest left. "Something is happening." Her generation was "gradually leaving the Middle Ages behind and catching up with science." There were still "men (as there are always) who [were] trying to stop it." But, as she told the ladies at the Christian association in front of which she spoke a few days later, "if the old folks . . . be quiet, the young people might work it out."[79]

Martha Ann Furgerson and Janet Brown were not alone in their sense of optimism that the educated young, with the power of knowledge, would usher in a better social and global order. Personal letters and journals of female college students from the immediate post–World War II period show that they shared the sentiment and participated in numerous progressive political campaigns.[80] By the early 1950s this momentum for social and economic reforms, as historians of the Cold War have shown, fell victim to growing anticommunist fervor. Against the background of the Korean War and high-publicity espionage cases, calls for a balanced analysis of current events were drowned out by fears that communist sympathizers would take advantage of any weakness in the American system.[81] In the writings of female students from this period, however, there is evidence that college still offered opportunities for the exploration of controversial ideas.

The distinctly mixed reception Senator Joseph McCarthy received when he spoke at Smith College in April of 1952 demonstrates that 1950s college women broke in major ways with sentiments held in the nation at large.[82] Addressing members of the Smith Young Republican Club, the American Legion, and the general student body, he found the audience divided. More importantly, after the fervent anticommunist left, students continued to discuss the validity of his position. At least some students could not help but see the senator in the same league as the communists he so adamantly persecuted. The friends of Ohio suburbanite Alice Gorton, for instance, called McCarthy a "true commissar" and ridiculed his rigid views: "Here's to . . . all the wise men of ages past who have lived and died and left us their wise words to read and enjoy. I'll drink to them. And to McCarthy too—for he is a true commissar."[83]

The use of the term "commissar" in reference to McCarthy hints at the intellectual source of students' critique. Alice Gorton's friends, mostly English majors like herself, were not involved in any Marxist or otherwise explicitly political organization. The books these women discussed with each other, which they at times encountered as part of a class assignment, at other times had picked up on their own, were highly political, however. The label "commissar," for example, was coined by British essayist Arthur Koestler in reference to people whose passionate embrace of a radical political agenda was based on unconscious psychological forces that they barely understood. Alice Gorton had encountered the same line of argument already in the work of one of her favorite authors, Philip Wylie. Any 1950s student would also find a similar thesis in Erich Fromm's *Escape from Freedom* (1941), Arthur Schlesinger Jr.'s *The Vital Center* (1949), and Theodore Adorno et al.'s *The Authoritarian Personality* (1950). What all of these books shared was a tendency to discredit political or religious radicalism as based on an irrational need or lack of education. Familiarity with this line of argument easily encouraged college students to be suspicious of the blustering style of Cold War partisans such as McCarthy. At the same time, students interested in the work of a controversial thinker could feel encouraged to do so by embattled liberals' portrayal of academia as a space in which intelligent and rational individuals engaged in scholarship and free inquiry. In the minds of students, the willingness to grapple with provocative ideas was thus a sign of intellectualism and a marker of an elite status. It was her familiarity with this line of reasoning that accounts for the nonchalance with which Alice Gorton in 1952 picked up the work of British literary critic Christopher St. John Sprigg without being disturbed by his known communist sympathies.[84]

The journal of June Calender serves as a further indication that exposure to the academic setting pushed and pulled college women—especially nontraditional ones—away from their communities of origin. June grew up in rural Indiana, and neither of her parents had received advanced schooling. Although her mother had graduated from high school, her father, who was born in rural Kentucky, only had a fifth-grade education. This notwithstanding, June's parents encouraged her avid interest in literature and writing. In 1956 the Indiana farm girl began a liberal arts course of study at Indiana University in Bloomington with the help of a scholarship. Over the course of the next few semesters, June would also come to see herself as a woman with insights and skills that most of her contemporaries lacked.

June, a high school valedictorian, avid reader, and frequent patron of her small town's public library, began her education at Indiana University already aware that small-town and farm families like her own had a reputation as being somewhat uneducated and backward. In fact, she was quite eager to distance herself from associations with these alleged traits of rural Americans. This shows poignantly in an entry she made when her high school senior class visited New York City. There in a department store on Fifth Avenue, a clerk teased her about her rural, midwestern, roots. June, according to her journal, retorted that even though she "was a farmer's daughter, [she] certainly didn't consider [her]self anything of a hick or bumpkin." This defense of her family background notwithstanding, however, with the start of her university studies, June became only more determined to transcend her family background.[85]

By the time June entered college, the effects of the G.I. Bill had abated. The low costs of public higher education by that time were bringing many women just like her to college. Yet June did not want to associate with others like her. She wanted to turn herself into a very different person. To "become a lady," she described her goal in her journal, and she actively worked to accomplish it. She wanted to learn "to hold [her] shoulders back and [her] voice down," [and to gain] an awareness . . . of [her] conduct."[86] Yet while her parents were still able to relate to June's desire to turn herself into a sophisticated woman, a source of friction opened because of the way college shaped the young woman's views on culture and politics.

Although June's diary shows her as an active participant in conventional campus life, college had clearly also turned her into a woman whose views clashed with the politics and values held in her home community. At Bloomington, she read psychology and history and met students from a broad variety of backgrounds. Eventually she made friends with a group that included Jewish Americans from the East Coast, with whom she discussed books, philosophy, and politics. This college culture caused her, like many of her peers, to adopt certain central beliefs. She saw prejudices against racial or ethnic groups as evidence of neuroses and believed that fervent anticommunism no less than other extreme positions endangered democracy. Yet when the young woman now visited her family in the small town of Versailles, Indiana, during breaks or holidays, she could not help but realize that her relatives accepted many of the beliefs she had learned to condemn. Recording her experience of a "terrible Christmas" at home in her diary, she vented her frustration: It made her "unhappy with men too dumb to deserve peace on earth, too morally, intellectually, and emotionally biased to understand good will," she recorded. "These are the people who can find happiness only in a delusion, only on the basis of ignorance of how matters really are. These are the majority of earth's population."[87]

June's frustration with her family could, of course, have various explanations. She might simply have been bored by the talk and turned to her journal to let off steam. But the entry demonstrates that June was beginning to see herself as a person who was cut out for a different life from that of her family members. Like the students quoted earlier, she believed that her education had turned her into an expert on current sociopolitical problems and a member of a new intellectual elite.[88]

Drawing on a number of case studies, this chapter illustrates that it was possible for college women to read the complex messages they encountered in higher education in ways that encouraged them to consider themselves part of an educated elite. This dynamic was particularly strong in the case of nontraditional students because the differences in outlook in their families of origin and in the prestige-endowed setting of higher education led them to think of themselves as a group apart. At the same time, however, these women also internalized the strong heteronormative pressures in their environment. College women thus had to balance countervailing messages. They had to take care to become well rounded, mature, and feminine at the same time that they also needed to develop their potential as independently thinking, rational intellectuals.

That many postwar college women did not consider femininity and intellectualism at odds shows in their choices. We have seen that they were exceedingly active participants in campus life. Yet if we look at women who decided to pursue an honors course or to prepare for postgraduate studies, we can find the same social butterflies. Merle Judith Marcus and Helene Harmon wanted careers in the arts. After graduation from Mount Holyoke, Janet Brown studied psychology at Yale. Alice Gorton chose to do honors work in English literature and, while at Smith, looked into opportunities for study abroad and graduate school.

June Calender also concentrated on literature and considered a career in politics or journalism. Although Cold War commentators actively encouraged college women to work for the social good in their role as wives, mothers, and volunteers, this was not—at least when they began their education—how students necessarily read the messages at their disposal. Although strong disincentives existed that would channel them away from specialized study, there was a substantial group of women who wanted to be experts in their own right and not helpmeets.

These students were culture-brokers in a very complex way. They introduced notions of conventional femininity but also of youthful independence into their families. In the collegiate environment, meanwhile, they helped spread notions of female intellectualism in a new form. They wanted to be new women of the nuclear age: feminine, and sophisticated, but with a voice in current affairs. And yet, by the time their studies came to an end, many of the women who spent time and energy talking about and preparing for careers after graduation chose the "humble role of housewife" as their métier. In the chapters that follow, we will learn more about the dynamic responsible for this development. Because personal records vary greatly in the amount of information about women's college experiences, I am not able to illustrate the experiences of all the actors mentioned earlier. From the case studies that follow, however, we will still gain a sense of why a number of women parted with plans for professional careers.

3

Not Part of the Crowd

CAREER-ORIENTED COLLEGE WOMEN
WRITE ABOUT THEIR GOALS,
IDENTITY, AND SIGNIFICANT OTHERS

In the fall of 1956, Susan Sperry Borman, a first-year Stanford University student, was working on an assignment for her English class. As a guiding question, she had jotted down, "how do I assert my individuality," and in her response she listed a series of traits as evidence that she was indeed a very individualistic person. Her choice of clothes, of interests, of actions, she wrote, were all motivated by genuineness, not by fashion or peer pressure:

> I do things because I want to do them, not because other people do them and they're the things to do. I wear nylons and flats because I like nylons and flats and I don't wear bucks and colored socks because I don't like white bucks and colored socks on me. . . . When I do things, I never consider whether my mother or my father or my friends would like it, I do it because when it concerns me, I never [stop] to think how anyone else would do it, I think only of how I would do it, and then I do it that way. When I think about something, I never stop to ask, how are they going to think about it, I just think about it and express my opinion.[1]

Although in this case, Susan's reflection about "individuality" was motivated by a class assignment, it was not the first time the young woman had pondered the extent of her independence from the opinions of others. Already "last year," she wrote in her diary, she had considered the issue and at that point she had been "proud" of being "an individual and independent and going [her] own way as far as opinions and desires." These desires included a genuine interest in academic work and a wish to use the skills and insights she was acquiring in college. Although she did not yet have concrete plans about what she wanted to do after graduation, it is clear from her journal that she was ambitious, that she had repeatedly told peers and family that she was "going to be a writer," and that she spent her free time volunteering with the Palo Alto chapter of the Young Women's Christian Association that was at the time active in civil rights work. Considering that neither literary ambitions nor civic activism were normative experiences for 1950s adolescent girls, Susan probably had these activities and interests on her mind when she prided herself for always doing things her own way. But in the weeks following the assignment, her diary entries kept returning to the subject of individuality. As it turns out, Susan was of two minds about it: "Holly came in and sat down and told me that I had impressed everybody on this corridor as being self-willed and independent," she wrote one day after having had a talk with a female dormitory mate and friend. Considering her earlier statements about her "pride" in her independence, this should have pleased Susan. That day, however, it had the opposite effect. In this instance, her individuality struck Susan as irreconcilable with her desire to also be feminine and attractive. As she put it, Holly's remarks suggested to her that she was no longer "little and cute and feminine anymore," and that she was changing from being "a girl" to being "a person." Quite apparently, Susan feared that this transformation might make her unacceptable in the eyes of others.

> I see a very sharp and striking and rather hard girl there [in the mirror], who is more a person than a girl. . . . And now I wonder how I strike other people and not only that, I'm afraid they're [sic] things inside of me that are coming out now that I won't ever be able to change. . . . I am afraid I'm too much of an individual and that I'm too strong of a person. . . . I'm afraid I'll be one of those people so much of an individual he [sic] can't adjust to society, that's what I'm afraid of. . . . I really don't know what to think. What else can I do but just go along and be what I am?[2]

The fact that Susan felt a conflict between being a "person" and a "girl" reflects her internalization of a particular concept of femininity, which any 1950s woman easily learned about by just reading one of the by-then numerous columns of mental health experts in magazines like *Good Housekeeping*, *Women's Home Companion*, *Redbook*, or *Colliers* that catered to a middle-class readership. Already in the 1930s social scientists had used the mass media to promote the value of adjustment to adult sex-role expectations, which included the willingness to enter into the family model of breadwinner husband and domestic wife. However, because the cultural authority of the mental health expert reached its apex in the 1950s, women who came of age in this period would have found it particularly hard to escape prescriptions of a gender-conservative nature. Although historians have recently emphasized that the discussion of femininity was actually more complex and diverse than we once assumed, much of the expert advice was nonetheless shaped by writers' interest in containing changes in the realm of gender and family relations.[3] Frequently informed by an adjustment psychology perspective, by neo-Freudian psychoanalysis, or by a functionalist sociological approach, the literature of advice held that a woman ought to dedicate herself to the needs of others. If she strove instead to find affirmation of her ego in the competitive pursuit of a career, she ran the risk of unsexing herself and become exactly what Susan feared she was turning into: a "sharp . . . and rather hard" person.

The postwar literature also included a particular theory of what motivated some people to part with conventional expectations of normal masculine and feminine behavior. Such men or women might claim they were just expressing their individuality. What actually caused their behavior, however, was probably a lack of self-awareness or intelligence resulting in an inability to adjust to society. Experts would increasingly argue that it was impossible to define "normalcy" as a universal standard. Instead, they now far more commonly used "normal" in the sense of "conventional" and "typical." The range of acceptable behavior was still rather limited, however, because experts operated on the assumption of a hierarchy of value according to which they labeled behavior that benefited the status quo as mature and intelligent, while they cast non-conformism as the result of a lack of impulse control, or as an immature rebellion. Deviations from commonly held expectations regarding a person's gender role, in this interpretation, were thus simply developmental flaws that suggested immaturity. Even in cases in which a genuine calling for an unusual life course lay at the root of a person's idiosyncratic behavior, experts still tended to warn that someone like this would probably have to pay the price of loneliness if, in Susan's words, he or she was "so much of an individual" as to be incapable of "adjust[ing] to society."[4]

In spite of the undeniable strength of gender conservatism, however, Susan remained ambivalent about the relative value of conformity versus individualism. In fact, her diary entries suggest that her internalization of the need to be true to herself was about as strong as her fear of what might happen to her should she fail to adjust to society. She had begun to feel rather self-conscious about her interest in her class work and her idiosyncratic goals, and she had to grant that she found the "pull" of campus life at times quite strong. She even (as a later entry suggests) sometimes faked uninterest in her studies in front of her classmates. Yet, in spite of the fears she had expressed in her journal only ten days earlier, by mid October of 1956 she emphatically declared that, no matter how difficult or painful this might turn out to be, she needed to stay true to herself. Referring to her literary ambition and her interest in class work, she wrote:

> You have got to believe, Susie, that something good and excellent and above all others is going to come out of what you are doing. Even though

you feel it pull you away, even though it makes you feel abnormal and insufficient and out of it, you have got to do it, because by not doing it, you are a nothing, and you're not working with what is inside of you. Maybe I feel as though I don't want to do it, but I've got a responsibility and I have to forge ahead and do it, do it, do it, because that's the way I do things, with all of myself and take the consequences as they come.[5]

The question of how scholars approach Susan's diary will depend on their discipline. Psychologists argue that introspective soul-searching typically occurs during adolescence and marks a phase in which a reorganization of the self takes place. Self-reflection at this stage commonly entails thoughts about what to become in life, a refinement of the gendered self-image, and a preoccupation with questions of authenticity. Especially when their social worlds expand, as is typically the case when youth start college, adolescents suddenly realize that parents, teachers, peers, and romantic partners approach them with different expectations, and they respond by adjusting their behavior accordingly. Awareness of this can lead to agonizing over the question of what constitutes the real self, which can at times takes the form of a crisis. Most of the time, however, a youth succeeds in formulating an organized concept of self.[6] From a developmental psychology perspective, Susan's concern about her individuality reflects a typical process for a person her age and in her situation. As a historian, however, I am interested in the link between cultural and political contexts and the coming-of-age experience of educated young women. Rather than seeing their writings as windows into a common psychological process of maturation, I will use these sources to explore to what extent it was possible for women with career aspirations to draw from the discourses at their disposal material that allowed them to formulate a stable sense of self.

A look at the context in which Susan's anxious reflections about her identity occurred suggests that her thoughts were influenced by a particular Cold War version of longer-standing anxieties about the larger social impact of a shift from a producer to a consumer society, and from scarcity to affluence. Since at least the late nineteenth century, the nation had seen a debate about how growing prosperity, the spread of popular culture, and changing gender and family roles affected society. Cultural critics during the 1950s wrote in this tradition while increasingly using theories developed in the fields of psychoanalysis and the study of the relationship between culture and personality. In its most complex and erudite version, this discussion took place in academia where sociologists, philosophers, and cultural critics from a variety of ideological backgrounds theorized about the state of "man in the machine age." The discussion also reached the public through articles in magazines, popular novels, and nonfiction books. Students who started their education right after World War II, moreover, encountered the discourse on "mass man" with particular immediacy because of the imprint it had left on the liberal arts curriculum.[7]

Mid-twentieth-century students of the liberal arts encountered variations of a particular argument in a number of their classes. Whether they took psychology, history, literature, anthropology, or a course in the relatively new field of American Studies, they had a good chance to encounter the argument that modern times had taken a psychological toll on the American people. As a great variety of works that were standard readings for students held, Americans, as a result of technological and economic progress, and as a consequence of their growing dependence on government-sponsored services through the New Deal state, had lost some of the ruggedly independent pioneer spirit that had allegedly shaped their character in the past. Not only had they grown physically "soft," they had also grown mentally more susceptible to conformist pressures. "The individual [had] cease[d] to be himself," wrote psychologist Erich Fromm in 1941. Modern man had "adopt[ed] entirely the kind of personality offered to him by cultural patterns; and he therefore [became] exactly as all others are and as they expect him to be." In the words of David Riesman, author of the influential *The Lonely Crowd* (1950), "inner directed" individuals had become "outer directed conformists" who molded their behavior according to the expectations of others in order to fit in and to get ahead.[8]

Anxieties concerning the impact of affluence on the character of the American nation and people were, of course, not a new phenomenon. The spike in prosperity in the post–World War II period, however, was unusually visible and dramatic, as a look at big-ticket consumer items illustrates. By the late 1950s, the proportion of families owning a home had reached 60 percent; 75 percent had a car, 87 percent a television, and 75 percent a washing machine. Considering that in the not-so-remote past, a blue-collar job and an apartment in an inner city neighborhood was the common experience for many Americans, and that, as late as 1939, most homes did not even have central heating or running water, these changes were indeed enormous.[9] Moreover, the expansion of the mass media and advertising made these developments highly visible. The dominant image of postwar America was that of a middle-class society in which virtually everyone, regardless of ethnicity, race, or sex, coveted the same lifestyle. The baby and marriage boom that accompanied the new prosperity, meanwhile, seemed a clear sign that the number of Americans who sought comfort and security in the midst of their families had also risen to an all-time, alarming high.

To understand the intensity of post–World War II concerns over the impact of prosperity on the national character, we need to put this debate in the context of concomitant anxieties. For one, the debate unfolded against the backdrop of a widespread perception that while men were losing strength and influence, women were gaining power. Writings about mass culture and the machine age clearly reflect concerns about this seeming gender convergence.[10] Although mid-twentieth-century writers generally used "man" in its generic sense, the debate about a loss of rugged individualism was gendered at its core. As an interest in children, home, and family was firmly in line with the female gender role, very few writers would have looked at women's longings for them as anything out of the ordinary. Evidence that an increasing number of men also craved approval, security, and the comforts of home, by contrast, was worrisome because it seemed to indicate a loss of manhood. At the same time that men seemed to grow weaker, moreover, women appeared to be turning the nation's suburbs into virtual matriarchies where they wielded exclusive authority.[11]

This trend of men becoming softer while women grew stronger struck observers as particularly alarming because it coincided with the escalation of Cold War tensions. Longer-standing "anxieties" about "affluence" only grew in intensity as a result of the international backdrop. In much of the mass media, the spike in consumption levels served as evidence of the superiority of capitalism over communism. Cultural critics, by contrast, found the consumer cravings of American men problematic not only because they reflected their turn away from a pioneer spirit but also because they might be indicative of dangerous unconscious desires. Influenced by the work of scholars who had studied the behavior of the "crowd" in authoritarian regimes, postwar critics of mass society looked with particular concern to citizens' apparent susceptibility to the relatively new field of commercial advertising. Americans who allowed billboards and glossy magazine ads to influence their purchasing decisions seemed to have the same unconscious craving to surrender their "freedom" as political fanatics who, in their search for moral absolutes, had signed their lives over to an extremist political party or a radical ideology. While most Americans were simply falling for the promise that buying the latest model automobile would satisfy their barely understood unconscious longings, the same psychological susceptibility could also lead them to political radicalism.[12]

The assumptions that influenced the writings of cultural critics are relevant because they shaped the college curriculum. In academia, fears that the nation's core values and founding principles were in danger at a time of crisis fueled the spread of a narrative of national development that was mapped on a romanticized past peopled by self-sufficient yeomen farmers and entrepreneurs. To recapture once again that old spirit of rugged independence, American men were urged to reject its opposite: the concern about the views of others, the tendency to seek security in consumer comforts, the home, or the crowd. With that, a narrative spread in academia as a whole of American national development in which either the experiences of women did not figure or in which values labeled typical of women inhibited progress.[13]

In retrospect, it is clear that the critics of mass society were affected by the same "middle-class myopia" as those who celebrated an end to class differences as proof of the superiority of the American way. Even against the backdrop of a real increase in per capita income, poverty remained a reality, among minorities especially.[14] For the purpose of this chapter, however, what is interesting is not so much the question of whether the assumptions at the core of the writings of cultural critics reflect reality but rather how the debate influenced the identity of female students.

The strength of ideals of individualism on college campuses shows in the emphasis on authenticity, on the need to reject peer pressure, and on sustained commitment to a goal regardless of the social cost that we see in Stanford student Susan's diary. After having experienced what struck her as a conflict between being a "person" and a "girl," she essentially declared her preference for the model of identity that her society valued most: that of a self-sufficient individual who did not depend on group approval. She did so in spite of the fact that the link between maleness and individualism was deeply embedded in her culture. A concern with the opinions of others and a longing to find approval from a group, however, connoted a weakness and neediness that was marked as distinctly inferior. Considering the high value attributed to a model of development mapped on a stereotypical and idealized male life path, it was almost logical for an ambitious young woman such as this Stanford student to prefer it to its alternatives. By doing so, however, Susan was trading in one "mystique" for another. Rejecting the "feminine" one, she aimed for an unrealistic model of radical individualism that entailed the devaluation of such needs as longing for community, security, love, or outside approval.

Neither Susan's concern with her individuality nor her attitude about it was in any way unusual. Rather, her journal reflects the clash of differently gendered messages in the Cold War student culture. On the one hand, normative pressures to adjust to female sex-role expectations had grown dramatically. On the other hand, concomitant pressures to develop independence of mind, to self-realize, and to resist the lure of security and comfort had also increased. Among the educators of women, this message was additionally enforced because they had to defend the value of a broad and comprehensive education to critics urging vocational training and a gender-specific curriculum.[15] Frequently exposed to the argument that their studies in the liberal arts fostered self-awareness and independence of mind, college women found encouragement to see themselves as members of a particularly individualistic elite.

Drawing on a number of case studies, this chapter explores how college women responded to the diametrically opposed messages to individuate and reject normative pressures on the one hand and to embrace a passive, self-abnegating female identity on the other. College women, in an effort to reconcile countervailing prescriptions, developed a language that allowed them to publicly justify ambitions still considered unusual for young women at the time. In addition, they created support networks with like-minded peers. Yet, although the success with which these young women managed to find confidantes, friends, and even dating partners in spite of idiosyncratic goals illustrates the diversity of outlooks in the student culture. The environment in which these educated women operated ultimately imposed huge limitations on their ability to arrive at a stable and comfortable sense of self. Central to women's coping strategy for the reconciliation of countervailing messages was their identification with the exaggerated concept of individualism, which essentially amounted to an unrealistic mystique. Their investment in this idea encouraged them to reject conformity to gender norms and to strive for academic excellence, but it also led them to buy into an ideology that denigrated life choices, desires, and needs stereotypically associated with women. As the unfortunate result of this situation, highly culturally literate and academically ambitious women strove hard to prove to self and others that they were unusually gifted and dedicated exceptions to their sex. With that, they tended to set standards of performance for themselves that were unrealistically high.

The analysis in this chapter is based on a close reading of a number of diaries women wrote while they were actively grappling with different ideologies. With this focus come certain limitations. Although diaries are often considered private writings about a person's innermost feelings, authors actually often use them to safely try out different personas. In fact, especially in the kinds of introspective journals that I use, writers frequently act as their own "mythmakers" who draw on literary models to put a positive spin on a situation experienced as painful.[16] This said, my reading of personal diaries still offers insights into possible coping strategies available to young women. Moreover, the way in which female undergraduates drew on the cultural material at their disposal illustrates the considerable literacy and intellectual resourcefulness of a population not usually considered as producers of ideology. The writings of a group of articulate young women illuminate the complexity of Cold War culture as well as the particular challenges that existed, especially for women who broke with traditional middle-class sex-role expectations. The chapter begins with an exploration of gender-conservative pressures in the postwar period, which, while in continuity with older ones, also entailed elements that were distinctive to the context at the time. It then shows that career-oriented college women deviated in their dating patterns from common trends and illustrates the influence of calls for individuation and self-realization on their thinking. After showing that many women, in spite of the fact that men were the primary targets of the discourse on individualism, also identified with the ideal, the chapter then turns to explore interpersonal relations between women and between opposite sex peers.

One factor that caused the quality of normative pressures in the mid-twentieth-century student culture to change was the transformation of courtship customs. Although "dating" had entered student culture already in the 1920s, in the course of only a few decades the practice had undergone substantial changes. With early roots in working-class, immigrant neighborhoods, dating had entered the urban middle class by the 1920s. College-educated youth especially, drawing on the writings of European psychologists and sexologists, fashioned themselves as a modern, sophisticated generation in distinction not only from their elders but also from less-privileged contemporaries. Flaunting psychologically informed theories became one way through which an elite tried to distinguish itself from competitors for status and influence at a time when the sociodemographic profile of the middle class was already broadening. In spite of its working-class roots, dating in the student culture therefore became linked to status. Successful participation connoted modernity and affluence. It served to set participants apart not only from an older generation's investment in Victorian mores but also from ethnic, racial, and religious minorities and small town or rural Americans who lacked access to a commercial leisure culture of dance halls, speakeasies, and movie houses frequented by college men and their dates.[17]

By the 1930s tighter Depression-era budgets put caps on the adventurism of youth. For this very reason, however, the ability to participate in the dating culture maintained its association with an elevated social position. Because young men were expected to pay for their own consumption and to foot the bill for their dating partners, it was expensive for them to date. Women, meanwhile, needed to be able to keep up with the latest fashions, which depended on the investment of not just money but also time. The costs associated with the activity thus meant that in spite of a continuous expansion and diversification of the student body, affluent students found it easiest to "score" dates. With college men and women affiliated with prestigious fraternities and sororities that dominated the social scene on many campuses, dating remained one of the ways through which class and gender hierarchies were perpetuated. In a 1937 article, sociologist Willard Waller labeled this informal yet influential system the "rating and dating complex."[18]

By the post–World War II period, student culture was once again changing. Affluence democratized the dating scene to some degree. Especially for women, however, social success still depended on meeting certain performance standards in the courtship arena. While under the "rating and dating complex" it had been their ability to consistently attract the attention of "class A rated" men, by the 1950s the new marker of elevated social standing was the presence of a "steady" partner. A marriage proposal was the ultimate pinnacle of success. As a preliminary step along the way, however, receiving a man's fraternity pin (or jacket) was highly coveted.[19] A cartoon that Smith College student Alice Silverman pasted into her scrapbook put a humorous spin on the increased normative pressures that ensued. The drawing shows two young women observing a group of their peers who are showing off their engagement rings. As the two single women walk by, one says to the other "I'm beginning to feel insecure."[20]

That college women whose ring fingers lacked adornment felt "insecure" illustrates the growing cultural authority of the mental health disciplines. Already in the 1930s social scientists promoted the value of adjustment to adult sex-role expectations, which included the willingness to enter into the family model of breadwinner husband and domestic wife. The cultural authority of the "specialists in marriage and family life," however, according to Kristin Celello, reached its apex in the 1950s because of a widespread rise in the public's demand for and "faith in expertise."[21] The influence of adjustment psychology only grew against the backdrop of postwar pronatalism and concern over family stability. Moreover, the writings of leading scholars trained in the field of Freudian psychoanalysis boosted gender conservative prescriptions. In *Modern Woman: The Lost Sex* (1947), the period's best-known antifeminist tract, authors Ferdinand Lundberg and Marynia F. Farnham cast the slightest stirring of ambivalence toward motherhood and domesticity as a sign of neurosis.[22] Farnham and Lundberg were on the extreme end of a more diverse discourse, but similar arguments could be found in the theoretically more sophisticated writings of Freud's pupil Helene Deutsch, who also argued that a psychologically healthy woman desired a child and longed for the security of marriage.[23] In fact, writers from a range of disciplines and ideological backgrounds tended to agree on the value of gender differentiation. Although many academic experts had grown uncomfortable with the biological determinism and tight circumscriptions of women's spheres in the work of Farnham and Lundberg, they tended to agree that the different reproductive roles of men and women inevitably put them on separate paths of development. Feminists and antifeminists actually found common ground in the assumption that the interwar women's movement had misconceived equality as "sameness." Yet, as anthropologist Margaret Mead put it, by trying to equalize men and women, a society inflicted as much harm on the members of each sex, as if it was pigeonholing them. Moreover, society would benefit the most if it used the "different gifts" each sex had to offer in its particular way. With each attempt to minimize sex differences, Mead argued, humanity was deprived of a contribution that would enrich it.[24]

The complexities of the post–World War II discourse on the nature of males and females aside, gender conservatism was noticeably spreading on campuses across the nation. Whether on coeducational or on single-sex campuses, college women celebrated their peers who had managed to attract a steady partner in ways that amounted to special kinds of graduation ceremonies. At Smith College, for example, a student not yet in possession of a pin or engagement ring in the winter of 1950 described the dynamic in a sarcastic letter to her parents: "Well, here we are again," she wrote: "Sunday morning breakfast with the . . . Oh, you (Oh, you-lucky-girl-to-be-getting-engaged) girls. . . .We have had one engagement this week, and K.S.'s is coming Saturday, much applauded by all." Another student recorded in her scrapbook: "At least eight juniors or seniors had either been pinned, become engaged, or made plans for marriage after school was out." In consequence, she added, her entire class descended into "sophomore slump." A few years later, another Smith student informed her family that the total number of her housemates who were engaged had risen to five, and a Mount Holyoke woman remarked: "About the 10th married girl in our class."[25] Stanford student Susan commented in 1958 that "a diamond on her left finger" made a senior "a significant and successful woman." It was "the ultimate . . . badge of achievement" after which she could "pat herself on the back" and "demurely accept the congratulations of her other ringed associates."[26]

The hint of sarcasm that shows in Susan's letter, however, also reflects that not all women were on board. In contrast to the pattern that was rapidly spreading around them, a look at their personal writings shows that women who considered postgraduate professional careers followed a different path. They did not plan to remain single forever, but they tended to fear that early attachment to a man would interfere with their goals. Judith Raskin, a Jewish American who had attended public schools in New York City and Yonkers, New York, for example, was clearly a career-oriented student. She had picked Smith College because of the good reputation of its music department. A highly talented singer, she knew from the onset of her studies that she wanted a career in the opera. She was socially active and dated a number of young men at the same time. In a letter home, she explained her dating choices to her parents. She wrote: "It's not that I'm fickle (oh no!) but I've seen Gary more recently than Mark + since I can't see them both, I really should see the one I saw least recently."[27] In January of 1946, she wrote her parents about a fraternity pin she thought she had lost at her last visit home. Yet even though accepting a pin from a young man usually went along with a mutual commitment to go steady, Judith kept seeing other men. About her peers' increasing eagerness for finding a husband, she had only words of mild mockery. About the offspring from family she and her parents knew well, she wrote: "Practically all those Birches are getting married soon Bern tells me—The fools!" A month later she wrote in reference to a peer who got engaged: "Must say Judy S. is pulling a fast one. Never thought she'd be the first to fall (Sucker!)." In contrast to these women around her, Judith Raskin remained determined to get in college the training she needed for her desired career. Although she was dating, she was not actively husband hunting.[28]

As Judith Raskin was writing immediately after the end of World War II, the lack of self-consciousness about the absence of a steady partner might indicate that pressures to go steady had not yet spread. There is evidence, however, that even in the 1950s, career-oriented college women were still not keen on committing themselves early to just one man. Alice Gorton, the aspiring writer from an Ohio suburb, for example, in early 1952 reflected in her journal on her goals for her social life. She wanted, she wrote, to "have many boys date me." She considered college weekends a success when men in the plural paid attention to her. "It was glorious," she wrote after returning from one party as a freshman. "I kissed many—+ wandered. . . . I charmed about 3 dateless boys. What an experience." She wanted "fun" but not "involvement" or "responsibility." "More men please," she wrote at a point when she was particularly content with college life.[29]

Although Alice eagerly accepted dating opportunities, she could not picture marriage as a particularly fulfilling condition. After talking to a newlywed peer, she called it a "horrible state" and in her diary described how the young woman had sounded "mildly bored" talking about "marriage & babies."[30] This might have been a defensive comment but it also needs to be said that the dreams Alice recorded about her future centered on having a glamorous job and the thrill of love affairs, not on marriage and children. Recording a daydream in her journal, she wrote in the summer of 1952 that she wanted to "write successful salable stories," land a "job on [The] New Yorker," have an "apartment, beautiful clothes," and a lover. "What a great life this would be."[31] Happiness, her fantasies imply, comes as a result of individualistic fulfillment, adventure, and fame; it is not brought on by being a devoted wife and mother.

The views on marriage and commitment that Alice recorded in her journal were not consistent. At times, she did admit in her journal that she found the idea of marriage tempting and that she would like to have a steady partner. This very longing, however, struck her as a weakness. Up to her senior year, journal entries in which she admitted a desire for commitment are almost always paired with, or closely followed by, reflections about the possible unconscious motivation at the root of the wish. In fact, as the following quotes from her diary illustrate, she linked marriage to a flight into security. "Got scared coming down thinking of planning my future," she wrote. "Post-grad work—a job. This business of life is pretty terrifying—new vistas, from which I will never retreat. Look at marriage as a safe hole?"[32] The link she drew between the marital state and conformity also shows in an entry she titled "Criteria for a 'Nice' Girl." The latter, in Alice's words, had "the goal in life to prepare herself as best she can to make herself worthy of some 'nice' boy and to bring up his children to be 'nice' people. . . . She believes a woman's place is in the home. . . . She has a set of strict ethical values gleaned from parents, church, and . . . social mores, to which she rigidly adheres to + will defend as the 'right way of life.' . . . She is in the main a conformist because she knows that she will in the end be happiest that way." Parallel to this description of a conformist "nice" girl, Alice then listed her "Criteria for Me," which included a listing of her goals. As she wrote, she wanted to be "admired—outstanding . . . intelligent—way above all."[33]

The frequent reference to what was considered "nice" and "the right way" indicates, of course, that Alice was aware that many of her contemporaries would not share her evaluation of the qualities that made a woman "outstanding." The label "nice," she expected, went to women who desired to become mothers and wives. She could not help but wonder, however, whether the choices of "nice girls" were not simply the result of their rigid and conformist mindset. Her journal thus suggests that in spite of the spread of commitment around her, she associated longings for love or desire for social approval with weakness. A lack of such desires, meanwhile, was proof that a woman was an "outstanding," "intelligent" member of her sex.

We can see in the writings of Margaret Hall that Alice's views were not unusual. When Margaret started her studies at Bryn Mawr in 1951, she was already engaged and expected to drop out of college before completing her degree. After a prolonged process of soul-searching delineated in the pages of her diary, however, she broke her engagement. "I cannot marry now. Perhaps this means never. Perhaps it does," she wrote. Yet, even if by breaking her engagement she would miss out a one-time chance for marital happiness, Margaret felt that this was a price worth paying because she believed that it was ultimately more important to strive for personal growth and to pursue her academic goals. She wrote about one night when she missed her former fiancé: "Last night I ached to run to him and feel the arms about me, and the love and goodness. But that is harbor, and I have just set out to sea. That is safety, and rest, and peace and the end of mutual striving with this passionate seeking, and that is the death of being *forced* to learn."[34]

Margaret subsequently received more offers for marriage. However, she turned down a total of nine candidates who proposed to her. This included a man whom she, by the time I met her in 2003, remembered as one of her life's great loves. That she refused marriage, although it caused her considerable personal turmoil each time, shows the strength of her conviction that there was something suspicious about early commitment: it would, she feared, hamper her development. No longer "forced" to learn, she would stagnate. She was able to imagine arriving eventually in the "harbor" that was marriage. First, however, she needed to concern herself with her own individual growth and interests.

Margaret, like Alice, was not consistent in her views. She, too, experienced bouts of longing for love, and she clearly felt normative pressures coming from her peers. Like her Smith College peer, however, she also justified her own choices as legitimate departures from a pattern that might be right for some women but ought not to be followed just for the sake of convention. In 1955, for example, she wrote to an aunt that more and more of the women around her were preparing for marriage: "All my best friends are getting engaged this month, it seems, the traditional pattern symbolized in lovely (tiny) solitaire diamonds and fixed futures. I am—eternally—slightly désengagée over the whole process. A nice position because it is so voluntary."[35]

Margaret's emphasis on the "voluntary" nature of her abstention from a common pattern is significant. What the young woman argued here was that she was single because she had consciously stepped on this path. While in her diary she did not dwell on the "conformist" values of her peers in the same way Alice Gorton did, her entry still indicates that she shared with the Smith student a desire to separate herself in a positive manner from the women around her. Her friends might prefer the safety of "fixed" roles. She, by contrast, was not afraid to embrace the freedom to make individualistic decisions. Like Alice, she noticed that a "traditional pattern" was having a renaissance, but she, too, tended to see in marriage a problematic flight into security that would end her personal growth.

For many college women, the decision not to go steady was certainly often motivated by practical reasons. This would have been particularly the case for those who lacked access to money. Scholarship student and English major Sandra Iger, for instance, was, like Margaret, already committed to one particular young man when she started her studies at Mount Holyoke. She had met Richard Kohler as a high school student in Queens. In 1957 Richard then went to Columbia University and Sandra departed for the small town of South Hadley, Massachusetts. Whenever they were united in New York City, both acted like a steady couple. For their separation, however, they had made a "little agreement." Both would meet other people of the opposite sex and "have fun." It is not clear who came up with this first. At least initially, Richard seems to have enjoyed the opportunities for varied dates more than Sandra. Although Sandra found many of her dates with "college boys" rather "dull," she continued to honor the agreement. Had she and Richard insisted on exclusivity, she would have lost out on most of the opportunities for excitement that campus life had to offer. Formal events, dances, and fraternity parties were reserved for couples. Although women often went together to movies or soda parlors, Sandra's lack of financial resources would have put even this option out of her reach.[36]

Financial reasons also factored into why Indiana farmers' daughter and scholarship student June Calender did not limit her dating opportunities to one partner. In 1958, she became engaged to a man named Don, with whom she had been going out for some time. This notwithstanding, she continued to see other men. In her case, no "little agreement" sanctioned her actions. Yet although she was self-conscious about her lack of commitment to Don, she also did not want to miss out on opportunities. As she mused in her journal at one point, she "suppose[d she] ought to quit dating Jack." She could not "see any reason to miss the number of movies [she] would miss," however. A few days later, she went out with yet another man whom she did not tell about her engagement. For this, she attracted the criticism of a female peer who found out about it. The scolding did not cause June to change her behavior, however.[37] Like other women, she, too, felt she had a right to fulfill a personal desire rather than to follow convention.

Although financial circumstances certainly influenced the dating behavior of these students, their ability to describe their behavior in positive terms in spite of rising heteronormative pressures reflects the strength of the ideology of individualism on campus. Sandra Iger, for one, encountered prescriptions for nonconformity almost immediately after starting her education at Mount Holyoke when she went to hear an address by the college president. "One of the things I like most up here," she afterward wrote to her boyfriend, Richard, at Columbia, was the "motto . . . that . . . the faculty would most like to instill" in their students: "The motto . . . is that of non-conformity, in its best sense: i.e. not being 'different' for its own sake, but having one's own ideas and being 'autonomous,' and of an opposition to all forms of mediocrity."[38] Sandra continued to say that not all the students fell into that category. Yet, luckily, she had "found more people here than . . . anywhere else who [were] above the mediocre," and who shared her "intellectual values."[39]

June Calender at Indiana University, meanwhile, had also clearly encountered a literature that cast domestic goals as a choice worthy of inferior women only. This shows especially in an entry she made at the occasion of a visit home to attend a friend's wedding during Thanksgiving break of 1956. In some respect at least, this visit was a disappointment. While June in college had felt she had made important progress to become a sophisticated, educated woman, the hierarchy of popularity in Versailles had not changed. She felt once again like an "outcast." Turning to her journal to vent her frustration, she focused on one young woman who enjoyed the reputation of being particularly "cute." Linking adherence to conventional gender roles to a lack of "drive" and intellectual potential, she wrote, "I don't like her. . . . She's strictly low class—the kind who has not training enough or has enough drive to do anything but get married. And she isn't cute at all!"[40] Like Alice Gorton before her, June here insinuated that women with gender conservative outlooks were inferior to a driven individualist like herself. Her peer had no drive to develop her potential. Because of her lack of stamina, her "cute" peer would never be able to join the ranks of the educated middle class. June, by contrast, would by virtue of her own superior intelligence be able to transcend her upbringing.

That career-oriented college women identified strongly with the notion that only a "mediocre" member of their sex would content herself with a domestic role is certainly in many respects simply a reflection of academic elitism. Although higher education was on its way to complete the transition from being an elite prerogative to a mass opportunity, the Seven Sisters especially but also the liberal arts programs of coeducational universities held on to the notion that they were training the best minds of the nation.[41] Yet there is evidence that young women selectively gleaned from the vast literature on nonconformism and individualism works that explicitly supported their views. This shows in the book titles these women mentioned in letters and journals. References were often brief and did not include a lot of details. But considering the large body of works students in liberal arts courses of study would have to read, those books they explicitly referenced must have provided them with important inspiration in their search for identity.[42]

One of the books many college women mentioned in their private writings is Erich Fromm's *Escape from Freedom* (1941). This is telling, because Fromm was one of the few writers in the literature on conformity who explicitly included women in his call for individuation and who discussed "marriage" in the context of his theories about "pseudo," as opposed to "genuine," freedom: A "man (or a woman for that matter)," he wrote, might consciously think "that he wants to marry a certain person," but in fact, at the root of the thought is man's "fear of isolation." As he warned, "a great number of our decisions are not really our own but are suggested to us from the outside."[43] Frequent references to Fromm's work suggest that it served at least some women in their attempt to put a positive spin on their idiosyncrasies.

Women looking for support to step on a different path in life than the one adjustment psychologists imagined for them also found fodder in Freudianism. The neo-Freudians who increasingly shaped the direction of psychoanalytical discourse in the post–World War II United States generally promoted the traditional female role. Yet while none of the college women whose personal writings I perused referred to, for instance, Lundberg and Farnham's archconservative *Modern Woman: The Lost Sex*, they frequently listed Freud's 1930 *Civilization and Its Discontents*, where they would have found a distinctly negative portrayal of allegedly typical feminine interests. Because they had historically been the main caretakers of the family, Freud argued, women had become more invested than men in creating loving, secure, and comfortable environments. This had been essential for the survival of the species. In more advanced societies, however, the "very women who in the beginning, laid the foundations of civilization by the claims of their love" now "come into opposition to civilization and display their retarding and restraining influence." Trying to keep the male members of the household tied to the security of the hearth, they interfered with their individuation and prevented them from being able to do "the work of civilization" that Freud saw as "the business of men."[44]

The Freudian idea of the retarding influence of women influenced a plethora of popular and often theoretically less sophisticated writings from the late 1930s through the 1950s. An author who was particularly successful in milking the trope of women and their harmful influence on

U.S. society, however, was Philip Wylie. Wylie is remembered today primarily for his venomous portrayal of middle-class wives and mothers in his 1942 nonfiction bestseller *Generation of Vipers*. Going through multiple reprints, *Generation* was assigned reading in many college classes at least up to the early 1950s. Wylie also wrote a series of popular novels in which he repeated central arguments from the bestselling book.

Among gender historians, Wylie has earned himself a reputation as a flaming misogynist for his coinage of the term "momism," a label he used as a shorthand to describe the rule of a "dynasty of dames" over American life.[45] Indeed, in Wylie's oeuvre, women as mothers and as wives appear responsible for virtually every problem ailing the nation. However, at a time when many advice writers reminded women to modify their expectations and to conform to conventional social roles, he also glorified individuals (both men and women) who saw beyond the prejudices and psychological hang-ups of the mass of their contemporaries and lived individualistic lives.[46] What career-oriented college women's interest in Wylie's work thus seems to suggest is that they were engaging in a process of selective reading to draw from the literature at their disposal arguments that cast their own interests and views in a positive light.

Mirra Komarovsky's 1953 study of Barnard College students corroborates that a substantial proportion of college women rejected one-size-fits-all prescriptions for the female gender role. In her survey, the professor of sociology found considerable diversity with regard to the postgraduate goals of students. "The largest group" of about half of the respondents, she writes, "looks forward to motherhood and home-making as the ideal design . . . without any misgivings or reservations." Only a minority of 20 percent of the respondents to her survey fell into the category of "determined career girls." Yet college women generally tended to "oppose any restrictions" regarding how a peer wanted to organize her life after graduation. "No woman," they argued, "should be coerced by law or public opinion to follow either [a] traditional or [a] modern [life path]." The decision of whether to have a full-time career, to combine a profession with marriage, or to lead an exclusively domestic life should be "left to the individuals concerned."[47] Komarovsky's findings thus confirm the influence of the ideology of individualism on college women's thinking about gender.

Komarovsky's study also alerts us to the fact that recourse to ideals of individualism alone might not suffice to encourage a greater acceptance of diversity of goals and identities, however. The sociologist wrote that career-oriented college women did not seem aware of the lack of material and structural support for their aims. As they believed, it was up "to the individuals concerned" to find a way to combine marriage and a career, should this be what they wanted. If these women ran into obstacles after graduation, their investment in the ideology of individualism might well cause them to hesitate before they considered lobbying collectively for the interests of career women as a group. Moreover, in spite of concession to individualist ideals among a broad range of college women, there still remained many who, while they might have tolerated a divergent viewpoint, were still not willing to accept the goals of "career girls" as equal in value. Asked about her opinion of peers who wanted careers, one of the young women interviewed for Komarovsky's study said, "Of course some women dislike housework and may be happy working, but thank heavens, I am not one of them."[48] Komarovsky did not elaborate further on why this student was grateful for her fondness for traditional female tasks. The quote echoes, however, the contemporary literature that linked a woman's distaste for their traditional responsibilities to a neurotic internalization of male values. It further suggests that at least some domestic-minded college women were no less judgmental in their assessment of peers with alternative views than the "career girls" who used the discourse on the pitfalls of conformism in defense of their goals. While gender norms might thus have been in flux, female adolescents seem to have responded to the situation by adopting the defensive stance of claiming superiority of their views over opposing ones. In this context, many women would have found it difficult to develop a sense of solidarity with others of their sex.

In spite of signs of tensions between college women, however, diaries and letters show that career-oriented students tried to build support networks with like-minded female peers.[49] Her honors course of study in English literature, for instance, put Ohio suburbanite and Smith College student Alice Gorton in touch with a number of women who shared her interests and who, like her, dreamt of professional postgraduate futures. She frequently wrote in her diary about a fellow student with the nickname "Poof," who wanted a career in the arts or in writing and was infatuated with literature critical of conformism. Poof was particularly fond of the 1943 novel *The Fountainhead* by Russian émigré Ayn Rand, which, according to Alice, she considered her "bible." In this work, Rand cast her chief protagonist, Howard Roark, loosely modeled on the modernist architect Frank Lloyd Wright, as the personification of the individualistic nonconformist, a man living life utterly unconcerned about gaining the approval or support of society, and Poof strove to live up to his example.[50] When Alice met Poof, she had not yet read *The Fountainhead* (although upon the friend's recommendation she would do so at a later time), but she was already familiar with celebrations of individualism from the work of her favorite author, Philip Wylie.

Like-minded female friends served as important confidantes and role models. Although when Alice met Poof, she already prided herself of her own independent mindset, she was initially intimidated by the outspoken peer. Gradually, however, Alice became more confident. She wrote in 1953: "Good talk with Poofy today . . . I talk to her as an equal finally, which is a very good thing." A little later, she gushed: "She is the star across the sky. She pushes me to think." She would even go so far as to say, "If it is possible to love a girl, I believe I love her."[51] At the same time, Alice formed a similarly close relationship with a woman named "Judy," who was also majoring in literature. Both felt a bond because of the interests and outlooks they had in common. They attended talks and classes together and discussed books and term papers as well as their social life. Judy fondly nicknamed Alice "Gort" and wrote her letters when separated from her during vacations. "Je vous miss muchly," Judy joked in a letter in March of 1953 and called her spring break vacation an "exile" during which she was separated from a peer she felt understood her like few others around her.[52]

Bonding with women who shared her interests and outlook also became an important element of Susan Sperry Borman's experience at Stanford University. Like Alice, she was drawn to women who shared her interests and who projected confidence to the outside. This becomes clear from a diary entry she made right after receiving a letter from a female peer in 1956: "It is a thing to realize, suddenly, in just talking with a person or through reading a letter that their minds are searching and working just as yours is." The woman she was referring to in this case was Mary Charlotte, whose writing clearly impressed her: "that letter sounded . . . wise . . . searching and discussing," she wrote and added that she "would like to sit and talk to [Mary Charlotte] at a round table or some other academic place." From the same entry we also learn about Holly, another female peer, who became very important to Susan as a friend and source of inspiration: "I'm talking about . . . how Holly and I have been talking about the letter," she wrote. She expressed some problems with Holly's personality and style. As other journal entries indicate, Holly had successfully cultivated the persona of a self-confident, career-bound woman, which the introverted Susan found a bit hard to take: "I don't think much of her manner of self-expression," Susan remarked, but she added that "what [Holly] expresses is true more than I know now, and . . . I'll never find a more faithful friend." At one point she showed Holly examples of her writing and was relieved when the friend delivered positive criticism.[53] Like Alice, Susan clearly saw in Holly a woman who shared her goals as well as a person who had already overcome some of the doubts and insecurities she was still struggling with. As such, Holly was not only a friend for Susan but also someone who set examples for standards to aspire to.

The way in which career-oriented college women wrote about like-minded peers complicates the arguments made by a number of historians who have looked at female students' same-sex friendships in the modern era and who highlighted the qualitative shifts that differentiate these relationships from their equivalent in the nineteenth century. As other scholars found, modern college women were more likely to use "female friendships as a means to access and discuss heterosexual pursuits," in contrast to their mothers, who might have turned to a female peer to discuss academic topics and their innermost feelings.[54] While this was certainly also an element in the relationships between 1950s female students, my own evidence shows that these women still bonded with each other over shared intellectual interests. They discussed books no less than they discussed boys, offered emotional support in times of insecurities, and served each other as role models.

It should not be underestimated how important it was for career-oriented college women in the immediate post–World War II period to have access to like-minded same-sex peers. In the formal curriculum and in the mass media, women were rarely, if ever, mentioned as relevant producers of culture, science, or art. Friends could fill this gap, however, and thereby become sources of inspiration for female adolescents who struggled to come to terms with their own identity. Outwardly self-confident students such as Holly or Poof projected to observers the persona of a successful and talented professional-in-the-making. As such, they suggested that it was indeed possible for women to be the equals of men in the public sphere. If this was possible for some women, then it might also hold true for others. Moreover, because women such as Poof and Holly did not present themselves as bookish grinds but as sophisticated individualists, they offered same-sex friends important assurance that intellectualism and feminine appeal did not have to exist in tension. The peers that career-oriented college women bonded with were, like them, active in the campus social and dating scene. They demonstrated by personal example that a smart woman could still be a popular date.

The style in which diarists described interactions with friends after moments of particular insecurity illustrates how important they were to them. One evening in November of 1956, for example, Stanford student Susan was dressing for a date. She was not entirely comfortable with the way she looked, but the admired Holly took care of her doubts: she had hoped she would "look nice tonight," Susan wrote. Her friend assured her that she had exceeded this goal by far: "She told me that I looked like an angel, and how gracious I was. She is so dear, so dear. . . . No one can make me feel so wonderful by saying things about me as Holly can."[55] Alice Gorton's friend Judy offered similar assurance. Alice struggled with weight issues throughout her stay at Smith. Constantly trying to lose pounds but never quite content with the results, she was assured by Judy that she was not only thin but downright "emaciated." Although a modern-day feminist familiar with the prevalence of eating disorders among female undergraduates cringes when reading such words, Alice was likely to take the comment as a compliment. She also clearly tried to serve as a supportive influence in Judy's life. As the latter wrote from her spring break "exile," she would find it "awful" if she did not have her "Gort" to "write and moan to."[56] Quite apparently, these women valued their friends by whom they felt understood.

However, the friendships between career-bound college students did rest on a shaky foundation. Alice's journal contains ample evidence that friends rallied to each others' support, especially after encounters with fellow coeds who disparaged the value of their goals or criticized their behavior. The arguments through which these students tried to reassure each other, however, point to important limitations of the mid twentieth-century cultural landscape for women with nontraditional goals. In conversations with friends and in private diary entries alike, career-bound young women repeatedly claimed that their interests marked them as exceptional and superior members of their sex. This strategy indicates that they felt immense pressure to defend their interests in front of challengers. It also is indicative of the devaluation, in Cold War culture, of allegedly typical female interests, goals, and values such as love, comfort, and security. The claim to have little in common with other women might allow female students to justify the wish for a career. It also, however, set very high performance standards and fed a negative image of women as a group.

Alice Gorton's journal poignantly illustrates the limitations of the strategy with which career-oriented college women tried to fortify their own identity in the face of challenges. In the case at hand, Alice was not herself the target of criticism. Rather, it was her friend Poof, with her unconventional goals and personality, who was being ostracized by other Smith College women. Alice tried her best to support Poof: Some women might have different outlooks, she argued. They might be happier and they might even enjoy greater popularity. But this, Alice emphasized, was just because they were herd animals who lacked Poof's potential. Quoting what she had said to the friend, Alice wrote she had "gestured towards the living room" of their dorm and said, "'Even though you may be . . . unhappy, be glad you aren't a vegetable like those . . . [followed by a list of names].'" In contrast to the "vegetables," Alice further argued,

Poof would one day "do something great."[57] How Poof responded to this statement, we don't know. Yet, if she gained consolation from Alice's words, relief would have rested on the idea that the loneliness and self-doubt Poof was experiencing at the present moment would someday be rewarded by the satisfaction of having made a truly "great" contribution to a profession or art. This, of course, was a lot to expect from her future and a very high performance standard to live up to.

That the way in which Alice tried to support Poof in the face of adversity might not have been exceptional is suggested by the journal of Susan at Stanford, who, in her first year at school also came under attack for her personality. While the diary is silent on what exactly transpired, Susan clearly felt that a number of female dormitory mates found her overly opinionated, competitive, and insufficiently social. Eventually, one student confronted her head-on. When Susan returned from a shower to her dorm room, the peer greeted her with the words: "'Susie, you are queer. You are really queer.'" Susan, who recounted the incident in her diary, was shocked and hurt. "I think girls can be the meanest things in the world," she wrote. She knew that girls tended to "say things like you're queer to make themselves feel better." Nevertheless, the comment did bring to her mind the danger that "all my thinking and everything will make me such an individual that I'll be alone."[58]

Susan does not seem to have kept her hurt to herself. Like-minded female friends quickly rallied to her support, and, as in the case of Alice and Poof, their arguments hinged on the idea that the young woman's outlook and personality were superior to those of her challengers. Because of this, the price of ostracism was worth paying. "Molly came in to talk to me," wrote Susan. As Molly assured her, she understood her conflict well: Susan was "afraid" to alienate her peers. Seeking their approval, however, would amount to selling out to a conformist mass. "And then she told me she was alone now," wrote Susan, "and that it was the most wonderful feeling." Susan's insecurities persisted. Yet she took Molly's words seriously. In the diary entries she made right after this incident, she pondered the possibility that she might in fact end up an isolated "queer." She consoled herself that as long as there were people like Molly who shared her outlook, she would not have to suffer such a fate. Moreover, she felt she owed it to herself to remain committed to her goals because she believed that she had the potential for excellence.[59] As in the case of Alice and her circle of friends at Smith, the bonds that tied together Susan and her female friends hinged on a shared sense of superiority over gender-conservative women.

Susan's encounter with a peer who labeled her "queer" also alerts us to an additional factor that complicated the friendships of career-oriented college women. By the 1950s, "queer" had been used as a derogatory label for gays and lesbians for quite some time. Yet it is not clear from Susan's diary whether she was familiar with the term. While Susan's peer might very well have used "queer" simply in the sense of "weird," Susan, like college women in general, would have been conscious of a spike of homophobia in the Cold War context. One of the comments in Alice Gorton's diary is telling here. As she wrote about her friend Poof, she would say she loved her "*if* it was possible" to have such feelings for "another girl" (emphasis mine).[60] Yet as Alice knew from the literature she encountered in college, intense feelings for a member of the same sex were suspicious. Influenced by psychoanalytical theories of sexual maturation, mental health experts by the 1950s tended to see intense feelings for a member of the same sex, or the lack of such feelings for a member of the opposite sex, as the result of arrested development most likely caused by a mother's inability to cope with a child's assertion of autonomy. Many pleaded tolerance for the people who, through no fault of their own, were trapped in an, if not overt, then at least "latent" stage of homosexuality. Most also felt, however, that because they saw same-sex leanings as the effects of developmental problems rather than as congenital desires, it was the responsibility of the individual to overcome the affliction.[61] Even though a woman might have pondered the possibility of love for an admired female in her personal journal, her consciousness of the stigma attached to such feelings would have caused her to be wary of allowing emotional bonds with other women from getting too strong.

That it could be difficult for a culturally literate young woman to be at ease with her feelings for a same-sex peer shows in a number of sources. After college, Mount Holyoke student Janet Brown came out as a lesbian. At no point in her correspondence, however, does one get the impression that she might have felt a particular infatuation with another woman. Social events she mentioned to her parents always included men. It is impossible to ascertain whether this was because Janet did not feel attracted to other women at this time or was censoring herself.[62] That a student would have been well advised to fake enthusiasm about heterosocial campus events even if she did not feel it, on the other hand, is clear. Already in 1945, Patricia Beck at Bennington College had been intensely self-conscious about the way in which her environment would label her friendship with the young wife of a faculty member if her frequent talks and visits were known: "Long talk about Barbara about things. She made me feel good. I admire her more than any woman I know. Psych. doesn't approve."[63] With growing dispersion of psychoanalytic advice in the mass media, the stigmatization of female friendships only increased.

The spike in Cold War fears of homosexuality meant that even young women who were not actively husband hunting had a strong incentive to cultivate relationships with men. The support they enjoyed from female peers, however, encouraged these women to expect a similar degree of acceptance from their male dating partners. When I reconstructed interactions between dating partners, I actually found that, personal doubts and conflicts notwithstanding, female students with access to friendship support networks believed that at least some college men would agree with them that a woman could be attractive and intellectual at the same time, that she could hold her own in banters and debates, and that she would be a desirable marriage partner.

A number of diaries allow us to reconstruct how the expectations of writers developed over time regarding their interactions with men. Alice Gorton, for instance, after only a short time in the dating culture, began to distinguish between first and second "rate" men. The men she ranked as second class simply "serve[d] [a] purpose." About the men she went out with in these cases, she wrote that she was "pleased" to receive their attention but she was not "thrilled or excited." She was actually "a bit bored" by them.[64] Mainly, she kept accepting them because she preferred them to the alternative of spending a weekend without male company: "Horrors!" she wrote when, at a rare occasion, she found herself without "a date for [the] coming weekend."[65]

While dating, especially at first, had an alibi function for Alice, she soon met men by whom she clearly wanted to be coveted as a consort. These were the men she labeled as intelligent and sophisticated. By the end of her first year at Smith, a Dartmouth College student named Richard had become a frequent subject in her journal. As she described him, he was "fascinating," and a "great light" and "brain" who "work[ed] on . . . many levels of subtlety" in discussions. She also wrote about a man named George that he was "extremely intelligent" and that she had enjoyed her date a lot. Meanwhile another man, Chase, had impressed her for his knowledge of Talcott Parsons, and she hoped he would take her out again.[66]

Alice's diary provides evidence about her own behavior on these dates. As she later quoted a friend who had observed her attitude, she was no "maternal and admiring [foil] for . . . lovers." Instead, she was "assertive" and "showed [her] own wit."[67] Letters by her dating partners confirm that this was also how her male friends perceived Alice. "Fascinating" Dartmouth College student Richard, for example, wrote: "You are one of the few people that interest me . . . and your letters interest me because I like to hear what's going on in your mind." Marc, whom Alice was seeing in the spring of 1952, also found her ideas intriguing: "Tell me about yourself, your dates, your school, your latest ideas, and above all, your . . . thoughts about life, sex, communism, death or what have you." At about the same time, Alice had also told a Princeton date that she had been "somewhat of a tomboy" and that she planned to "be a writer." The man was intrigued: "I would be most interested to read one of your compositions," he wrote her.[68] Although it is possible that Alice only pasted letters into her journal that showed her in a flattering light, she apparently went on a good number of dates during which she was not trying to hide her own interests, goals, or intelligence.

Margaret Hall at Bryn Mawr had dating encounters of a similar quality. Although she arrived on campus prepared to don the role of an educated wife-to-be, Margaret's ideas about what she expected from her inter- actions with men changed over time. Until the end of her sophomore year, she remained engaged to Bill, a student at the U.S. Naval Academy at Annapolis. When starting her education in 1951, she wrote about him that he was her "very dearest friend."[69] In the course of her studies, however, Margaret began to doubt that her fiancé and she were intellectually com- patible. As she remarked in retrospect about him, he thought that the main purpose of her stay at Bryn Mawr was to turn her into an educated wife and mother. While meeting men other than Bill, Margaret gradually developed that this was not what she wanted her education to yield.

Ironically, Margaret's fiancé introduced her to the first of a number of college men who suggested to her that a man and a woman could be on the same page intellectually. In 1951 Bill introduced her to Frank, another Annapolis student, at the Princeton–Navy football game.[70] Frank had also brought a date. Yet although his female partner sat right next to him in a crowded diner, Frank talked mostly to Margaret, who was intrigued by his wide-ranging literary interests. Her first impression was only con- firmed when Bill informed her that Frank was "a star man," the Annapolis term for a student who ranked "in the top 5%" of his class. How impor- tant this information was in Margaret's mind shows in her memory of the conversation. Years later Margaret still remembered that Bill told her about Frank's "IQ of 175." Then Frank sent her a notebook of his favorite quotations. After reading what she described as "succinct quotations con- cerning ethics, aesthetics, philosophy, and human relations," she felt as if she had met "a kindred spirit, a soul mate." As in Alice's case, letters by male dating partners show that she was not trying to hide her intelligence or conceal her interests. She and Frank would not see each other again for three years. When they met again, however, they instantly reconnected. The letters Frank wrote her right after their reunion shows that her intel- ligence and her broad interests had been the main reason why he had not been able to forget the meeting. It had been "clear to him," he described his first impression, "that [she] had . . . a brain (and used it)."[71]

Margaret broke her engagement two months after once again meeting the "star man," Frank. To turn their reunion into the reason for why she ended her relationship, however, would be simplistic. In fact, Margaret's expectations of relationships with men changed over time because of her overall college experience. She had developed a sense of herself as a person with scholarly potential. As a result, she was no longer content to use her skills solely in the capacity of "educated wife and mother." Moreover, she met other college men with whom she had conversations about intellectual and literary topics, which she never had with Bill. With evidence piling up that it was possible for men and women to converse as intellectual equals, she found more and more faults with her fiancé. He could not keep up with her, she now felt. "This year has been a constant growing" for her, she wrote, but "somehow it just no longer seems as though [she and Bill] were growing in the same direction." The weekends they spent together now struck her as "stop-thinking times, which [was] not what [she] want[ed] [her] life to be."[72] Margaret thus ended her engagement not because she found a new romantic partner but because college had changed her expectations of her own potential and of what she expected in her relationships with men.

Stanford University undergraduate Susan Sperry Borman's dating career resembles those of Alice and Margaret in essential aspects. Like her East Coast peers, Susan wanted to find companions who were intelligent and whose interests matched her own. This shows in the development of her relationship with an upperclass man she met in her first year. In her journal, Susan described Harry as a "smooth" college man, and she was instantly smitten. Yet she was not sure whether he was a good match. His personality and penchant for parties and drinking made him popular on campus, but these attributes did not automatically turn him into Susan's idea of a desirable companion.[73] A journal entry she made during this time shows us the qualities she wanted a dating partner to possess: "Lord, if I have him over-estimated," she wrote after one of their early dates and felt herself reminded of a story she once read. "He is struggling, he is; and all I can think of is that man in that story who went to look at his wife's I.Q. before he married her, because that's what I wonder about with Harry."[74] Like this fictional spouse, Susan did not want to get attached to a man who lacked intellectual potential. Shortly after, however, Harry took her to a philosophy lecture that left a lasting impression on Susan. Then, in the summer of 1957, the two Stanford students were both invited to join a research project in psychology funded by the Ford Foundation. As a proud Susan wrote her parents, work of this kind was normally reserved for graduate students. That she and Harry were allowed to join although they were still undergraduates seemed to have assuaged her doubts about her companion's intellectual potential and their compatibility.[75] Harry continued to be a topic in her journal for almost another year.

Multiple factors influenced these three career-oriented college women's focus on the intelligence and interests of their potential partners. Concerns about social standing were certainly among them. For instance, Alice Gorton tends to highlight in her journal the Ivy League backgrounds of dating partners, and throughout her stay at Smith avoided going out with students from the University of Massachusetts, the nearby public university. This attention to a dating partner's background, however, was not simply an attempt to match standards of popularity in the student culture. Rather, Alice felt that the attention and admiration of prestigious partners affirmed the legitimacy of her individual goals in the eyes of others. This shows, for example, in one of the comments the Smith College student made about Dartmouth College man Richard: She liked "to be seen with him," she wrote in 1952, because she felt she "could defy anyone with him behind [her]." In this journal entry, Alice did not say whom she was seeking to defy and why. Considering the frequency with which she pondered the legitimacy and value of her goals in her diary, however, it is likely that she was trying to show potential challengers that she was indeed an exceptionally intelligent woman and not a gender deviant. With an Ivy League man at her side, she had evidence that, instead of suffering from a developmental flaw, she was getting closer to her goal of becoming "admired—outstanding . . . intelligent—way above all."[76] Although Alice thus sought to shine in the reflected light of a man of high status, the ultimate goal of this was to affirm her identity as a woman with untypical goals.

An interest in the intelligence of dating partners, of course, also suggests that women were thinking about the attributes of future husbands. The postwar upsurge of pronatalism, coupled with the spread of standardized testing in higher education, drew heightened attention to the IQ scores of the educated young. In the student culture, this changed the definition of membership in an elite. Whereas before World War II family background and social affiliations of college men had formed the basis for status, criteria for membership in the postwar elite were changing to include intelligence ratings. Career-oriented college women's attention to IQ scores reflects their eagerness to gain prestige through association with members of high status groups. It might also indicate their acceptance of notions steeped in eugenic thinking that as members of an elite they needed to pair up with similarly gifted reproductive partners. That said, the evidence about what career-bound college women wanted from male partners still suggests that they were trying to establish a new foundation for their heterosexual relationships.

In their attention to the status and prestige of dating partners, Alice, Margaret, and Susan certainly reproduced elements of the rating system that sociologist Willard Waller saw at work in the late 1930s. Yet while the collegiate members of Waller's high-status groups reproduced traditional middle-class notions of gender, the reflections I found in at least some women's journals suggest that progressive notions of more egalitarian relationships had spread among students. If Margaret, Alice, and Susan are any measure, career-oriented college women wanted relationships with men with whom they had intellectual and cultural interests in common. As suggested by the fact that they were not trying to hide their own intelligence, they expected such like-minded men to accept them as thinkers and experts in their own right. As long-term dating partners, they coveted men who treated them as partners in intellectual as well as romantic adventures.

That attitudes such as those displayed by my three diarists were shared by at least a substantial proportion of college women is once again supported by sociologist Mirra Komarovsky's 1953 study. Among the 20 percent of her respondents who came to college already sure that they wanted careers, she found a pronounced sense that men would no longer contest a woman's right to have it all. To such women, "men" she writes, "are not the antagonists in a contest but are partners." They fully expected to one day "marry a man who recognizes that a woman, too, needs a vocation" and to support them fully in the realization of their aims.[77] Considering that I found similar views, we can safely assume that we are confronted here with a substantial minority. At least a significant proportion of postwar college women was thus actively engaged in the reconceptualization of companionate partnership.

The anecdotal evidence culled from diaries and personal letters suggests that in their conception of marriage, a vocal group of Cold War college women wanted to push for intellectual and economic egalitarianism. Despite their undeniable confusion and insecurity, they believed that at least some members of the educated young would support these goals. Here female peers aware of the same theories and books offered ideological and personal support. Meanwhile, dating relationships with men who seemed genuinely curious about women's professional aspirations indicated that the time had come when a male spouse would accept a woman as his intellectual equal and economic partner. Thus, there was a window of opportunity on the post–World War II campus to redefine gender and family norms. The next chapter focuses on how the sense of self of career-oriented young women is affected by their intimate experiences with men in an increasingly sexualized dating culture.

4 Individualism and Sexuality

In the early 1950s Philip, the son of a Harvard-educated lawyer from Charlotte, North Carolina, left the United States for a year of study abroad in Paris. Philip, who was twenty-two years of age by then, was an introverted, intense, and studious young man, and from the diary he kept, the reader soon learns that he felt ill at ease around other college men who found his love for literature; his interest in psychology, history, and anthropology; and his habit of journaling odd. Philip himself opined that his academic interests had long been simply "a great part of the life and heritage of civilizations to which [he fell] with others into lines of succession." What did cause him a lot of distress, though, was his dating history, which he found quite inadequate. Even though Philip's diary entries are often rather short and at times even cryptic, it is still apparent that he hoped that he might arrive at answers to the questions that concerned him by means of journaling. He recorded dreams, attempted to interpret them, and in general spent a lot of time and effort scrutinizing his emotions and the possibly unconscious motivations for his actions. He also eventually underwent psychological treatment. As he put it, "Analysis is a necessary evil that may bring about my good."[1]

Philip had male and female friends, and he seemed to have had long, friendly discussions with members of either sex. Yet in spite of good relations with some women, his reflections about female dating partners reveal an undercurrent of hostility. Shortly before embarking on his study abroad year, for instance, he stood up three female acquaintances with whom he was supposed to watch a movie. From the entry he made the following day, it almost seems as if he cherished the idea that he had been a bit cruel to the women. They had hurt his pride during previous dates, and he wrote that he had resented that each of the women had felt that "she had gotten control" over him. However, when he stood them up for the movie date, he had shown them that their sense of control had been "false."[2]

Philip continued to keep his diary after departing for his study abroad year. He might have looked forward to his time in France as a chance to reinvent himself, but his internal conflicts clearly did not stop. He worried a lot about the question of what profession he ought to pursue after graduation. He also agonized about the proper balance between "reading" and "living," especially because, in Paris no less than in North Carolina, he appeared to have had to justify his penchant for literature in front of male peers who told him that "a person shouldn't read a lot" but "rather live his own life."[3] But his anguish about the question of his vocation, or the proper balance between the contemplative and the social life, paled in contrast to the distress he felt about his difficulties to decide once and for all the question of how to act on a date. Repeatedly, during his stay abroad, he castigated himself for being insufficiently aggressive. Reflecting on an encounter with a young woman the previous night, he wrote, "I should have moved in, short of rape for which she is too strong anyway. Besides, she said at the first of the evenings it looked like she was in for assault and battery. I was a rude gentleman!? . . . C.—You know my desires. . . . I do not know yours. Do you know them?"[4]

Philip's diary entries are rarely sufficiently detailed to allow for a reconstruction of the context. Yet it is quite apparent that he had expected from his date with "C." a higher level of sexual intensity than the young woman was willing to consent to. As suggested by Philip's use of the word "rape," he was pushing for intercourse, yet his partner was holding the line. She might even have argued that only a betrothal would make her change her mind, as Philip recorded only a little later that "Of you . . . wedding poses are characteristic." Philip, however, was looking for experiences and not for a wife.

With its casual reference to "assault and battery," and "rape," Philip's diary entry comes as a shock to the reader. Raised in the South, with its hierarchical social and racial structure, he might have felt entitled to the bodies of working-class or nonwhite women, "short of rape." Because such a cross-class or cross-racial encounter was not what seems to have transpired here, Philip's dating partner probably expected him to respond in a chivalrous, "gentlemanly" fashion toward her. Yet that Philip felt that he ought to have "moved in," even against the explicit wish of his date, reflects a particular understanding of male and female sexuality. What his female partner consciously and clearly said regarding sex, Philip believed, was not likely to be an authentic expression of her wishes but a product of social conditioning: "The girls do unadmittedly like roguishness. But their super-egos permit them not to tell of it," he recorded after the date with C. Yet, while this young woman had internalized her society's prescriptions against premarital sex, Philip felt that he was in the process of transcending his upbringing and reaching a higher level of understanding. What he had learned in his years as a college student was that "sex mores" went "back and forth" throughout history. At times more permissive, at others less permissive, they "had little to do with the growth of civilization." Even in the "eyes of God," Philip continued, the sexes were equal in their desires: "Man and woman have no sex in the eyes of God—That greater force is concerned only that the race should continue to be."[5]

Considering that Philip's dating behavior had just earned him a rebuke from C., his reflections on sex mores might simply be a rationalization for actions that had crossed the line of acceptable behavior. But Philip was not simply trying to take a date for a ride. That he wrote with some conviction shows in the fact that his perceived failure to act on his insights on the flawed nature of "sex mores" and "civilization" caused him real distress. If his thesis was indeed right, then he had failed miserably on his date with the young woman. He "[had not] even straddled her," he castigated himself. "What could [he] expect" but a rebuff. Had he only been more "roguish," he and C. might both have reached a higher level of maturity. Unfortunately, Philip believed, he had not yet freed himself entirely from certain inhibiting influences that acted upon his psyche: his "extraconscious concern centered on the 'superiority of women.'" Accepting a traditional notion of women as moral arbiters, he had remained stuck in an outdated mindset and repressed what he in his journal repeatedly referred to as "the Drive." His "conscious mind" was still held captive like a "prisoner" by "the illusion" that it needed to "control" his sexual instincts. Philip felt he would need to free himself from the influence of women and their values for this sorry state of being to end. That same year in Paris, however, Philip seemed to have found the right partner in his own developmental quest. He wrote about her: "B. . . . in search for truth, we unite our intelligence in less conscious restrained (human) experimentation. . . . Hold me (sexual)/See all of each other."[6]

Philip's diary is an accidental find. When I came across it in the Southern Historical Collection at the University of North Carolina at Chapel Hill, I was actually looking for the papers of his sister Margaret, also a college student at the time. Because women have historically used the diary as a medium of expression more frequently than men, I had not systematically searched databases for journals by male students. In the course of perusing archives and collections, however, a few more journals by men came to my attention. In addition, I found a number of letters written by men in the personal papers of women. Over the course of my research, I found enough corroborating evidence from other male students to be able to say that neither Philip Kennedy's view of sexuality nor his tendency to scrutinize the workings of his inner self was exceptional.

Young men who attended college after World War II might well have scrutinized their thoughts and feeling about sexuality with particular intensity for a number of reasons. For one, they were increasingly exposed to a framework of male gender and sexual performance that emphasized assertiveness and aggression and that disconnected sex from love and romance. These "vernacular" sexual attitudes that were conveyed in interpersonal contacts between men and through jokes and innuendos had long coexisted with an official middle-class morality centered on the need for self-control and delayed gratification that was articulated in advice literature, the print media, and by the Church. In the context of the expansion of the military apparatus and the reestablishment of the draft after World War II, however, an unprecedented number of young men from a variety of backgrounds were initiated into a framework of male heterosexuality that often clashed with the mores and values on which they had been raised.[7]

While vernacular masculinity and sexuality had long carried an association with the sexual cultures of the lower classes and nonwhite races, the growing influence of Freudian theories of development increasingly naturalized these traits. In works of psychoanalysis, the male role in the sex act is that of an initiator of reluctant women. As Helene Deutsch argued in her influential two-volume *The Psychology of Women* (1944/45), for example, a normal woman's role in intercourse was passive and her desire had a strong masochistic streak. It was thus a man's responsibility to awaken his partner's desire. Bestselling books such as Ayn Rand's *The Fountainhead* (1949) and Grace Metalious's *Peyton Place* (1956) both reflected the spread of this masculine ideal of a man who, by breaking the resistance of his female lover, enabled her to enjoy her heterosexuality. In both works, the sexual initiation of a female character takes the form of a rape-like scenario in which a resisting woman is conquered by a man who knows better than she the true nature of her desire. The popularity of working-class male heroes in Hollywood movies and the launching of *Playboy* in the early 1950s also indicate the spread of vernacular sexuality as a new yardstick against which middle-class male adolescents measured their own performance.[8] In the post–World War II context of an expanding mass media and military apparatus, an increasingly homogenous set of expectations of heterosexual masculinity was therefore spreading. This masculinization of middle-class culture, combined with the psychoanalytical literacy young men acquired in the course of studying for a liberal arts degree, made this demographic particularly likely to scrutinize their sexual feelings and to experience insecurity about their development.

Cold War political and social developments only heightened the potential for male students to experience sexual anxiety. A debate about an alleged crisis of masculinity was escalating by the early 1950s as a result of increasing homophobia. The publication of the first of two studies by the research team around Alfred C. Kinsey, *Sexual Behavior in the Human Male* (1948), raised awareness of male homosexuality among Americans of all walks of life. Kinsey's revelations of the higher-than-expected number of men attracted to members of the same sex was covered in all the major magazines of the time and even discussed on the floor of Congress. Once alerted to the subject, the mass media further heightened awareness of homosexuality. In the sex-segregated units of the World War II military, many young people had experienced a gay or lesbian coming-out. After demobilization, this generation contributed greatly to the expansion of a homosexual bar culture. This subculture blossomed particularly in port cities on the East and West coasts.[9] Because of media exposés, however, the existence of what seemed like a virtual sexual underground became common knowledge. Then, in 1950, Undersecretary of State John Puerifoy released information about the firing of ninety-one allegedly homosexual employees. In response, a full-fledged sex panic ensued.

While "sex panics" in themselves were not new, the Cold War intellectual and political context made the situation unique. Americans' growing awareness of homosexuality was particularly significant because in a climate of national insecurity, sexual nonconformity and political unreliability became tightly linked. Within the expert community, the evaluation of homosexuality ranged from diagnoses of psychological immaturity and maladjustment to congenital perversion and mental illness. Inherent in any of these labels, however, was the idea that a homosexual lacked the personal integrity and character structure necessary to function in a social or political leadership position. This association made it possible for conservative partisans to capitalize on Puerifoy's revelations to discredit the New Deal establishment. The undersecretary seemed to prove that the masculinity—and hence the political reliability—of the East Coast liberal elite was wanting. In its most extreme form, this link between sexuality and political dependability was exploited by Wisconsin senator Joseph McCarthy in his venomous attacks against "bright young men . . . born with silver spoons in their mouth" who with their "Harvard accents" and "lace handkerchiefs" walked the halls of the State Department and the Capitol and posed as the "prancing mimics" of Moscow. Claiming that a critic of his demagogic approach had "to be either a Communist or a cocksucker," McCarthy outdid everyone in vulgarity.[10] However, he did not have a monopoly on the trope of emasculated elite manhood. Arthur Schlesinger, in his 1950 *The Vital Center*, a book that would become one of the founding documents of postwar liberalism, also linked political unreliability to gender and sexual performance. Writing against the backdrop of espionage allegations against former New Dealer Alger Hiss, Schlesinger tried to rescue the reputation of postwar establishment liberals. While previous cohorts, he claimed, might have been malleable "doughboys" whose spineless masculinity and unprincipled, weak, posturing in response to communism had endangered the nation, the new type of liberal was a "tougher breed" who had the "juices" to approach politics in a realistic and take-charge fashion and would issue in a return to the radical tradition of an America as it had existed before the machine age "emasculate[d] the political energies of the ruling class."[11]

The political and cultural context of the early Cold War created a very difficult environment for the sexual coming-of-age of educated youth. In this chapter, I look at encounters between dating partners to examine how public debates shaped the private experiences of career-oriented college women especially. These women chose as their dating partners men with strong academic interests and aspirations for social leadership. In the political culture of the Cold War, however, exactly these traits earned these young men the label of effeminate "egghead." Moreover, because they spent large amounts of time in the sex-segregated atmosphere of Ivy League classrooms, student dormitories, or fraternities, they also felt that they easily deviated from the increasingly popular model of the take-charge, assertive, virile, go-getter. Especially against the backdrop of their acute awareness of Freudian psychoanalysis, college men tended to grapple intensely with questions of their own gender and sexual performance. Proving one's sexual prowess in sexual encounters with dating partners in this context was a way to deal with normative pressures and self-doubts. The expectations of college men who took from their reading of Freudian psychoanalysis that only penile vaginal penetration was real sex, however, easily clashed with those of the women they dated who had encountered no less urgent messages to abstain from intercourse until marriage. Countervailing normative pressures acting on college men and women thus turned the student dating culture into a field marred by the potential for conflict, suspicion, and misunderstandings. And while the struggle to balance "boys" and "books" is not specific to the dilemmas of female undergraduates in the early Cold War, the historical backdrop made dating a particularly time and energy-consuming affair.

This chapter and the next focus on examples of students who were (hetero-)sexually active before marriage and whose private records offer insights into how they experienced their intimate encounters. I want to emphasize that I often do not know what acts women actually engaged in. Because sexuality was a highly controversial topic during the Cold War, the sources yield more silences than explicit evidence. Even in their introspective accounts, women broached the topic of sex only hesitantly, a reticence that at once reflects the writers' socialization into the middle

class and their lack of access to reliable information. The conflicts that
(hetero-)sexually active women were experiencing were thus not necessarily the consequence of premarital intercourse. Rather, they stem from
the fact that they were dating and at least at times engaging in a range of
activities that they and their contemporaries experienced as illicit. Two
women in particular, Alice Gorton and Sandra Iger, stood out because of
their unusually detailed personal papers. In each case, I know that the
women had premarital intercourse at some point in their college career,
and while their situations were different, their experiences, as this and the
next chapter will show, were similar in important aspects. Although I cannot generalize on the basis of these women's stories, I can situate them
in a larger context. Considering the discourse on sexuality, the curtailed
nature of college women's social autonomy, and their limited access to
reproductive information, my subjects' experiences were a logical result
of their situation and therefore likely to have been shared by others.

College women who began dating in the collegiate setting of the 1950s
did so in an environment in which standards of morality and expectations
of sexual behavior on a date were in transition. This transformation of
"manners and mores" had been under way for some time, but World War
II accelerated the pace of change by loosening the traditional bonds
between youths, parents, and home communities. Mobilization pulled
Americans away from the towns in which they had grown up and into
factories, military bases, and even overseas. Targeted as defense workers
and military personnel, women experienced unusual geographic mobility
and made substantial financial gains. The proportion of jobs available to
women rose from 21 percent before the war to 55 percent after 1941, and
many of these paid significantly higher wages than the white- and pink-
collar occupations women had traditionally filled. Last, but not least,
women joined the armed forces as auxiliaries, volunteers, and eventually
as official members of the military.[12]

The possibility of carving out spaces and lives independent from
families and spouses also opened up new erotic opportunities. The way
in which young women took advantage of new vistas is particularly
reflected in the phenomenon of adolescent girls flocking to military
bases to meet servicemen. Deemed "khaki wackies" and "good-time
Charlottes," they became the focus of an intense and concerned public
debate.[13] They were not the only young women, however, whose behavior concerned children's agencies and juvenile court judges. More and
more girls also smoked and drank in public, joined gangs, or acted in
other ways that suggested defiance of traditional family authority and
gender norms. Arrest figures for statutory offenses reflect the determination with which civic authorities and public health experts attempted to

contain these changes. Nonetheless, it was undeniable that in the context of the social disruptions of the war the social and sexual autonomy of young women was increasing.[14]

Although college women did not make the same financial gains as their working sisters, they were still affected by the social and economic upheaval of the time. As the wartime contributions of female students tended to take the form of volunteer labor, their autonomy did not increase as a result of financial gains. However, the war did make it increasingly difficult for college officials to maintain genteel conventions of supervised courtship. The nature of the challenge shows nicely in the correspondence of Mount Holyoke College student Alice Rigby who, one evening in 1944, right before the onset of spring, received a visit from a serviceman. The G.I. who called on the young woman found himself frustrated in his desire for a date with Alice by the housemother, Miss Smith, who turned him away. Miss Smith had followed a standard procedure. Since colonial times, on the basis of English common law principles, American institutions of higher education had acted as moral guardians of their charges. Honoring this responsibility to watch over the morality of a student in loco parentis, Miss Smith certainly expected her actions to find the approval of the Rigby family. Alice's parents, however, and Mr. Rigby in particular, complained. He would not claim that anyone in uniform was automatically a "gentleman," wrote Alice's father in a letter to the college, but a man serving his country did not deserve a rude rejection from a housemother.[15]

Alice's father's angry response should not be confused with moral laxity on his part. In fact, this case was one of mistaken identity. The reason why Mr. Rigby was so outraged that the young man in question was denied access to his daughter was because he trusted the man's credentials as a respectable "gentleman." A cousin had introduced Alice and the G.I. Yet, although the way the young man was treated by his daughter's moral guardian offended Mr. Rigby, Alice was more aware than her father of the context in which Miss Smith had acted. The suspiciousness of her housemother was based on a phenomenon many college officials and students perceived as a problem. Men from nearby military bases had repeatedly shown up on campus grounds in search of female company. This challenge to the sheltered atmosphere of a rural women's college was not something college officials took lightly. "What Miss Smith did wasn't wrong," Alice tried to explain the situation to her parents: "You can't blame her for being suspicious—they have had trouble with 'cruisers.'"[16] The nature of the problem was also explained to the Rigby elders in a letter from Dean of Residence Catherine P. Robinson. In defense of Miss Smith's actions, Robinson tried to convey the dilemma that Mount Holyoke faced in the attempt to balance patriotic support for the troops with its responsibility as guardian of the morality of its female charges:

> As you may imagine, running a girls' college located four miles from a flying field and eleven miles from an Army training center and being hospitable, but not too hospitable, is like charting a course between Scylla and Charbydis. . . . We have, on the whole, had very friendly relations with the men at Westover [Airbase]. . . . After a dance, however, we have occasionally had trouble with service men who come to the College not to call on a particular girl, but to pick up an acquaintance with anyone around the campus. This we try to discourage.[17]

The correspondence between the Rigby family and Dean Robinson poignantly illustrates a dilemma that existed for not just Mount Holyoke. Educators of young women in general faced the unintended consequences of officially sanctioned policies. Assuming responsibility for the moral integrity of their female charges was part of institutions' official mission. As part of their patriotic duty, however, they also encouraged female students to spend their free time volunteering as junior hostesses at events organized by the United Service Organization (USO), an agency established in 1941 to meet the social and spiritual needs of the members of the armed forces. The fact that older women were present during these events as chaperones illustrates that the breaking of standards of respectability was not included under the definition of service. But women were encouraged to make themselves available as companions and show servicemen a good time. Moreover, the media portrayal of hostesses blurred the distinction between "coeds" and "khaki wackies." In articles about the patriotic duties of college women and sorority girls, women who boarded trains and buses to meet a serviceman in the context of chaperoned USO events were commended for their service to the nation. Yet a few pages further, a reader often found magazine features about women who traveled on their own in search of erotic adventures.[18] That some G.I.s hoped that encounters with college women would also go beyond dancing and polite conversation shows in the letters of yet another Mount Holyoke student.

The letters of zoology major Grace Gray offer insights into the atmosphere at officially sponsored USO events at her college. Writing on the day of the 1943 Victory Ball in a letter to her parents, Grace described how the dance affected campus life. Long before the official start of the event, men from the nearby Westover air base flooded college grounds. "Tonight is the Victory Ball," wrote Grace, "and already there are a lot of men on campus." She did not intend to go because she had "lots of work to do," but most of her peers, she informed her parents, had different priorities: "All the kids are going," she wrote and "most" young women did so "with blind dates."[19]

Grace spent the night of the Victory Ball in the science lab. When her "gang" of female friends returned from the event, they let her in on what had transpired. Apparently the maintenance of official standards of morality had been difficult. Grace shared her information with her family:

> It seems that the boys in the service . . . are pretty demoralized. . . . They aren't one bit sure that they are fighting for anything worthwhile. . . . Therefore, they are determined to get as much pleasure out of every moment as they can, as long as they are still alive. A good number of them brought their own liquor along and got drunk during intermission. Many . . . attempted . . . to persuade the girls that since everything else was accelerated at this time, it was necessary that court-ship be accelerated too. . . . So ended the effort of Mt. Holyoke girls to be patriotic and show our fine and noble service-men a pleasant evening.[20]

Grace's description of the dance was hardly an unbiased account. As she had told her parents before the event, she was content with just watching her friends have a good time. It made her feel "proud" to watch her peers take off for a night of entertaining men, like "ducklings [going] for [a] swim." The words she used in her letter, however, also show that she felt old-fashioned and inexperienced by comparison to her peers. The "ducklings," she informed her parents, participated in mixed-sex campus events regularly: for them, the Victory Ball was "far from their first swim!" Writing in a self-deprecating tone that belied her self-consciousness about her choices, Grace said that she was a "rather senile fat old duck" who preferred lab work and studying to socializing with servicemen.[21] Grace might thus have exaggerated the negative aspects of the Victory Ball in an attempt to make herself feel better about turning down a social opportunity. When "the kids" returned from their adventure with shocking tales, she could feel validated in her decision. "Well, I'm just as glad I didn't go!" she wrote her parents.[22] She might be old-fashioned, but at least she did not have to put up with drunken servicemen who tried to take her for a ride.

While it is possible that Grace exaggerated those aspects of the ball that affirmed her choice not to attend, it is apparent that Mount Holyoke College struggled to enforce moral standards on campus. Describing in her letter to her parents the experiences of her clique of female friends, Grace had put the onus for the breakdown of morality on the shoulders of the "boys in the service." Other accounts make clear, however, that college women were not necessarily damsels in distress. That they, too, were trying to carve out new erotic opportunities shows, for example, in the correspondence of Alice Rigby, who told her parents in 1944 about two female peers who got in trouble for violations of moral regulations. As Alice wrote her family, the students were suspended for four days, a punishment she described as "tough." She felt "awfully sorry for them," but she also supported the decision. She felt "very Puritan" about her attitude, she wrote her parents, but she did believe that her fellow students had "brung [sic] [their punishment] on themselves."[23] In this letter it is not clear what exactly the women in question had done to attract official attention. At the very least, however, they had tried to evade the college's attempt of control of their social and sexual behavior. This by itself, we can see from Alice's letter, already concerned not only the administration but also parts of the student body. By independently looking for social and possibly erotic opportunities, the students were blurring the boundary between patriotism and immorality. As such, they constituted a danger to the reputation of all women at Mount Holyoke College.

The evidence for a breakdown of moral standards at Mount Holyoke College is particularly significant for our understanding of the war's impact on the collegiate setting. Of all the Seven Sister women's colleges, Mount Holyoke was the most isolated one.[24] That even in a small community like South Hadley, Massachusetts, mores and standards were slipping thus suggests the extent to which wartime developments created problems for institutions dedicated to the higher education of women.

We should not underestimate the extent to which contemporary observers perceived the wartime slippages in discipline and morale among college women as a problem. Boundaries of permissible sexual activity in middle-class youths had been expanding through the interwar period. Older courtship conventions such as "calling" and the practice of chaperonage increasingly gave way to "dating." Even in the conservative advice manuals written by Emily Post, the chaperone was labeled a "vanishing . . . convention."[25] College campuses were anachronistic spaces in this context. Charged with the supervision of morality in loco parentis, they held on to the genteel model of supervised courtship.[26] Young ladies were allowed to gain experiences with the opposite sex in the context of organized mixers or by meeting gentlemen "callers" in the semipublic space of their dormitory's parlor. When coeds accepted the invitations of cruising servicemen, they therefore accelerated the speed with which a traditional upper middle-class model of courtship was dissolving. This development was alarming, on the one hand, because it fed wartime concerns about the convergence of male and female behavior. Coeds who tried to evade their alma maters' attempts of moral supervision displayed a sexual agency at odds with traditional notions of feminine passivity in courtship. In the sexual realm, they seemed to be acting more and more like men. The extent of the problem, however, went beyond the challenge to female gender norms.

Mid-twentieth-century educators of women were alarmed not only by the changing behavior of women but by the fact that this development occurred at a time of challenges to middle-class homogeneity in general. That coeds violated moral rules and regulations was, after all, not a new phenomenon. Depending on undergraduate tuition payments and faced with growing numbers of women who saw in the collection of experiences independent of the supervision of adults a part of their well-rounded education, colleges had to make concessions to accommodate modern youth. The introduction of deans of women and the adoption of rules and regulations served to enforce official morality. Yet campus life also offered considerable leeway.[27] The angry letter of Alice Rigby's father shows that as long as parents trusted that their daughters would meet "gentlemen" on their dates, they accepted college dating as a matter of fact. Yet the correspondence between the Rigbys and Mount Holyoke College also illustrates the particularities of the situation in the 1940s.

In assessing the nature of the morality problem during the war, the distinction between gentlemen callers and "cruisers" is crucial. As Dean Robinson's letter to Mr. Rigby shows, the college was not opposed to the visits of young men in principle. When hosting patriotic events for servicemen, however, the college opened its doors to G.I.s from a variety of backgrounds. In this context, the maintenance of middle-class culture and values became a more urgent matter. From the many servicemen that wartime coeds met as part of their role as patriotic helpmeets, gentlemen callers were still welcome as potential beaux. Respecting the official rules of courtship, they demonstrated their knowledge of and respect for genteel college convention. "Cruisers," however, did not. Whether out of ignorance or defiance, they lacked the proper reverence for traditional mores and might give young women the wrong idea. In an attempt to maintain class homogeneity, Mount Holyoke College attempted to shield its charges from men who might introduce to them behavioral models and moral examples that were irreconcilable with genteel values.

If educators of women had expected that the end of the war would also bring back the times when coeds met only with "gentlemen" callers, the G.I. Bill crushed their hopes. Veterans helped transform not only the academic aspects of college but also the behavioral conventions and expectations in the student dating culture. After their experiences in the World War II military, middle-class men were no longer as likely to conform to collegiate conventions as did preceding cohorts of college men. Moreover, of the many men who took advantage of government-subsidized higher education, a substantial proportion came from a non-elite background.[28] Once again, developments at Mount Holyoke College, the most remote and least easily accessible of the Seven Sister colleges, illustrate the extent of change.

The letters of Mount Holyoke student Mary Browning offer a window into how the influx of new students changed the campus dating culture.[29] Mary, who was born in Baltimore, Maryland, and started her education in South Hadley in 1947, kept up a regular correspondence with her mother. From the information about Mrs. Browning's background, it is clear that Mary came from an upper-middle-class family. Her father held a Ph.D. in psychology from Johns Hopkins. Her mother, born in Mystic, Connecticut, was a Wellesley alumna who had graduated in 1916 with a major in English. Maybe Mrs. Browning shared with her oldest daughter stories about her own collegiate experiences. In any case, when Mary was about to go to her first freshman mixer at the private Amherst College, she expected to meet proper young gentlemen in a genteel setting. There would be, she wrote her mother, a "big Freshman dance" to which "all the Freshmen from Amherst [were] invited . . . to meet the Freshmen from Mount Holyoke." She continued that she was hoping at this dance to line up an escort for the main social event of the semester: "This dance is supposed to let you find one that you could ask over to the big fall formal dance put on by the Senior year book committee." Mary was looking forward to both: "I want to go awfully badly." When the young women returned from the freshman dance, however, she was disappointed. The male students did not match her expectations of eligible and appealing beaux. "Most of the boys were quite peculiar," she wrote her mother. Their behavior had shocked her; they "had been drinking," she wrote. She also found them unappealing in their looks: "Some of them were pretty horrible looking," the disappointed young woman informed her parent.[30]

It is of course possible that Mary had the bad fortune to attend a dance with an unusually high number of unattractive college men present. It is more likely, however, that ethnic and class backgrounds other than the Protestant gentility that she had anticipated tainted her impression. Apparently Mary had expected that as a student of one of the prestigious Seven Sister Colleges she would meet men who matched her own background in culture and class. She found, however, a surprisingly diverse body of male students. In explanation of the young men's peculiarity, she wrote to her mother, "not only were . . . fellows from Amherst present, but also some from Mass. State and Springfield." Had Mary been aware of the demographic and social developments in the East Coast valley that had become her temporary new home, she would not have been surprised. Massachusetts State (renamed University of Massachusetts in 1947) was originally founded as one of the first public land-grant agricultural colleges in 1863. Already in 1931, it had outgrown its original limited mission and broadened its curriculum. The most significant spur in growth, however, occurred as a result of the boost in enrollment through the G.I. Bill. By 1954 the institution featured a student body of more than four thousand.[31]

While the G.I. Bill opened up educational opportunities for many young men, their chances to find a dating partner in the classroom were a different matter. Although coeducational since 1892, Massachusetts State, just like other universities in the nation, rejected many of its female applicants to make room for veterans. In the face of this uneven ratio of male to female students, women from the nearby Seven Sister colleges beckoned as potential dates. The G.I. Bill thus introduced men from nontraditional college backgrounds to the circuit of formal mixers, parties, and dances that had long been a staple of collegiate culture. This mixing of classes in the public relations battle of the Cold War represented the success of United States democracy. If Mary's letter is any measure, however, genteel college women were not necessarily infected with the spirit of democracy when it came to finding dancing and dating partners. Mary was not just appalled by the drinking and the looks of the students she had met. She drew a link between their behavior and demeanor and their status as public university students. By virtue of what she assumed was a family background different from her own, she rejected them as potential beaux.

That in the Browning household there was in fact a certain cultural snobbery against men from ethnic and class backgrounds other than their own shows even more poignantly in the letters of Mary's sister, Louise, who went to Wellesley. Writing to Mary about a dance at her school in 1947, she at first gushed about a "Harvard senior" who had saved her from having to finish a dance with a partner she did not like. It was "just like in a fairy tale," Louise told her sister. "He cut in on me just when I was dancing with the most horrible drip going." Unfortunately, the man soon disappeared again, exposing Louise once again to unwanted attentions: "And . . . then I met another person who appeared to have a crush on me. . . . It was horrible,—especially since all his friends were Jewish. So I suppose he is one, too, even though he didn't look like one. . . . What do you suppose is the matter? I don't look Jewish, do I?"[32]

While Louise's concern with looking "Jewish" suggests disturbing prejudicial attitudes, we need to consider the Browning sisters' age, lack of experience, and the fact that they had only just left behind their parental home before we condemn them too harshly. Having been brought up in a sheltered Protestant middle-class household, neither sister had been exposed to diversity before. The sentiments that emerge in their letters therefore say more about the older Brownings than about the young women who wrote the words. In fact, Mary's attitude soon changed. She started going steady with a young man from another vocationally oriented institution, Worcester Polytechnic Institute. Yet, as we will see, her difficulties of adjusting to a campus life that no longer operated along the norms of genteel mores were just beginning.

The letters of the Browning sisters offer only snapshots of experiences. However, they do hint at the ways in which the diversification of the student body in the wake of the G.I. Bill affected the campus dating culture. Young women who had experienced a sheltered upbringing now met men who were older than traditional college men, more experienced, and less likely to stick to official courtship standards. Having been exposed to military culture, they displayed behavior that sheltered young women found difficult to reconcile with their expectations of "fairy tales" in which chivalrous gentlemen treated them like ladies. The drinking Mary referred to already hinted at one facet of this development. Veterans on the G.I. Bill were hardly the first college men who brought a flask to a date or dance, however. Far more significant in the context of postwar higher education was the way in which their sexual expectations changed campus life.

Veterans who went to college or university on the G.I. Bill entered a social milieu very different from the one they had just left behind. The culture of enlisted men in the World War II armed forces was highly sexualized. Although officially, control and containment were the policies adopted regarding the sexual behavior of G.I.s, lenience and accommodation was increasingly the reality. Monthly lectures and films encouraged servicemen to abstain from sex but at the same time counseled them in the use of condoms. G.I.s openly displayed pictures of pin-ups and received cheesecake magazines through the mail. Sex was a frequent topic among enlisted men and visits to prostitutes a common way to spend time on leave. The general atmosphere in the U.S. armed forces was that men needed sex and that they were entitled to find these needs met.[33]

When former G.I.s returned to civilian life, they brought with them attitudes toward sex that they had learned in the military. Veterans often resented obstacles to their erotic and dating opportunities. Moreover, their refusal to accept the curfews and regulations that impeded their access to dating opportunities was contagious. By the early 1950s, male discontent on college campuses across the nation took the form of sporadically occurring panty raids. Ostensibly in protest against their curtailed access to dating partners, college men on these occasions stormed into women's dormitories and sorority houses to capture female underwear as trophies. Beginning first on the campuses of larger universities, these raids soon entered the collegiate setting as well. In the spring of 1953 Princeton University students could be seen marching through town to chants of "We want girls, we want sex, we want panties."[34] By the time the U.S. government discontinued veteran benefits after the Korean War, the dating and sexual expectations of these older, more experienced men had left a trace on the student dating culture for good.

College women noted the changes in the sexual climate of campus life. Similar to their wartime predecessors, many put the responsibility on the shoulders of men. However, their letters also allow us to see that some coeds were exercising a sexual agency of their own. As Mary Browning's letters inform her mother in 1950, Mount Holyoke was suffering the effects of a series of "scandals." For one, there was the example of a young heiress who used her trust fund money to elope and explore the country: "During the past 2 or 3 months she has been traveling around," wrote Mary. "She got as far as Florida." By the time Mary told her mother about this incident, the heiress was petitioning the college to allow her to re-enroll. In the meantime, however, "another senior [had] packed up and took off."[35] Moreover, Mary's letters also suggest that the "scandals" on campus were not just limited to an increase of wanderlust among young women. Female students also actively violated boundaries of appropriate sexual conduct: "Other [sic] scandal is the fact that another girl had an abortion—and then the campus cop found 4 or 5 contracepts [sic] around the grounds after Snowball weekend. . . . All this is very upsetting to the administration. We're supposedly going to have a required assembly on this serious subject."[36]

When Mount Holyoke College required students to attend a hearing on the topic of behavioral standards, it was not acting alone. Responding to the visible changes in the courtship behavior of college men and women, Bowling Green State College, for instance, condemned what it saw as "emotional exhibitionism" on campus. In the student newspaper, the school tried to define the line that separated acceptable from unacceptable actions. As the writer opined, good-bye kisses and handholding were acts "quite normal and within reason" and did "not violate the moral code properly expected of college students." However, the current trend was an increase of unreasonable "demonstrations" of affection. As the writer stressed, "unnecessary prolonged embraces while kissing good bye," and "uninhibited indulgences" would not be tolerated. A student engaging in such conduct should expect to become "the target of administrative action."[37]

In their attempts to change the behavior of individual students, administrators in higher education were fighting a growing trend. The

1953 publication of the second Kinsey report, *Sexual Behavior of the Human Female*, made particularly clear the extent to which norms were changing. After Kinsey's earlier findings about men had already come as a shock, the impact of the female volume was virtually explosive. Close to 50 percent of American women, the study exposed, had coitus before marriage. Not only were many women no longer saving themselves for marriage, they masturbated, petted, and engaged in same-sex activities at rates that were unexpected to all but the most jaded of observers.[38] Regarding college-educated youth, the one thing that might have consoled cultural conservatives was that, despite Kinsey's figures, the persistence of a double standard of behavior still motivated young women to limit the intensity of sexual exchanges on a date.[39] Yet over the course of the 1950s, signs of an unraveling of this dynamic were building up. As sociologist Ira Reiss would put it by the early 1960s, educated women had become "half-willing" as boundary setters at best. Americans, he advised, should expect "a continued trend toward . . . permissive codes."[40] In the immediate post–World War II period, however, college administrators were not ready to accept the increasing sexualization of campus life just yet.

In an attempt to keep a future elite committed to traditional middle-class sex mores, institutions of higher education imposed increasingly stringent rules and regulations on their students. Practices, however, differed according to gender. Curfews in most schools limited only the social mobility of women. Rules for visitors and callers in single-sex colleges specified in often excruciating detail how a young man and a young woman ought to interact with each other. Rules required doors to remain open and feet to stay on the floor. Attempts to maintain control by providing scripts of moral and appropriate behavior became only more pronounced in the course of the 1950s.[41] The treatment of college men, however, was different. Although some institutions maintained official curfews for men into the 1960s, male students in general faced fewer obstacles to their social mobility. An Amherst College student described the permissive attitude of his alma mater: "We have lots of freedom here. . . . About the only restriction is no kegs of beer in the dorms."[42]

The different treatment of the sexes reflected the persistent influence of a sexual double standard that held women up to higher standards of respectability. But it also illustrates the fact that it seemed increasingly impossible to insist on restraints of the sexual energies of male students. As panty raiders and disgruntled veterans had made clear, more and more male students saw it as their right to express their sexuality in active and assertive ways. Although administrators no longer felt they could insist on constraints on the physical urges of men, they still hoped to channel the libidinous energies of the educated young into appropriate channels by restricting men's access to those women they would ideally one day marry. Raising the obstacles to premarital sexual encounters would keep middle-class youth committed to the institution of marriage. Keeping young women from exercising sexual freedoms in ways similar to men would maintain complementary gender roles. And as long as the women whom the men of the expanding middle class married remained paragons of morality, traditional middle-class values and ethics would survive even in the face of the challenges posed by the cultural changes and the influx of new groups into academia.

Judged from their official responses, the educators of women seemed to have moved very close to the camp of post–World War II religious conservatives. Insisting on the necessity of holding on to a firm official standard of morality, proponents of a fundamentalist position were gradually growing in influence in the Cold War nation. Their beliefs and philosophy showed particularly clearly in the response to the publication of the two Kinsey studies of the sexual behavior of humans (1949 and 1953). The evidence of frequent rule breaking and of a diversity of moral codes suggested to Kinsey and his team of researchers that an adjustment of official prescriptions was in order. Religious conservatives, however, disagreed. Articulating his stance on Kinsey in a book-length publication, Roman Catholic Archbishop Fulton John Sheen argued, for instance, that Kinsey merely gave an "air of scientific goodness" to "exaggerations and perversions" that would be clearly recognizable as "evil" if it was not for the mantle of social science.[43] Sheen here responded to the publication of the first Kinsey report on men. His outrage at the study paled, however, in comparison with the reaction of American religious leaders to the follow-up volume on women. Linking notions of female purity and national identity, the editor of a Catholic newspaper wrote about the 1953 report that it was "the most direct and devastating attack upon Christian civilization" since the "Revolution in Russia in 1917" and a "dirty, beastly attack upon American womanhood." An Indiana chapter of the National Council of Catholic Women, meanwhile, in a letter to the president of Indiana University where Kinsey was teaching, likened Kinsey to the perpetrators of the Nazi Holocaust against the Jewish people. "We have seen in Nazi Germany what can happen to men when the traditional idea of moral law is questioned and then scoffed at." Among religious conservative Americans, this evaluation was widely shared. These Catholic voices were of course on the conservative edge of American religious thought. Yet when it came to the subject of female sexuality, even liberal mainline Protestants took a hardliner position. That Kinsey's report reflected "moral anarchism" and "absurd hedonism" was Reinhold Niebuhr's verdict in *Christianity and Crisis*. The tone of the national debate was clear: moral standards and behavioral expectations might be changing. The trend, however, needed to be resisted rather than condoned.[44]

While the higher-education setting certainly reflected elements of this resurgent religious conservatism, evidence from the students themselves suggests that the question of morality was not answered through recourse to an absolute standard of right or wrong alone. The correspondence of Mount Holyoke student Janet Brown, who discussed Kinsey with her parents, illustrates the point. Janet's parents had sent her a clipping of an article by Archbishop Sheen. In her reply, Janet summarized his view: "although no one does right, there is still an absolute right," she wrote. This, she added, was "the accepted viewpoint." Yet, significantly, Janet did not stop her musings here. In reference to Sheen's article, she wrote she found him "rather good" but also labeled "some of his points . . . rather doubtful—like [his] attitude towards the validity of Kinsey." Janet here was referring to the archbishop's uncompromising condemnation of the scientist. Yes, she admitted, most people would agree with him that there was "an absolute right." But she could not quite reconcile that with what she was learning in her social science classes: "most social sciences take the stand that right is conformity with group mores." Janet was clearly confused. She asked: "May I keep the article a week or two until I get other's opinions on it??"[45] Janet did not return to the subject of the Kinsey study in her letters. But her correspondence illustrates an important point. Exposure to higher education challenged arguments based on fixed, universal truths. Their awareness of theories about the naturalness of the libido for both sexes and of the cultural specificity of values and mores had the potential to turn educated youth into religious skeptics.

Although arguments based on religious fundamentalism were not likely to win many students' hearts or minds in the intellectually sophisticated setting of higher education, mid-century social scientists managed to reconcile cultural relativism and modern sexology with a conservative moral agenda. The main influence here came from the functionalist school of social analysis. The way in which this paradigm influenced the advice literature directed at middle-class teenagers shows nicely in one of the period's most popular examples of the genre: Evelyn Millis Duvall's *Facts of Life and Love* (1950). Having earned her Ph.D. in Human Development from the University of Chicago, Duvall had studied in an academically cutting-edge interdisciplinary department in which students drew on insights from anthropology, biology, sociology, and psychology. She also had a background in liberal Christianity. A scholarship from her local church for which she had taught enabled Duvall to graduate from Syracuse University in 1927. She started to write about family and marriage issues first in magazines such as the *Christian Home*. During the war, she helped organize Marriage and the Family courses for enlisted personnel for the United States Armed Forces Institute. Subsequently, she joined the newly established National Council on Family Relations and wrote some of the most widely distributed high school textbooks. She lectured frequently in front of young audiences and on these occasions collected questions by and responses of adolescents concerning sexuality, dating, and marriage. In *Facts of Life and Love*, she presents her evaluation of this material to the American public.[46] The book clearly reflects the influence of the functionalist paradigm on her thinking and the way in which it enabled her to reconcile Protestant morality and social science.

Duvall's emphasis on maintaining traditional sexual mores and family structures shows in her warning against premarital sexuality. Although she presented the presence of strong sexual urges as a "normal" fact of adolescence, she warned youth against permissiveness. Once floodgates of instinct were opened, she emphasized, physical urges would be hard to stop. Immensely "strong and insistent," the sex drive would "press for completion." Because of this, premarital sexual contacts easily culminated into "a problem [which] in our country [was] popularly known as 'getting into trouble.'" Although many such troubles confronted youth of today, Duvall informed her readers, when people used the phrase, they were virtually always using it in reference to "the pregnancy of an unmarried girl." For any young woman who finds herself in such a situation, she writes, the consequences will be severe. "Getting into trouble . . . at best . . . is disillusioning, often painful. . . . At worst it can wreck [a girl's] whole life."[47]

Duvall conceded that the stigma against out-of-wedlock pregnancy was not based on a universally valid moral imperative. It was a cultural convention. Yet the way a culture evaluated a behavior could not be separated from how a person experienced it. Combining relativism with cultural determinism, she wrote that the "attitude of the general public" would inevitably "increase the seriousness of the problem." Considering this context, rules against certain conducts served a functional value. Offering safe standards to live by, they protected the individual and shielded society from the costs of deviant behavior. "When a girl defies these safeguards she places herself in a highly vulnerable position. Better by far is willing conformity to the standards of one's culture, based upon one's intelligent awareness of why such restrictions are important." *Facts of Live and Love* thus clearly illustrates functionalism's contribution to the perpetuation of the status quo. Duvall combined an acknowledgement of the relativity of standards with an emphasis on the functional value of conformity. While youth today might possess considerable freedoms, she argued, a mature and intelligent person understood the consequences of deviance and would therefore abstain from defying social mores.[48]

The conservative direction of Duvall's analysis notwithstanding, it is important to note that she urged both men and women to conform to traditional sexual mores. In line with a longstanding dichotomous view of the meaning and quality of sexuality for the sexes, she argued that women were "less easily excited by sex stimulation and more slowly moved to demand sexual contact" and could therefore "stop love making more easily than the average male." For this reason, it has "down through the ages . . . been considered the female's responsibility to keep relationships under control." Duvall did not see male biology as an excuse to express urges and desires at the expense of society and the individual, however. The need to comply with conventions extended to the males of the species. Boys, no less than girls, she wrote, would spoil their chances for "a happy marriage and family life" by defying their society's rules and regulations. "Sowing of wild oats so often means the harvest of a crop of thistles," she warned. A mature and intelligent boy recognized "that sex behavior is a matter of responsibility for both sexes."[49]

Duvall thus suggested to youths of both sexes that they had a responsibility to not give vent to their individual desires at the expense of others. While she here presented conformity as the sign of a young person's intelligent comprehension of what would ultimately be best for him or her, she painted the alternative in distinctly unattractive colors. Youth who refused to play to society's rulebook, she wrote, were hardly laudable nonconformists. Rather, their behavior was the result of their upbringing in dysfunctional families, of ensuing psychological problems, and of a lack of education. These factors Duvall saw as potential dangers in families across the social spectrum. Yet she also linked low class status to an individual's inability to conform. Her frequent mentioning of "certain neighborhoods" in which problem families and individuals congregate draws a clear connection between sexual nonconformism and social marginalization. A low class position in Duvall's functionalist paradigm was the result of a lack of impulse control. Here the consultant of the National Council of Family Relations drew on a larger literature that applied individualistic and psychologizing interpretations to analyze the social position of lower class and nonwhite populations.[50] The growing popularity of this line of argumentation in the postwar period suggests that in the face of widespread challenges to traditional middle-class values, an emphasis on the importance of traditional standards of sexual behavior and gender performance was becoming more pronounced. Duvall illustrates this link poignantly through the example of "Viola."

The character of Viola in Duvall's book serves as a powerful illustration for the consequences awaiting a woman who fails to maintain control over her "appetites." "Viola was a creature of strong desires and lusty appetites," writes Duvall. She went through life following her impulses "without considering the consequences." When she entered adolescence, "she gave complete reign to her feelings and could not stop the behavior that led to" the expected result: "her pregnancy." Only now that she was dangerously close to ruining her chances for happiness forever did she finally "get the counseling guidance that helped her come face to face with herself and start the process of growing up emotionally." Yet while eventually Viola saw the errors of her ways, a person who rejected expert help in becoming a "reasonable, sensible person" would have only himself or herself to blame for the consequences. As Duvall closed a section on the sexual challenges of youth, "your sex life," and hence your social position, "is yours to choose."[51]

The paradigm that underwrites Duvall's highly popular book accounts for a lot of the power and influence of official morality in the collegiate setting. While a fall from grace and social status was the stick that kept students committed to their administration's standards of morality, the air of mature responsibility bestowed on those students willing and able to comply was the carrot. Student publications and personal writings clearly reflect that the emphasis on personal responsibility and the social utility of regulations left an imprint in the collegiate setting. Student self-government organizations emphasized the need for the individual to control personal passions and individualistic desires for the benefit of the whole. As the Smith College Student Government Association put it: "maintenance of . . . social honor is the responsibility of each member of the student body."[52] This was not just an official line. Female students complied with official regulations and actively policed and enforced them. Some served on judicial boards while others supervised their peers' compliance with curfews and other dating regulations in an unofficial capacity. As Beth Bailey argues, college women who served on honors and judicial boards in the 1950s through the early 1960s did not hesitate to use the power of their office to the full extent. Disciplinary measures students imposed on peers were often more harsh than administrations would have demanded.[53]

Occasionally, isolated students attempted challenging moral rules and regulations. This was the case at the Women's College of the University of North Carolina in 1953, for example. Yet, despite these students' argument that the rigid requirements clashed with the ideal of individualism and contradicted the school's claim to educate them in the values of social responsibility, their protest of official regulations went nowhere.[54] Either because they wanted to protect their own reputations as female students or because they identified with their institution's agenda, a majority of coeds accepted the need to adhere to codes of conduct that had been agreed upon as beneficial safeguards and yardsticks. Unfortunately, the

official codex of regulations and the behavioral expectations women confronted while on an actual date at times diverged quite significantly.

The discrepancy between official morality and behavioral expectations on a date became apparent to Alice Gorton when she started
dating "fascinating" Dartmouth College man Richard in 1952. Alice clearly
wanted a close friendship with Richard. In her diary, she still described
him as one of the most important acquaintances she had made at Smith,
even after they had had a falling out. Richard, as mentioned in the previous chapter, was important to her because the fact that the suave and
intelligent Ivy League man was interested in her raised her self-
confidence and increased her standing among her peers. In addition, she
sincerely enjoyed the conversations and intellectual banter. Her enjoyment of the friendship was dimmed, however, when Richard wanted her
to consent to sexual acts for which she was not yet ready.

Insights into sexual activities of postwar college women are hard to
come by. As noted earlier, even in their diaries women often make only
vague references to acts they engaged in. The underlying reason here was
often fear that peers, parents, or other authority figures might get hold of
private journals. In addition, however, women also lacked a language to
describe their actions. "Love making" is the almost universal term they
applied when referring to activities on a date. But which acts, specifically,
they included under this term tends to be obscure. This lack of access to
a terminology implies that postwar college women, just like previous
generations of middle-class female adolescents, lacked information about
sex. Although lectures and courses on marriage education were increasingly part of their reality, women's inability to describe body parts and
desires suggests that they were learning more about morality and the
need for role adjustment than about the physical and emotional aspects of
sex. The lack of a language to talk about desires was an additional causal
factor for the silences around sex in women's writings. In cases in which
women did broach the topic, their writings point to further consequences
of their sheltered upbringing. These students did not know for sure which
kinds of sexual activities carried a high risk of leading to pregnancy and
which did not. They were either not able to name the birth control
methods used at dating encounters or misspelled their names. Coming
from women who were unusually literate and educated about topics not
related to sexuality, such spelling errors suggest that they rarely encountered discussions of contraceptives in print. College women's education
about sexuality and morality thus prepared them only inadequately for
the time when they were alone with a man on a date.[55]

Considering the silences that surrounded sexual encounters, Alice
Gorton's diary entries are a very important source. As already mentioned

earlier, Alice habitually pasted letters from dating partners into her journal. Among them is one that Richard wrote her in response to a disagree-
ment about the question of how far to go sexually. Here, the young man
had pushed for a level of sexual intensity with which Alice was not
comfortable. She had refused her consent. Not wanting to lose the man
as a friend and consort, she then tried to explain her reasons in writing.
Unfortunately, this letter has not survived. Because Richard paraphrased
Alice's arguments in his reply, we can see how she had tried to justify her
actions. Women, Alice had argued, could not just "go around fooling
with [any] man" because they had their "reputations to protect. . . . There
[were] other, cheap, girls that [did] that" (have sex), but women like Alice
would not want a man like Richard "to get the wrong idea." Moreover,
"there's a danger too." Richard could not "expect" her "to enjoy" sex
when there was the "possibility of conceiving [a child]."[56]

Whether the question of how far they should go centered on the question of intercourse cannot be answered conclusively. Considering her lack
of access to information about sexuality, it is unclear whether Alice mentioned her fear of "conceiving" because Richard had wanted to sleep with
her. What we can say with surety, however, was that he wanted to engage
in sexual activities that were more intense than anything Alice was willing
to do. To justify her stance, Richard's summary of her arguments shows,
Alice drew on a catalogue of prescriptions that were firmly in line with the
thrust of the postwar advice literature. Reminding him that only a "cheap"
woman would consent to sex outside the context of a committed relationship, she referred to the official moral standard and the link between
female sexual behavior and social status. Considering that society would
judge her actions based on conventional mores, she had no choice but to
conform. If she did not, she risked losing her reputation.

If Alice thought that by refusing Richard's advances his opinion of her
would grow, however, she was wrong. The tone of his letter was
downright sarcastic. About her argument that she needed to heed social
conventions, Richard thought little. "Really," he wrote, he "just couldn't
care less about the 'we girls have . . . ' line," he told Alice. Ignoring what
she said about her fear of pregnancy, he attributed her refusal of consent
to sexual repression. "Go rape a bedpost, girlie," he bluntly suggested. He
even accused her of contributing through her behavior to the higher than
expected figures of male homosexuality which the first Kinsey study had
made public only a few years earlier: "Its [sic] you [repressed women]
who make the homosexuals, especially when you become a parent."[57]
Anticipating here an argument that psychoanalyst Robert Lindner would
popularize in the widely read *Must You Conform* (1956), namely that male
homosexuality was a response to the "rigid" mores of a "sex denying

culture," he denied any legitimacy to Alice's expressed wishes. Rather, he labeled her arguments a conventional "line" and charged that her behavior was ultimately a root cause for broader social problems.

Richard's impatience and irritation with his partner's sexual reticence was not exceptional. Social science data from the postwar period shows clearly that many college men were dissatisfied with the amount of sexual activity on a date and pushed increasingly hard for intercourse.[58] My own sources, whenever they yield insights into the perspective of men, affirm this. Male students appeared aggrieved and frustrated when women tried to set limits. Like Dartmouth College student Richard, they lacked patience with their partners. In 1950, for instance, the Worcester Polytechnic Institute student who had by that time offered Mount Holyoke student Mary Browning his pin broke up with her. Questioned by her mother about the reasons for the break-up, Mary named their differences regarding their sexual expectations. Her boyfriend had felt that she and he "had 2 entirely different concepts on love + sex." Elaborating on the issue further, Mary wrote that she "wouldn't go in for all the necking he wanted" and that ultimately, this was the main reason for why the relationship did not last.[59] Another male student in 1950 wrote to the boyfriend of a Mount Holyoke student that he was already frustrated at the thought of his upcoming Friday night date. He was determined to "press harder than usual," but he was sure that he would be "hit by the usual barrage of no's." He was clearly fed up: "Goddam it!! Just the thought of going through the old bullshit for the umpteenth time. What a wear + tear on my poor testicles."[60] As these voices show, college men increasingly wanted to go further sexually, and at earlier stages of their relationships, than the women they went out with were comfortable with.

While the lack of patience and sympathy displayed by college men does not endear them to a modern-day feminist, we need to put their voices in context. These men received confusing messages about the sexual behavior of women. From the public media, they gleaned the impression that female sexual behavior was in transition, and on college campuses, at least some women were defying traditional prescriptions. With female sexuality changing across lines of class, the distinction between girls who were nice and those who were "cheap" was becoming blurred. Conservative cultural commentators saw this phenomenon as symptomatic of a cultural crisis. In the collegiate setting, familiarity with Freudian psychoanalysis gave it an air of normalcy. In fact, Richard's sarcastic response to Alice's objections suggests that he felt she was acting in violation of her own needs and desires when she refused his advances. Not only would her behavior turn her into a repressed woman who reproduced her own pathology in the next generation once she became a mother, heeding convention would not be to her benefit, either. Sexually frustrated, she would be left to "rape a bedpost." Richard's impatience with Alice's sexual reticence thus suggests that college men's growing psychoanalytical sophistication was causing them to reformulate traditional definitions of female respectability. A bad woman, in their eyes, might no longer be the one who gave in to her desires but the one who out of cowardice or neuroticism insisted on reproducing an official morality that was out of step with the insights of modern science.

Before we look at postwar college men as a vanguard of sexual egalitarianism, however, we need to consider the data provided by surveys of student opinions. Studies conducted among college students make clear that a double standard persisted into the early 1960s. For women, defiance of official morality still yielded a high cost. Women who did not act as the limit-setters in sexual relationships and who consented to sex or heavy petting with casual partners often found themselves abandoned.[61] Once labeled as "cheap," they lost their ability to attract economically upwardly mobile young men, and with that lost one of the main gateways to middle-class status for women. Men's responses to the sexual reticence of their partners therefore cannot be interpreted as a dramatic switch in attitudes toward female sexuality. Male students struggled to reconcile perceivable changes in female conduct with older notions of morality. The insistence with which college men pushed their partners in sexual encounters, however, was not just a response to the actions of women. Rather, the hostility with which male students reacted to reticent female partners developed in the context of these men's heightened level of self-consciousness and insecurity about their own sexuality and gender performance.

College men's responses to their female dating partners need to be seen in the context of the close link in Cold War culture between personal health and political reliability on the one hand and male sexual and gender performance on the other. Young men intimately familiar with the trope of emasculated manhood would easily feel that by accepting the limits a partner tried to impose on sexual exchanges on a date they were allowing women to domineer and control them. Not surprisingly, young men who were themselves trying to come to terms with identity and sexuality lacked the ability to relate to the concerns of their female partners. From their perspectives, sexually reticent women were no longer "good girls." Instead, they could be looked at as culprits. As Richard accused Alice, it was they who "made the homosexuals." It was they, rather than men, who could be held responsible for the weakness of men and for the nation's woes.

Cold War ideological developments thus resulted in normative pressures on men and women that were diametrically opposed. Even though the advice literature linked the ability to maintain impulse control to maturity and adjustment for both sexes, partisan attacks and cultural anxiety about softness made it especially difficult for culturally literate college men to identify with these prescriptions. Dating encounters between insecure young men who scrutinized their inner selves for signs of weakness, on the one hand, and women who tried to insist on an official, albeit contested, standard of morality, on the other, easily turned bitter.

When college men held women responsible for keeping the nation committed to conservative sexual morality, they had a point. The majority of college women resisted increased pressures for premarital intercourse. As we know from Kinsey and other social scientific studies, female rates of premarital intercourse remained stagnant until the mid 1960s.[62] Indeed, my evidence shows that some coeds resolved the question of the right course of action on a date with relative ease. This was the case, for example, for Lelah Dushkin, a young woman who started her studies at Smith College in 1949. One of the first things she noticed when she attended a social event at nearby Amherst College was the extent to which student leisure activities centered on sexual activities. A "usual Saturday night," at Amherst fraternities, she wrote her mother, involved a limited number of activities: "beer, singing, beer, dancing," and most of all, "sex, sex, sex." A "darkened room" was set aside for the sole purpose of necking and petting, and, as Lelah pointed out, couples took full advantage of the accommodation. Because Lelah had stayed away from the darkened room, she did worry whether this had earned her a reputation as "a terrible prude." A "long, long talk with [fellow student] Tooky," however, assuaged her concerns. As "Tooky" assured her, a girl did not "have to neck, drink + smoke to get a man." The "nice" ones would even expect her to say no. Reassured in her attitude, Lelah was confident that she did not have to change her moral outlook for the sake of staying involved in campus life.[63]

The way in which Lelah broached the topic of sexuality in her correspondence with her mother is unusual.[64] While most mid-twentieth century college students answered in opinion polls that they could not talk about sexual matters freely with their parents, the exchange between Mrs. Dushkin and her daughter is remarkably open. Lelah freely discussed the "boys [she had] been out with" and her "luck" to have so far been able to avoid particularly "wolfish" ones with her mother. This openness had a lot to do with Lelah's background. Unlike many other women of this study, she was not a first-generation college student. Lelah's mother had herself attended Smith College, graduating in 1925 with a degree in music. Mrs. Dushkin had also spent time studying in Paris, where she met her future husband and Lelah's father. She still occasionally came to campus to perform her compositions. As a professional artist familiar with campus life, and who had in her own youth enjoyed considerable independence, Mrs. Dushkin may have been predisposed to respond in a nonjudgmental way to her daughter's struggles to adjust to student culture. Having thus met in her mother a woman who was a sympathetic and helpful source of advice, Lelah might then also have been encouraged to express her confusion in front of a female peer.

Lelah's access to a sympathetic mother, however, was unusual in the mid-century context. As a previous chapter illustrated, few families could relate to the social challenges daughters faced in campus life. Female students from families without college culture believed that their education gave them access to knowledge and information their lesser-educated parents lacked. Considering this, they were unlikely to seek out parental advice in questions concerning appropriate behavior. When it came to a touchy subject such as sexuality, moreover, the fear of parental sanctions only added incentives to be silent. Family backgrounds thus influenced the extent to which a woman felt comfortable asking for clarification in the confusing environment of the student dating culture.

While family backgrounds predisposed first-generation students especially to experience confusion over sexual morality, their responses to dating pressures were also shaped by their cultural literacy. How familiarity with contemporary debates about the state of American nationhood and culture influenced the way a college woman saw her sexual role and responsibility in a relationship shows forcefully in the papers of Sandra Iger. Sandra, who had grown up in Queens, New York, wasted no time after starting to study at Mount Holyoke College in 1957 as an English major. Recognized by the faculty as especially talented right away, the scholarship student was exempted from freshman English and during the same year joined the staff of the literary magazine, *Pegasus*. Sandra's strong interest in cultural and political debates shows vividly in her correspondence, in which she broaches topics reaching from civil rights to colonial independence movements. Before her freshman courses even had a chance to get her busy, she was already reading David Riesman's *The Lonely Crowd* (1950).

While Sandra was starting her education in small-town South Hadley, her high school sweetheart, Richard Kohler, was beginning his studies at Columbia University. He, too, read *The Lonely Crowd*.[65] Like Sandra, he found Riesman's thesis that, in the contemporary corporate economy, individualistic and "inner-directed" values had given way to "other directedness" a poignant social commentary. That Sandra and Richard soon interpreted their own experiences through the lens of Riesman's analysis shows in the attention they paid to the question of being sufficiently "inner-directed." Neither wanted to allow peer pressure to cower them into conformity to group norms and both took care to emphasize their individuality. It was Richard, however, who first drew a link between the problem of "outer directedness" and sex. As he wrote her by late September of his freshman year: "Love you, my virgin indignant," and he called his label a "combination . . . of Riesman's analysis and Kohler's [his own] frustration."[66]

The basis of Richard Kohler's frustration becomes clear from the letters the two students sent back and forth to each other. At regular intervals, Sandra visited her boyfriend in New York. During these visits their erotic encounters became gradually more intense. Yet when Richard wanted to sleep with Sandra, the latter felt that things were moving too fast. The act would have great "significance," she argued. "If we were older and more sure of what would become of us, I would not feel wrong in loving [Richard] fully, in every way."[67] The way things were, however, she did not feel she should consent to intercourse. The reasons she listed, which were in part practical, in part emotional, vividly reflect her internalization of the notion put forward by experts that the act of coitus carried grave meaning and consequences and ought not to be engaged in as part of a casual relationship: "We are seventeen years old; we still don't know if we will be married. If we had relations now we would feel tied to each other. . . . I know that it would be just about impossible for me to love anyone else without deep guilt and unhappiness. Also, carrying on an affair from now on till the time we married, which wouldn't be till we finished school, would be torturous."[68] These arguments, however, failed to convince Richard.

As Richard's response to Sandra's well-reasoned objections shows, he took from the discourse at his disposal different lessons than his girlfriend. Referring to psychoanalytical theories, he accused Sandra of having a "virginity complex." Utilizing the literature on mass society, he argued that his wish indicated a laudable individualism. Contrary to the "170,000,000 people" who just followed what they were "watching [on] T.V.," he proudly asserted that he had "lost my reservations and have little guilt to dredge for final mental freedom about sex." Sandra, he implied, was a herd animal. Eventually, he gave her an ultimatum. If she "[would not] have intercourse with [him] willingly, [he would] look for girls who will."[69]

When reading the letters between Richard and Sandra, it is easy to see them as behaving in predictable and stereotypical ways. While Richard pushed, Sandra held the line. The dynamic is more complicated, however. For one, it is not a logical development that Richard would turn into a man who tried to pressure his partner into sexual activities. When he and Sandra parted for college, the two self-ascribed "virgins" had both been committed to a "wholesome" perspective. Both wanted to finish their education, including graduate studies in literature, before taking their sexual relationship to the next level. When their erotic encounters became more intense, Richard in fact struggled with feelings of shame no less than Sandra. How intensely Richard himself felt conflicted about his sexuality shows in the fact that, prior to presenting Sandra with his ultimatum, he had written her about his fears that, should she continue to hold the line, he would eventually have intercourse with a girl he had no feelings for. We can see in the outline for a novel he was planning to write, which he sent Sandra, that he saw something highly immoral and potentially dangerous in sex devoid of deeper feelings. In his novel, a "guy like [him] loves a girl like [Sandra] who goes to a Holyokeish college." Because "Sandy" refuses to have intercourse, however, the male character "gets infatuated" with another woman who consents to the sex act with him. Afterward, the male protagonist realizes that his infatuation had been but "momentary physical passions" instead of "true spiritual love." The consequence is his downfall and ruin: "horrified and ashamed . . . he drops out of his college and becomes a bum, bitter and wretched." Eventually, he "plunges from a first-story window and . . . dies in huge torment."[70] Although Richard called the idea for his story "hypothetical in toto," we can see in it clearly how deeply the young man was still steeped in traditional middle-class concepts of morality. Sex just for the sake of physical gratification was not something he could easily imagine as a positive thing. Only a few months after he had sent Sandra his outline for a novel, however, Richard called sex "an amoral expression of instincts" that could "be indulged with more than one provided one is sure of contraceptive efficiency," and that was "a natural desire for one sex toward the other and alone [was] not love."[71]

That Richard "revised [his] thinking about sex" over time illustrates the extent to which exposure to student culture had the potential to homogenize assumptions about male sexuality and gender performance. Introverted and literary-minded, Richard suffered personally in the masculinist atmosphere at Columbia where, as his letters show, he met men who boasted about their sexual experiences. Increasingly perceiving his "virginity" as a handicap, he grew more and more self-conscious. The extent to which he felt out of place among his male peers shows in the fact that he called himself a "misfitted egghead." In this situation, Richard must have felt consolation in the writings of critics of mass society who lambasted the spread of a herd mentality. Yet, while this literature enabled him to situate his own dilemma in a context, his cultural literacy would also heighten Richard's sense that he needed to find a way out of his dilemma.

The way the literature on mass society affected Richard shows in the increasingly emotional nature of his letters. Right after he had devoured Vance Packard's *The Hidden Persuaders* (1957), a book about the manipulative techniques in the advertising industry, he wrote a letter to Sandra. He hated "commercials and their associations," he vented in capital letters. He repeatedly expressed his disgust and frustration with society, and the way in which he jumped from rants about consumerism to complaints about sexual mores shows clearly that he had come to see sexuality as central to the problems that affected him personally and the nation as a whole: "Sex is neither holy or impious. . . . Sex is so gruesomely treated and stupidly dealt with. . . . The U.S. in particular, I think, is nuts in this fashion. . . . America must lead or be led. Today she stinks. . . . Russia is admirable. Cruel, worse than Hitler, but admirable. . . . The people are enduring. They seem so crushed to Western eyes but I'm sure we're worse off. 170,000,000 people watching T.V. shit. Poor US."[72]

Confronted with her boy friend's anger and frustration, Sandra felt embattled. His accusations that she did not love him fully hurt her. His charge that she had a complex put her on the defensive. But she also found it increasingly difficult to mount counterarguments in response to his. Answering one of the letters in which Richard presented to her a "thesis on sex," she wrote: "The most difficult problem in answering your letter is the fact that I in theory agree entirely with the ideas you expressed." She once again brought up the fact that she felt handicapped by social norms. She was "afraid—of the feeling of guilt that [she] might and probably would have . . . of becoming pregnant, and of the emotional chaos that would cause in [her]." She added, however, that she did not think that these objections were legitimate: "I don't think I *should* feel that way," she wrote. Richard, she added, struck her as "ready for things that I am not mature enough to take yet." She was "ashamed of myself for my cowardliness."[73] In spite of the clear line on official morality in the female collegiate setting, Sandra took to heart her partner's arguments. Despite the fact that her gender put her in a more vulnerable and more closely scrutinized position, she did not feel that these factors were sufficient as a justification for her continuous refusal of intercourse.

Sandra's statement to Richard that, despite her internalization of prescriptions against premarital sex, she was in theoretical agreement points to the existence of a strong counterdiscourse to sexual conservatism in the student dating culture. Indeed, Sandra's case was not anomalous. We can also see from the diary of Alice Gorton that even though Alice had rebuffed the advances of her Dartmouth date, Richard, the practical and emotional factors on which she had based her objections were increasingly losing legitimacy in her mind. After Alice lost Richard as a result of what she eventually called her "puritanical" side, the Smith College student continued to confront the question of how far to go sexually on her dates.[74] The entries she made at this early phase of her dating career reflect her internalization of the stigma attached to premarital intercourse, but they also show that she was struggling with countervailing pressures. Increasingly, she was beginning to think that she had a personal responsibility to defy conservative prescriptions. "Dating fulfills both a physical and a mental need in each sex," Alice pondered at some point between December 1950 and May 1951. Considering this physiological reality, she mused, cultural mores needed to be redefined. Evaluating a dating encounter during which she had stopped short of actual coitus but nonetheless crossed a line of permissible sexual behavior in her own mind, she wrote: "A subjective definition of the word 'bad' is now in order. Old fashioned morals, the 'it just isn't done' type is gone for unfortunately it is done. Also 'just because' is out for inquiring minds. I think each should develop his own ideas—not a rigid code."[75]

This entry in Alice's diary suggests that she, too, found in the student culture strong incentives to doubt the legitimacy of official prescriptions and to link the subject of sexual morality to the pitfalls of mass society. The young woman evaluated conservative mores against the backdrop of an intellectual discourse in which "rigid" belief systems were thoroughly discredited. Moreover, she mused that especially educated people like herself—those in possession of "inquiring minds"—would have a responsibility to arrive at a new morality individually. In this notion she had at least in part taken her cues from the young men she went out with. Referring to one of her dating partners, she wrote that he lived by the motto "do what I want and not what I don't want." This, she concluded, ought also to become her own attitude. Unfortunately, she "always" experienced "an exhaustive self-searching process to find out what I really want."[76] Alice's greater struggles to come to terms with her needs and wants were of course grounded in the fact that, as a woman, she was exposed to greater risks and more stringent regulations. Her "self-searching" was therefore the result of a double standard. Like Sandra, she accepted the example of her male dating partner as her model. Interpreting her personal struggles as shortcomings and doubting the legitimacy of her feelings, she felt she should be able to have sex like a man. She was even considering that it might be her personal responsibility to challenge the status quo so that society could progress.

That Sandra and Alice felt that they ought to model their own behavior after that of their partners implies a deference to the needs of men that was firmly in line with a conventional female sex role. However, we also need to see their identification with their partners' arguments in the context of their own intellectual pursuits. In fact, when we once again look at the authors and books that left a particularly vivid impression on these young women, it is no longer surprising that they found their partners' arguments convincing. Both women were immersed in a literature that linked the fate of modern man to sexual mores. In Sandra's case, her own study of the work of British author D. H. Lawrence, which she conducted independent from the direct intellectual influence of her partner, enhanced the credibility of his arguments. "Have you read 'Sons and Lovers' by D. H. Lawrence?" she asked her boyfriend after he sent her his "thesis on sex" from Columbia. "There is something very similar to [your] idea . . . in it." Sandra here referred to Lawrence's critique of "the machine age." Under conditions of modernity, Lawrence argued, men and women found it difficult to express all facets of their being and become "whole" as spiritual, albeit sensual, beings. Alienated, they were forced into an existence demanding the denial of certain aspects of their selves. Some banished physical passions completely and concentrated on the life of the mind. Others went the opposite extreme and indulged in lust devoid of meaning. To experience life authentically, Lawrence argued, men and women needed to combine all the facets of the self in "phallic" love relationships based on physical and spiritual intimacy. Unfortunately, the persistence of conservative sexual mores in the modern West made it difficult for both sexes to achieve wholeness.[77]

While Sandra found the link between a cultural crisis and conservative sex mores confirmed in the work of an author she was studying on her own, it was also here where she learned about the way in which women contributed to the perpetuation of this dismal state of existence. Although Lawrence saw both sexes as victimized by the machine age, his work featured prominent female characters who negatively influenced the physical and psychic health of men because of their attitudes toward sex. These were women who allowed their minds to dominate their being, who repressed their instincts, and who tried to impose their own will and values on the men who loved them. The latter meanwhile, were driven into misery by the domination of such cold and purely ego-driven females. Either because they denied themselves sensual pleasures or because they went to the opposite extreme, they were doomed to never reach happiness and wholeness.[78]

The fact that Alice Gorton in the early 1950s was intrigued by books that expressed the same thesis illustrates that we are dealing here with an important influence. Alice, too, would eventually start reading the work of D. H. Lawrence in the context of her honors course of study in English. Long before that, however, she had already found ideas similar to those expressed by Lawrence in the work of an author she read in her free time: popular essayist and fiction writer Philip Wylie. Here she also found a particular version of the role she as a woman could play to help alleviate the cultural crisis. Wylie nowadays is particularly remembered for his writings about "momism." As mothers and partners of men, he argued, women controlled the definition of morality as well as their families' "purse-strings," and thereby kept the United States wedded to emasculating consumerism and conformism. "Moms" had only been able to gain their undue influence over men, Wylie claimed, however, because as young and alluring versions of themselves—as "Cinderellas"—they had used their sexuality to entrap men to marry and support them. Yet Wylie's novels also feature female protagonists whom he portrayed as new types of women who would be worthy mates for an invigorated breed of man. This new model woman rejected the "fetid incrustations of ages" on her "sexual instinct." Unlike conformist "Cinderellas" and domineering "moms," she was a female version of the glorified individualist unaffected by the moral admonitions of peers and elders.

It was this new model woman whom Alice Gorton found immensely appealing. Determined to change her behavior in sexual encounters, she adopted Wylie's work as her dating manual. After one of her dates as a freshman in 1951, for instance, she wrote in her journal that the night had been "good in Wylie's terms." She had "followed [her] instincts and got rid of much nervous repression."[79] A little later she was "rereading" Wylie's novel *Night Unto Night*; a book that was released as a motion picture starring Ronald Reagan in 1949. Alice recorded that she read it "with great profit" and found especially helpful "naturally" what she learned here about "the technique of making love." Inspired by what she read in Wylie, she felt that she was finally learning the right lessons about sexuality. While others might "learn from early attraction + experience," she had to learn from "reading + late practice." She closed the paragraph by saying "Thanks P. Wylie."[80] She encountered an even stronger incentive for sexual nonconformism at a later point when in the course of her readings she came across an essay on "free love." In it the author linked the ability of individuals to engage in love relationships outside the security of marriage to the superior mindset of rational-minded people free of psychological fears and hang-ups. "Hey!" she wrote and quoted from her readings: "Free love is possible between truly free people . . . who have . . . complete control over irrational . . . impulses."[81] As demonstrated by the exclamatory remark she made upon finding this statement, she was glad to find additional support for her developing theory about sex.

Because Sandra and Alice read a great number of books in college, it is telling that they paid particular attention to authors who emphasized a link between sex mores and cultural conditions. This, of course, might be because their dating partners had suggested that they read exactly these books. Yet, in the absence of evidence for this, it seems likely that both were drawn to the literature because they felt an affinity to it. Indeed, if read selectively, even Wylie's acidic attacks on women as a group includes a sympathetic look at the restrictions and contradictions faced by the young generation. In the current United States, he argued, they were constantly bombarded by sexually inciting suggestions. But because the values in the nation had not yet caught up to new realities, an old-fashioned morality demanded restraint. Kept in a constant state of nervous excitement, it was not surprising that contemporary youth felt troubled. Such a portrayal would undoubtedly appeal to students who were confused about their own feelings and the social demands of their environment. Meanwhile, the stereotype that women were responsible for the perpetuation of a conformist and conservative culture also matched the daily reality of female students. To young women familiar with official restrictions on their social and sexual autonomy, the charge that old-fashioned mores and norms were keeping the individual from coming to terms with sexual needs would not have appeared far-fetched. Moreover, in the context of a peer culture in which there existed competing ideas about the particular value of their nondomestic goals, the model of a woman who was idiosyncratic, albeit superior to the majority of her sex, would have appealed to students like Alice and Sandra.

That both young women did indeed feel that the cultural criticism they read described their own situation is supported by their own words. The way Sandra described her life as a Mount Holyoke student, for example, increasingly resembled Lawrence's portrayal of man's existence in the Machine Age: In college, she wrote in 1961, it was impossible to live as a "whole person." Here she had to be "a brain . . . rather than whole, rather than utterly me. The complete me." She did not "want to be separate things at different times." Yet, "three quarters of [her were] dissolved and left behind with [Richard]."[82] Alice Gorton at Smith, meanwhile, in reaction to female peers who delivered conservative moral advice, cast them as conformist and inauthentic moms like those she had encountered them in the work of her favorite author. In response to criticism from one of her housemates, she wrote: "Finally [Nancy] broke out with the motherly advice with which her dramatic little heart has been overflowing." The woman had struck "many admonitory poses" and delivered her advice. "Ye Gods," commented Alice, "I couldn't help smiling—hard fight. But she was so serious + so enjoying her role."[83] In both women's writings, the personal appeal of the theories their male partners were pitching at them is apparent.

Although I do not believe that Sandra or Alice picked up the books they read merely as a result of manipulation by the men they dated, their writings clearly show that they internalized the idea that their sexual behavior and the manhood and well-being of their partners were directly linked. That other culturally literate women interpreted their roles in similar ways is suggested by the frequent expressions of guilt that accompanied refusals of intercourse. Bryn Mawr's Margaret Hall, for instance, wrote in her diary after one dating encounter that she "hate[d]" feeling that she was "doing wrong with another person, against both natures."[84] Although her journal does not offer a lot of context or background, it seems apparent that she was castigating herself for meeting neither the needs of a partner nor her own. Stanford University student Susan Sperry Borman in her diary also increasingly questioned her motivation for wanting to save herself "for one man." She found sexual encounters that exceeded a certain limit "debasing." Yet she wondered what really caused her to insist on limits: "Do I really do this because I want to keep myself pure," she wondered, "or because I know it is a cruelly ensnaring way of leading some guy on and subordinating him to me?" As she sometimes feared, she might just be trying to exercise power in an illegitimate way. "My criteria [sic] is," she pondered self-critically, "you've got to be so crazy about me buddy, that you'll do anything for me before you get anywhere with me." "Doggone it," she concluded, "it's just another way of completely dominating somebody, of making myself the complete master, isn't it?"[85]

The fact that many college women continued to abstain from premarital intercourse vividly illustrates the influence of postwar conservatism. The self-incrimination and guilt that shows in the introspective writings of some of them, however, shows the strength of a parallel discourse that not only incited women to express their sexuality but also erected a forceful new imperative. If developmental progress depended on the expression of heterosexual desire, then how could one possibly continue to say no? At the same time, however, the gap that separated daring nonconformism and cheap vulgarity was a small one. In the context of clashing messages about their sexuality, young women were not surprisingly confused. Because public commentators widely agreed that the psychological problems of individuals, the state of the nation, and homeland security were connected, especially culturally very literate young women would have felt under special pressure to resolve their confusion. How their difficulties in negotiating the sexual terrain of the dating culture shaped their college careers over the longer run will be the subject of the next chapter.

5 College Women and the Clash of Mystiques

For Margaret Kennedy, the year 1949 marked not only the start of her studies at Duke University but also separation from her boyfriend Ken. By virtue of her background, Margaret had all the trappings of the model coed. She clearly came from money. Her father, Harvard graduate Frank Hunter Kennedy, was partner in a law firm in Charlotte, North Carolina. Her brother, Philip, was about to embark on the exciting, albeit costly, adventure of a study-abroad year in France. Margaret's social coming-out was featured in one of *Life Magazine*'s special debutante editions. Despite the facts that she bore all the markings of a Southern belle, however, Margaret developed during college nontraditional aspirations for a woman of her class.

That Margaret had developed career ambitions is suggested by a letter she wrote in 1951 to a male admirer. Now in her junior year, she told the man that she had "always wanted to write" and had been told that she was talented. It is clear that when she wrote these lines, though, Margaret still lacked confidence in her abilities: "I've been told that I should write, and I want to. But is that enough?" she asked her pen pal.[1] That she had the courage to discuss her ambition at all, however, was the result of her recent experiences as a student. Duke University had awarded her the Angier B. Duke regional prize. Founded in 1925 to enable financially disadvantaged North Carolina students to study at the university, the award was redesigned as a merit-based scholarship in 1948 and granted annually to two women and four men of outstanding academic promise. Margaret was one of the recipients in 1950. By decade's end, she was still unmarried and enrolled in a graduate program at the University of California at Berkeley. Moreover, if we believe what a new boyfriend wrote in a letter to her brother, Philip, she had by then turned into a committed "career girl." But when she was still an undergraduate student at Duke University, her then-partner Ken had tried to keep her committed to a rather different kind of career.[2]

The collection that includes Margaret's letters does not offer a lot of information about the men she dated. It is clear, though, that when she was starting her studies in 1949, she and Ken were thinking about a future together. Where Ken went to college is not clear, but the letters he sent

Margaret between 1949 and 1951 show that he saw the purpose of Margaret's education as different from his own. For himself, Ken imagined a career as an academic. In a letter to his sweetheart, he shared with her his vision of their marriage: he could not wait to live with her in "a small house on a university campus." He imagined spending long nights "reading and looking at [her] over a book," of "watching her sleep, snuggled close to [him]."[3] Although he saw his own studies as leading to a career as a professor, it was not part of his plan that Margaret would develop academic or professional ambitions of her own. As a passage from a letter to Margaret illustrates, he believed the main value of her studies were that they would turn her into an ideal wife: "Your work is that of preparation—of becoming a woman—of cheering me up—of continually pointing out our goal to my near-sighted eyes—of keeping me from becoming self-centered— . . . and most important of all of becoming an individual—I am so very demanding—and tend to be dominating—You must preserve your personal integrity. Never commit suicide. Always make your own decisions and always make me think I made them."[4]

Ken's conception of female individuality here is interesting. Although he clearly felt that Margaret, no less than he, needed to preserve independence of mind, his agenda was ultimately a gender-conservative one. Although he encouraged Margaret's individuation, he expected her to do so mainly for the purpose of serving his own ego needs. Ken wanted a wife who was a helpmeet, not a woman who challenged a traditional role division in marriage. His gender ideals become even clearer in a letter he sent Margaret after she wrote him that some of her friends had criticized him. Annoyed by this, Margaret had defended her partner. While Ken was flattered that she would risk alienating her friends, her anger was not something he could reconcile with his view of his future wife. After calling her his "poor darling," he used the occasion to outline in detail his theory of male and female nature: "Do not alienate yourself from your friends because of me. . . . It is a man's duty to protect those whom and those things which he loves. A woman is too delicate to do this. Your courage is wonderful, but courage without armor is futile. . . . Be more sympathetic. It is your nature. Love [your friends] for their gullibility and pity them for their ignorance. . . . Never struggle against nature, seek your goal within her limitations."[5]

Because Margaret's half of the correspondence has not survived, it is not clear how she thought about Ken's vision of her role. There is evidence, however, that her partner's reflections about gender roles were at least in part motivated by a fear that Margaret might be changing. As Margaret told a male acquaintance in the fall of 1950, she was beginning to feel that her stay at Duke was putting a strain on her relationship.

Her friend assured her that surely she was just imagining this. But Ken's fears that her education might turn his girlfriend into a woman whose independent-mindedness included career designs of her own are apparent when he sought reassurance that she would still be content with the role of helpmeet: "Once you said you would be content to achieve through me," he said in one of his letters after Margaret had just started her studies at Duke: "Do you still feel that way?" His insecurities regarding this question explain the urgency with which he emphasized his need for her: "Remember me and my Love," he wrote: "You are my Reason and my explication logically for this mess we call a world. I need you and always shall." In a follow-up letter, he assured her that she was "the fulfillment of [his] soul" and without her, he "would be condemned to unhappiness—a man tormented by his soul." Ken's fear that his partner might develop new ideas about her role shows further in his frequent reminders of the value of a complementary division of roles. "A man and a woman combine to form a whole—a plurality," he wrote. There should be no competition between partners. If Margaret thought that either one of them could "even win a contest," it would be as if "the two hands of one body tried to prove the predominance of one."[6]

Interesting parallels exist between the correspondence of Ken and the letters Richard Kohler sent to his partner, Sandra Iger at Mount Holyoke. Although Richard had bonded with Sandra over their shared interest in literature and politics during high school in Queens, he was treating her less and less as an intellectual equal as his college education progressed. Instead, he presented himself increasingly in a superior role. When Sandra picked up a few faddish words and phrases used by her peers, he criticized her writing style as "other directed." When she sent him her poetry, he condescended that they were "nice enough" but not sophisticated and he added that "I love you in spite of your poems." No longer seeing his "girl" as an intellectual equal, Richard instead became enamored with a view of Sandra as someone who, by virtue of her sex, occupied a sphere entirely separate from his own. She lived, he informed her, in "a magical world of whimsy and enchanted fancy which often startle[d] [him], and always amuse[d] [him]."[7] When the couple had decided on marriage, he spelled out exactly how he conceived of their respective roles: "I want to give you a nice home and a wonderful family. I want to protect you and be a male husband, not an intellectual companion. . . . You are so truly a woman I feel shy with you, even while wishing to master you as a male."[8]

There is evidence that Sandra was uncomfortable with the changing dynamics in the relationship. From a visit to New York during which she had gone out with Richard and some friends, she returned to Mount

Holyoke College dissatisfied with the way her partner had treated her. The extent of her irritation shows in the fact that the scholarship student, chronically short on funds, invested in a long-distance call. While we have no way of knowing how this talk transpired, Richard felt he needed to continue the conversation in writing, and it is from this letter that we can glean the nature of Sandra's complaint. Richard, she felt, had monopolized the conversation and ignored her. Defending himself, Richard did not deny the charges but he said that she should not take his behavior as a sign of disrespect. "If I seem, unfortunately, to ignore you publicly, it's simply that I bask in your presence, and, feeling it around me, am able to turn, my attention more to the others who may be present," he wrote. Without her, however, he could not function. She was, he stressed, "the treasure of my life and all my thoughts revolve around you." He "desperately" needed her. "Thinking of you," he pleaded, "redeems me," and he needed her "to save my own soul." For evidence that his devotion was sincere, he even provided quotes from letters he had written to male friends. He was "mentally, spiritually, and emotionally dead," he quoted himself, whenever he was not around Sandra. It was only "when, on weekends" he saw her that he "enter[ed] time, and therefore, life."[9]

The letters Ken and Richard sent to their sweethearts illustrate more than the long-distance romances of teenagers. The rhetoric they used reflects their awareness and internalization of central elements of the post–World War II discourse on masculinity, mass culture, and the family. In liberal and conservative family discourse alike, complementary family roles were cast as central to the survival of democracy and national stability. As Adlai Stevenson had put it in 1955, the home offered an educated woman a chance to create a sphere protected from the contamination of mass society in which "Western man" could maintain his wholeness and integrity. This model of the ideal couple not surprisingly appealed to young men in Ken and Richard's situation. As students exposed to a masculinist campus culture, both of these young men encountered performance pressures regarding their sexuality. Moreover, both aspired to, and could reasonably expect to enter, a comfortable middle-class existence after graduation. Their longings for the comforts and the security of home, however, connoted susceptibility to conformist pressures and the taint of effeminacy. Likewise, their aspirations for academic careers could be seen as indicative of a somewhat deficient masculinity. While the expansion of the apparatus of higher education was opening up professional positions, the growth of colleges and universities also meant that these institutions increasingly resembled large impersonal corporations in which employees needed to perform in an "other-directed" fashion. Considering the self-consciousness that Ken and Richard in all likelihood experienced, it is hardly surprising that they were attracted to the ideal of a marriage based on mutually exclusive gender roles. Positioning their partners as models of femininity would enable them to assume the properly masculine complement: they would "master" them as males. Yet while it should not surprise us that college men identified with this version of the ideal couple, the question remains whether it appealed to their partners, and if so, why.

The model of partnership that Richard and Ken presented to their girlfriends clashed in important aspects with their girlfriends' evolving identities as academically accomplished women. Naturally, it was flattering to be called the person a man needed for the survival of his soul. But a supportive role as the helpmeet and muse that both men were imagining did not match their partners' budding sense of themselves as potential professionals and intellectuals in their own right. There is no evidence that either Sandra or Margaret argued for an alternative definition of their role, but it is also clear that neither Ken nor Richard felt that they could take for granted their lovers' compliance. More than just the romantic hyperbole of teenagers, the rhetoric in their letters suggests that both felt the need for a sales pitch for a model of partnership they found appealing but to which their partners might have responded with ambivalence.

Due to the lack of access to the thoughts and voices of Margaret and Sandra, the question of how they felt about their partners' ideas about gender role divisions must rest on speculation. The diaries of Alice Gorton and Margaret Hall, however, offer insights into the distinctly mixed feelings these talented young women had about their partners' conception of modern marriage. Smith College's Alice Gorton met her future husband, Korean War veteran George Hart, the summer before her senior year. When they met, George was a philosophy major at Yale, but he was already disillusioned with the course of study and considered a corporate job as an alternative. As such, he did not match the profile of the kinds of men Alice had been drawn to up to this point. About his professional plans, for instance, she at one point dismissively wrote that he would be a "button puncher."[10] Moreover, from the start there were warning signs that marriage to George would entail a great degree of compromise on Alice's part. His response to his girlfriend's adventures when a group of bohemian men from New York City's Greenwich Village paid a visit to the small town of Northampton, Massachusetts, demonstrates that George held much more conservative ideas than Alice about how an educated young woman should conduct herself.[11]

That the Beat subculture that was taking shape on the West and East coasts would appeal to a career-minded English major such as Alice makes a lot of sense. As Wini Breines has shown, young, white, middle-class women who rejected suburban life as conformist and stifling were drawn to ideas of "wildness and originality" embodied in the figure of the Beat poet and other social outsiders.[12] When representatives of the New York Beat scene arrived in the college town of Northampton, Alice eagerly took advantage of the opportunity to get to know them. That she was doing so, although she was already going out with George, reflects her belief in her entitlement to a considerable degree of social autonomy. Her journal conveys her excitement after meeting people she called the "slicker" types from "the village": "They are fabulous people," she gushed, "we talk—what an experience!" With the men, Alice drank, smoked, discussed literature, and her own goals in life. The latter, it seems, struck her acquaintances as rather conventional: the "only way to find yourself," one of the Beats told her, was by dropping out of society and traveling. Alice playfully adopted the jargon of the visitors. When the campus police stopped her for riding her bike without a light on, she joked that she, too, now had her own Beat story to tell: "Man! fuz busted me! Riding with no light!" she quoted herself as telling a friend.[13] Yet this joke also indicates that, despite her fascination with the visitors, Alice had no intention of becoming Beat. She might ride her bike without a light on, but the thought of getting "busted" for a more serious offense appealed to her no more than the idea of dropping out of college. In a diary entry that followed a night of partying with the visitors, she wrote that just like her "books, imagination," and her "written words," adventures with "types" like the Beat poets fed her "thirst for life." Alice did not see her brush with bohemia as a dangerous transgression but as a legitimate social adventure. In consequence, she did not have qualms about sharing her experiences with George. Now, however, she learned that her dating partner adhered to stricter notions of appropriate female behavior. After Alice told George about what to her had been an exciting exploit, he got "mad." He did not like her "adventuring" at all. At least for a short time, Alice considered that he might have turned his back on her for good. After a while, he phoned. "Glad he called—not mad anymore," wrote Alice. The incidence had taught her, however, that George had different ideas about how an educated woman ought to conduct herself.[14]

George's disapproval of Alice's adventurism reflects discomfort with young women's growing social autonomy and mobility that was typical of postwar Americans of his class and generation. Yet it clashed with the ideas about an ideal partnership that Alice had formulated in her diary so far. This incident was not the only warning sign that George might hold more conservative ideas about gender roles than she did. George expected to "take the lead," she wrote. He did not expect his partner to be an intellectual equal. Rather, he expected her to play a passive and supportive helpmeet role. It is clear from Alice's diary that she was aware of this. In fact, she deliberately and consciously adjusted her behavior to conform to his expectations. After she had already started to see George regularly, for instance, she went out on a movie date with one of her older male acquaintances and another student couple. After this double date, the two females exchanged opinions. From Alice's record of this conversation, it is clear that both women were at this time changing their dating behavior: "Joanie said that this sort of thing was a different type of fun than with George + Dick. We were more assertive and showed our own wit instead of being maternal and admiring foils for our lovers."[15]

Alice added to this entry that she preferred the "George-type fun." She also insisted that "George is it." Yet despite these remarks, it is also very clear from her journal that she felt ambivalent about him. Alice wrote that she would have to "adopt a pose" and "[force herself] into the conventional marriage pattern" for her relationship with George to work.[16] As she noted herself, she was "vacillating, wanting George + missing him, . . . + at the same time thinking perhaps I don't love him." In another entry, she wrote she was "finding fault with George." She reminded herself that she did not want to become just "a rubber stamp" of a dominant male. She kept seeing other men and continued to toy with different options for work and study after graduation. Eventually, however, Alice shoved her doubts and apprehension aside. On September 11, 1954, she married George Hart.[17]

Only a few years later, in 1956, Margaret Hall met her future husband, Robert "Blake" Reeves, at a Radcliffe Graduate Center dance. Margaret had by then graduated from Bryn Mawr and was pursuing a master's in education at Harvard. On first view, the couple seems ill matched: Blake and Margaret had little in common. Once he proposed, Margaret's diary shows that she articulated her concern that their lack of shared interests might cause problems in the future: "I remarked that he had lots to say about physiology, and I about English and education, but what had we to say to each other? He said that that would solve itself when we had done a lot of things together, and developed a communal past."[18]

That Blake was less worried than Margaret about their lack of shared interests reflects the fact that he adhered to a different definition of complementary marriage than did Margaret. Since she had broken her engagement with her first fiancé, Bill, Margaret had wanted the significant men in her life to share her passion for literature. She had been drawn to men who were intrigued by her ideas and intelligence. Blake neither shared her passions nor treated her like an intellectual equal. Intellectual compatibility, in his view, was not essential for success in marriage. A shared leisure life would give spouses sufficient material to talk about. As Margaret's journal entry shows, she was aware of this fact.

However, she also adjusted her behavior to the different expectations of this man. She was "not very brilliant and just rather amenable" when she was with Blake, she wrote. Just like Alice, Margaret responded with a great degree of ambivalence to Blake. At one point she wrote that she could "imagine so easily getting engaged to Blake. Getting married to him . . . cooking for him. Bearing his babies, . . . and loving him so very much." On other days, however, she doubted that he was "very bright." Although he seemed "sturdy and reliable," he might also be very unsuited to her intellectually. In 1956 she applied for a Fulbright grant. She kept going out with other men and continued her studies, but she married Blake in June of 1957. Margaret continued her coursework in education for a while but ultimately did not finish her degree at Harvard.[19]

The question why these two women agreed to marry men for whom they clearly had ambivalent feelings begs for an explanation. Already before Margaret and Alice met their future husbands, however, changes in their outlooks became apparent in their journals. As both women's studies progressed, they became increasingly intrigued by notions of an archetypal or instinctual femininity that they gleaned through their in-class and extracurricular readings in the fields of anthropology, literature, and psychology. To Alice Gorton, these ideas about femininity were introduced in the context of her honors work in literature during her junior year in 1952–1953. Searching for a thesis topic, she encountered the work of British literary scholar Gilbert Murray, and she was instantly intrigued. Quoting Murray, she wrote that there was a need to analyze literature for the "undercurrent of desires and fears and passions, long slumbering yet eternally familiar, which have for thousands of years lain near the roots our most magical dreams." Subsequently, she homed in on a thesis topic. "This is the great subject," she wrote. She would write about "the archetype from the collective unconscious."[20] Alice had come across the work of Swiss psychologist C. G. Jung. Although Murray himself had not read Jung, literary scholars counted his essay "Hamlet and Orestes" as one of the first analyses that applied the concept of a transhistorical archetype to the interpretation of literature. From her honors course of studies, Alice was familiar with the writings of these scholars.[21]

The title of Alice's senior thesis—"The Artistic Use of Myth in Certain Poems of William Blake and T. S. Eliot"—shows she did indeed follow through on her scholastic plans. Even more significantly, she began to apply the theories she encountered to make sense of her own experiences during her junior year. With growing frequency, Jung's concepts appear in journal entries about Alice's own life and identity as a woman. "Archetypal patterns: . . . woman, femininity, fertility," she jotted down at one point, and at another described her belief in "the collective unconscious + the possibility of a priori knowledge."[22] While these entries might still have been inspired by her thesis research, the way in which her readings influenced her thoughts about her own life show in the way Alice was rethinking central tenets of her identity.

Alice's infatuation with the idea of a female archetype entailed a significant change in her attitude toward motherhood. Alice liked to dream about her future after graduation, and she frequently recorded these fantasies in her journal. She imagined herself as a successful writer and saw working for the magazine *The New Yorker* as a particularly fascinating career. Often, she dreamed about moving to New York City where she would have exciting love affairs with men in addition to having literary fame. When Alice was a sophomore, for instance, she recorded the following scenario: "New plans about my future . . . disappearance . . . to a steel town. Work in a bar, love . . . of a. . . . Streetcar named Desire type. . . . Loss of baby. Perfect . . . happiness for two years. I continue to write successful salable stories. . . . No kids. He is killed, I am completely desolate . . . I go to New York, apartment, beautiful clothes, a gorgeous desirable sensual satisfied wise + loving woman. Job on New Yorker, honored, respected, a literary light."[23]

Obviously, this entry does not reflect a realistic plan for a postgraduate career. It is a fantasy that was in all likelihood triggered because Alice saw the actor Marlon Brando in the 1951 movie version of Tennessee Williams's *A Streetcar Named Desire*. Countless other young women probably engaged in similar fantasies. The entry nonetheless illustrates Alice's desire for independence and individualistic fulfillment. The young woman dreamt of literary fame and an exciting love life. Motherhood, by contrast, does not figure as an appealing option in the scenario. That in her fantasy Alice allowed her offspring with her glamorous lover to die shows that she was aware that the presence of children would make it difficult to combine a career and a marriage. Alice's discovery of "the great subject" of the female archetype, however, entailed a reassessment of motherhood.

The development in Alice's thinking becomes clear in a journal entry she made during the spring of 1953 while spending a college break with her family in Ohio. To work on her thesis, she had taken a book by C. G. Jung. Her reading of *Psychology and Religion* (1938) was interrupted, however, when her slightly younger brother returned from a party. Having had too much to drink, the young man got sick and Alice cleaned up after him. Afterward, she turned to her journal. The actions, she mused, had a deeper meaning: "I know dimly now the love + dedication and the joy that mothers know. It is a wonderful thing—this doing things for others without expecting or requiring the slightest thanks. . . . I am proud of myself and proud to be a woman. . . . An archetypal feeling—I am now part of the tradition of motherhood."[24]

The desire for literary fame and individualistic fulfillment that had characterized the earlier daydream is clearly absent from this entry. Instead, Alice emphasized the satisfaction she had gleaned from acting in a selfless way. Not even expecting gratitude from her inebriated sibling, she insisted that she was content to rest in the sense that she had become part of a long tradition of women who devoted themselves to the well-being of others instead of to their own ego needs.

Striking parallels exist in the way Alice Gorton and Bryn Mawr's Margaret Hall came to write about themselves. Margaret's journal is less detailed than Alice's. She neither commented extensively on her readings nor did she record her dreams. It is still clear that over the course of her studies her reproductive role became more central to her identity. In May of 1953, for example, she described an experience in which she had felt particularly in touch with her femininity. In this entry she expressed a concept of women's nature as instinctual, "primitive," and maternal: "My bra was loosed for once, and for some odd reason it caused me the most primitive feelings . . . a sharp identification with land, and being a woman and a bearer of children." Being a potential mother here clearly struck Margaret as one of the most key components of her identity. She also, like Alice, emphasized that because of her reproductive role, she possessed particular traits, insights, and interests that set her apart from men. Women, she wrote to a friend in 1955, "never see as men do; they aren't made to fight their battles as men do; they don't understand as men do." If they were a "good member of [their] own sex," she believed, women had intuitive insights. They could "use woman-sensitivity for others' good," or apply a particular kind of "woman wisdom."[25]

The parallels in the journals of Alice and Margaret suggest that over the course of their studies they were increasingly won over to the idea that they differed in essential aspects from men because of their potential role in reproduction. Considering that this emphasis on divergent gender traits and interests also informed some of the most conservative expert writings of the postwar period, it looks as if a "mystique" of essential femininity had finally caught up with these women. It is important to note, however, that neither Alice nor Margaret experienced this interpretation of their nature as an imposition from the outside. Both experienced their ideas as authentic. To Margaret, it seemed that her own physical sensations affirmed the central importance of her potential as a "bearer of children" in the make-up of her self. The extent to which Alice, too, identified with these notions, meanwhile, shows in the determination with which she held on to them even after an expert authority belittled them.

In 1953, to gain some advice on the material she was planning to use for her honors thesis, she approached a Smith College psychology professor about C. G. Jung. From his response, it was clear that the professor thought little about Jung's work. It was not scientific, he dismissively stated, and appealed only to women and artists. Alice's response shows, however, that by this time she trusted her own insights more than those of her professor. She vented that he was a "stupid Man!" and had "absolutely no imagination." She declared with pride that she was now finally "beginning to formulate my own beliefs, including the collective unconscious + the possibility of a priori knowledge."[26] Even though the man had, by virtue of his sex and position, authority that Alice lacked, her confidence suggests that she gained more satisfying answers from her new beliefs than from alternative ones.

To understand why the concept of an archetypal femininity appealed so strongly to Alice and Margaret, we need to look at the events that pre-occupied them at the time when they formulated these thoughts. Once we take into account their situational context, we notice that in each case the notion that their reproductive potential equipped them with distinctive qualities grew in appeal at a time of mounting stress in their intimate lives. Even though Alice Gorton had stopped seeing Dartmouth College student Richard, for example, she was soon confronted once again with the question of whether to have intercourse. She was still dating multiple partners in her junior year, but Jim, a young man she knew from her home town in Ohio, now appeared frequently in her journal. The son of an art critic for a local newspaper, Jim struck Alice as the kind of intellectual, nonconformist, and sophisticated dating partner in whose company she liked to be seen. Regarding his sexual demands, Jim presented a challenge similar to that of Dartmouth College's Richard. But by the time she was going out with Jim, Alice was no longer as strongly committed to holding the line as she was a semester earlier. She did not want to lose another dating partner because of her "puritanical" attitude. Moreover, her own readings and deliberations had eroded her belief in the legitimacy of a sexual double standard. She was no longer able or willing to argue that only "cheap" girls expressed themselves sexually. Rather, she had begun to believe that an exceptional and nonconformist woman owed it to her own development and the men she went out with to, as she had put it, shed "nervous repression."[27]

Alice and Jim's sexual relationship became progressively more intense. By the start of her junior year, although she still had not consented to intercourse, she was clearly performing acts she knew many of her contemporaries would consider illicit and about which she felt ambivalent. In her diary she described her growing sexual experiences as progress. Aside from her close circle of female friends, however, she concealed her activities from her Smith College peers. She was clearly concerned that her reputation would suffer if the extent of her sexual experimentation became common knowledge. Yet it is also apparent that she and Jim were not basing decisions about their intimate lives on convention or official morality. This shows, for example, in a letter from Jim. Alluding to a recent occurrence, he wrote, "What you have done or will do has nothing to do with the fact that I will always receive you with the pleasure you have given me. What I have done or will do has nothing to do with the fact that my silence will always be dedicated to your best interest."[28]

Jim's letter makes possible a number of insights into Alice's sex life. Already, she and her partner had engaged in acts she was not comfortable to admit to in public, and they considered going even further. Alice's response to the letter also enables us to glimpse how deeply ambivalent she felt about her activities. She wrote that she was "overwhelmed" by "emotion." She "reread [the letter] several times." It is clear that she was not entirely sure what to think about it. "It was a good letter—exactly fitting our situation," she wrote, but Jim's promise to keep his "silence" in her "interest" also irritated her. She "could get mad" when she thought about "the crack about keeping silent for my own best interests." Yet she could not quite explain her reaction to herself. "This is *so* strange" (her emphasis), she wrote in reference to her anger and to the fact that she felt "drained" and "without . . . joy." The question of how to respond to Jim's letter now took all of Alice's attention. Even though she was in the midst of working on a paper, she dropped her academic work and set to the task of composing a response: "I will now write the best letter that I am capable of—all the honesty, the maturity that I possess. Also dignity and warmth. It must be the perfect opus in construction, subject matter and penmanship. All shot are plans for study. . . . His letter was a masterpiece, let's make mine one too."[29]

Alice's response to Jim's letter offers us an important snapshot into how difficult it was even for culturally highly literate women to cope with the ambivalent climate surrounding female sexuality. In her irritation, we can see that she was becoming critical of the gender dynamics of her sexual encounters. It is also clear that she lacked the language to express herself. We see here the extent to which the perspective of women was denied legitimacy in the student dating culture. Alice was used to an environment in which female students were regularly reminded of their social obligation to meet the needs of others, where the views of men were endowed with special prestige, and where references to the sexual double standard were seen as a "line" of repressed or manipulative women.

Her "strange" inability to locate the exact source of her irritation shows us poignantly that she had internalized these messages.

Although in the dating culture of self-fashioned sexual liberals, which Alice frequented, students argued that the sexual double standard was no longer a legitimate argument against intercourse, the effort the young woman put into composing her response also illustrates the persistent stigmatization of female sexuality. She was not exaggerating when she expressed her wish to write "a perfect opus." She composed multiple drafts before she sent a final version of her letter. The level of attention she devoted to the task shows that she assumed that Jim's opinion of her depended on how he would interpret her motivation for giving in to her sexual desire. Alice knew that a woman could get away with acts that middle-class society generally considered illicit only under certain circumstances. Against the background of an expert discourse that linked the lack of impulse control to the vulgar sexual behavior of low-class women, she would have to maintain the impression of acting in a self-aware fashion and of being in control of her desires. Alice's attention to detail is thus her attempt to distance herself from the kind of woman who got herself "in trouble" and to present herself instead as a rational free-lover. If she succeeded in proving her dignity and maturity, Jim would see her as a laudable nonconformist. If she failed, however, he would see her as a vulgar specimen of her sex.

We do not know how Jim responded to the letter, but he and Alice continued to go out. At times when she felt at her most confident, Alice experienced herself in control and insisted that she was collecting important experiences. During these times, she rejoiced in the sense that she was becoming the kind of "fascinating" woman whom an "old worldly wiseman [*sic*]" like Jim would be attracted to.[30] Eventually, she also agreed to take the relationship to the next level. When she consented to intercourse, however, she became even more vulnerable to suffering personal conflicts because of the cultural ambivalence about female sexuality.

Thanks to Alice's high level of self-scrutiny, her journal provides an unusually detailed account of how she experienced intercourse. She and Jim devised a plan. Officially, Alice was spending the weekend at the New York City home of her college roommate's family. One night, however, she spent with Jim in a rented room in Brooklyn. The morning after, Alice turned to her diary to evaluate the experience. Her entries show that her initial interpretation was positive. She was able to portray her actions not as a fall from virtue but as the act of a woman who had successfully freed herself from the influence of tradition and convention. Physically, she had enjoyed the experience. Psychologically, she had been able to separate lust from love: "This is fascinating," she wrote into her journal. She had felt only "happiness," she insisted, "no panic, nervousness, possessiveness."[31] The following day she continued to present her actions as exciting, daring, adventures on the path to self-awareness: "Feel no different on this day of reaction except very tired. . . . It is an experience + I am learning much. Perpetually surprised by the ease + simplicity. Why the hell do people make such a damn fuss. . . . Let me live in awareness. 'Alice fell from virtue somewhere in Brooklyn.' Marvelous. . . . So happy!"[32]

Unfortunately for Alice, the context in which she was experiencing her first coitus made it exceedingly hard to maintain a sense of delight in the "ease" and "simplicity" of the encounter for long. A gender gap regarding information about sexuality worked to her disadvantage. Alice's ignorance about birth control soon caused her to agonize about the possibility of being pregnant. Although Jim used a condom, Alice did not trust its effectiveness. Returning to Smith College, she spent hours alone brooding in her room. "Nervous from smoking too much," she wrote: "wonder if I conceived." Once her period set in, Alice recorded in her diary that "birth control sure is a marvelous thing." But Alice's internal conflicts did not just stem from her inability to control her fertility. They were also a result of the self-imposed isolation in which she tried to come to terms with her actions.[33]

From Alice's diary it is quite apparent that at a time when she clearly needed support, she did not turn to her female friends. She usually kept a detailed record of conversations with friends in her diary but because there is no mentioning of a talk about her postcoital anxieties, I assume that it never took place. This is all the more remarkable since Alice had involved her friends in her plans in the days leading up to her trip. At a minimum, she needed the cooperation of her roommate to meet her lover in Brooklyn. Moreover, Alice knew from a number of her female friends that they, too, had slept with men with whom they did not have an exclusive, steady relationship. She also had discussed with friends the example of another Smith College woman who dropped out to have a child and refused to marry the father. In their private conversations, Alice and her friends had admired this woman's actions.[34] Therefore, fear that her friends would condemn her could not have been the reason why Alice did not seek their counsel or advice. Rather, her silence would suggest that even self-ascribed nonconformists were able to look in a positive light at a woman who had sexual intercourse outside a committed relationship only under very particular circumstances.

That Alice seems not to have sought the help and advice of her friends may be due to the linkage between a woman's sexual performance, her intellectual abilities, her personality, and her social status in general. The onset of self-doubt and shame in the aftermath of her affair raised the specter in her mind that she did not possess sufficient maturity and self-awareness after all. If she was not a rational woman in control of her impulses, she could only be a vulgar bad girl. Shortly after the Brooklyn trip, she described herself in her diary as "unclean" and "weak" and as a woman who resembled an "animal" and a "throwback" in evolution. She was "bad, bad," wrote Alice, and should not be allowed to even "touch clean" women anymore. In the aftermath of her Brooklyn affair, the tenor of Alice's diary changed. She increasingly felt that she was on the wrong developmental track. She was "just drifting into messes"; she had "no honor, no maturity."[35] She also at this time became critical of the literature of individualism popular within her circle of friends. She emphasized the interdependence of all social groups on one another, and she described herself frequently now as a person who was tender and giving and ready for love.

The diary entries of Margaret Hall reveal less about her dating encounters, but a careful reading shows that she, too, was unable to experience her sexuality in a positive way. At the start of her college education, Margaret's engagement to Bill had protected her from sexual conflicts. Bill was sexually conservative and did not pressure her to go beyond her comfort zone. Margaret lost this safe space, however, when, after having broken up with her fiancé, she was pushed and pulled back into the dating culture. As she described herself in a letter to a friend, she became quite "a sucker for a good-looking man, or an interesting mind. Preferably both." Like Alice, she preferred partners who shared her interest in literature and who seemed able to accept a woman as an intellectual companion. These culturally liberal men, however, also expected Margaret to agree to a level of intensity in the sexual realm with which she was not comfortable. Moreover, because she was not in a committed relationship, the sexual acts that occurred in the context of her dates were by definition casual. Just like Alice, Margaret experienced her dating life as a moral challenge. As she at one point remarked in a letter to a friend, she had been getting into a number of "man predicaments" after leaving Bill.[36]

While at Bryn Mawr, Margaret seemed to have managed to keep her affairs from growing too intense. Strict guidelines regarding moral behavior at this women's college might have aided her in her effort to avoid situations in which she was alone with a man. As she wrote about this time in retrospect, she adopted as her motto to "stay out of trouble, stay out of bed."[37] It became more and more difficult to avoid sexual entanglements, however, once Margaret started graduate school at Harvard. "Why do dorms permit young men to have young women in?" she asked at one point. "Oh dear," she continued her journal, "it does sound as though there had been a scandal. There wasn't. Kissing, and hugging, and some petting. . . . Hands outside one's clothes, across one's breasts." These actions, Margaret knew, could not be judged as "evil" according to a universal moral standard. Culturally no less literate than Alice, she was familiar with a literature on the cultural and historical relativity of sex mores: were she "in a different society," her actions would not be considered taboo. Nonetheless, her sexual encounters clearly left her with a nagging sense of shame. Her own desire alarmed her as an indication that she might be incapable of controlling herself. In addition, her confusion about the appropriate course of action suggested a lack of maturity.[38]

A fear of what her personal conflicts might reveal about her character prevented Margaret, just like Alice, from turning to other women for advice. If others only knew of her difficulties, she wrote in her diary, they "would dispise [sic] [her for her] lack of wisdom and control." Like Alice at Smith College, she did not turn to a female peer for advice. She continued to refuse consent to intercourse, but even the donning of a conservative stance toward sexuality did not protect her from conflict. From whatever angle Margaret looked at it, her performance in sexual encounters raised fears that she might lack the "wisdom and control" expected of a member of the educated middle class. That even this professor's daughter from a rural country estate agonized this intensely about the question of appropriate sexual performance illustrates poignantly how central sexuality had become in the demarcation of membership in the educated middle class at a time when its composition was in the process of changing.

The difficulties culturally literate women experienced in the attempt to come to terms with their sexuality are highlighted by their responses to the Kinsey reports. Because these studies offered statistical data that demonstrated the frequency with which moral codes were violated, one might assume that college women welcomed the news and appreciated the information. Curiously, though, very few women even mention the Kinsey studies in their personal papers. Margaret and Alice are two of only a few women who talked about them at all.[39] Even though both took note of the publication of Kinsey's material, they found it of little help. The way in which Margaret responded in her journal is telling: "There are as many conflicting standards among my fellow Bryn Mawrs as among the young men who feature so prominently in Dr. Kinsey's pages," she wrote. "This I suspected—but did not know for sure."[40]

Considering the impact the Kinsey studies had on the nation at large, this is a surprisingly curt response. But Kinsey was not really offering Margaret new information. The 1949 study on men confirmed that Americans conducted their intimate relationships in a variety of ways. The information supported the notion that in the final analysis it was up to the individual to decide on the right course of action. "One tries to decide What is Right . . . and learns that . . . Right is a relative thing," Margaret commented on the report. She clearly wanted to hear something else by this point, however. From the comments she made immediately after this sentence, we can see what she was looking for. If one was "lucky," she wrote, "one learns what the flexible, inevitable Right is for one's self. That which must be. That self-made cave within which one is at peace with self and soul."[41]

As indicated by this comment, Margaret had gained little from Kinsey's aggregate data. She was not interested in what was typical or average but in what was "Right." As her mentioning of the flexibility of standards shows, she was not looking for a universal norm. Morality was "self-made" and individualistic. Her craving for peace, however, illustrates the strains caused by sexual encounters that left her either with a sense of guilt for not meeting the needs of partners or with a sense of shame for doing so. The fact that Margaret at this time took up yoga and meditation further illustrates the intensity with which she craved some kind of yardstick other than the refrain of individualism. She was actively looking for answers to questions that affected her sense of well-being and challenged her identity.

It is telling that Alice Gorton also found Kinsey's studies of human sexuality of little help. Published in 1953, *Sexual Behavior in the Human Female* came out the same year she went to Brooklyn to consummate her affair. Not surprisingly, considering her preoccupation with how to interpret her actions, Alice read the report. She learned from it that her behavior was not unusual: "The Kinsey report on women makes me typical, but a bit more 'sexy' than average. Good." This brief comment, however, was the only reference in a diary composed of often page-long reflections on readings and how they relate to the author's life. It seems, therefore, that Alice, too, did not find in Kinsey's report what she was looking for. As the entries that increasingly appear in her journal reveal, she was reeling under a sense of having to live up to other people's ideas and expectations. "I have the idea now that I am not much of my own," she wrote, "just a hodge podge of other peoples ideas + desires + drives—from books + friends." Like Margaret, she wanted a respite from the experience of moral conflict: She wanted "there to be a core of me-ness somewhere!" She, too, began to practice yoga. Only a few pages after she described her desire for a "core," she wrote that she wanted to be more attentive to her own well-being: "I am me," she wrote, "responsible only to myself. And I've got to learn to take care of that self." Alice here was clearly starting to feel that she was being shortchanged. She wanted her own needs to be honored and respected.[42]

The evidence for how urgently Alice and Margaret craved a respite from personal conflicts puts their infatuation with notions of female distinctiveness in a new perspective. Alice and Margaret were both becoming aware that the gender dynamics in their environment put them at a disadvantage. When it came to sex, college women carried the brunt of the burden of risk for defying conventions. They were the ones who had to fear pregnancy or who risked official sanction for violations of moral regulations. Moreover, because of a persistent sexual double standard, the loss of impulse control carried a heavier stigma for women than for men. Women's arguments based on practical objections, social norms, or fear of consequences, however, had routinely been denied legitimacy. As we have seen earlier, college men tended to interpret their partners' difficulties to express themselves sexually as personality flaws. In this context, it is no longer surprising that Alice and Margaret experienced the notion that a woman's identity and sexuality were inextricably linked to her reproductive potential as authentic.

If we consider the possible benefits of summoning biology or archetypal patterns in dating situations, the strategic value of an emphasis on difference becomes clear. Not only did this argument offer women opportunities to exercise agency, it also promised a respite from personal conflicts. For one, the idea that a woman's sexuality was linked to her reproductive role explained to Margaret and Alice in positive terms the roller coaster of emotions that routinely ensued because of sexual encounters. It allowed them to see their difficulties in coming to terms with their desire not as a sign of repression or a personality flaw but as the logical consequence of their nature. Moreover, they gained an argument to counter male demands to meet their needs. If women as "good members" of their sex were not made to be "like" men, they ought not to be expected to live up to male expectations.[43] Yet, in contrast to explicit references to gender-specific needs, the argument allowed women to plead an altruistic motivation. Alice and Margaret could argue that they were acting in the best interest of the nation and the human race. They were not stringing men along. They simply could not help being sexually more reticent than their partners, and this, for the sake of the future generation, was a good thing. When these young women adopted the notion that their reproductive role was central to their identity, they were thus picking selectively from a variety of different discourses the one that best seemed to serve a particularly urgent need. Considering the frequency with which college women encountered male demands to act against their own self-interest, we need to see their embrace of notions of gender difference not as selling out to conformist pressures but as an attempt to influence the power dynamics in their encounters with men and to exercise authority.

Looking once again at the events that coincide with Margaret and Alice's emphasis on their female distinctiveness, we can see that they indeed used the notions of an archetypal force beyond their control to legitimate their own needs and interests in dating encounters. Margaret Hall in a letter to a friend, for instance, attributed it to a growing "woman wisdom" that she had not gotten herself into any "men predicaments" for a while. The usefulness of this notion of her intuitive femininity also shows in another journal entry. Reflecting in 1955 on her reasons for refusing consent to coitus with another graduate student, she expressed her guilt and sense that she was violating her own and her partner's natures. "I wish I could resolve this feeling" of "doing wrong with another person, against both natures," she recorded. She also wrote, however, that she had no choice. It was "the inevitable result of my emotional make-up." The impulse to say "No" came to her "like a night force. . . . There is no appeal; I cannot quite ignore it."[44] Alice Gorton similarly saw in the "possibility of a priori knowledge" a potential yardstick in dating encounters. After discovering the "archetype from the collective unconscious" for her honors thesis, Alice emphasized only a page later in her diary that "sex and physical love" should be engaged in only in "secret loveliness." Later in the course of her studies, she specified that "the sexual act is to be carried out only within a context of regard and concern for the good of another." In this she saw an answer to an urgent need. She had found a rationale for a valuable and ethical course of action. As she recorded, she had come "knocking on the door of a higher plane of existence."[45]

Strategic or not, women's recourse to notions of gender difference did of course entail the glorification of motherhood.[46] Yet in spite of this, Alice and Margaret had not turned into gender conservatives. In Margaret Hall's case, the complexity of her thoughts on gender becomes clear in a letter she wrote to one of her male partners. The immediate point of reference in this case is not clear. Clearly, however, Margaret was writing to insist on the legitimacy of her own perspective. She "never was a feminist," she begins her explanation. Shortly after distancing herself from a stigmatized label, however, she delineated a concept of masculinity and femininity that can be seen as an articulation of "difference" feminism. "Women are not men," she wrote. "They never see as men do; they aren't made to fight their battles as men do; they don't understand as men do." Yet she did not emphasize these points in support of a traditional gender role. Margaret's allusion to female distinctiveness was meant as a challenge to her friend to take her seriously. He should not hold her up to a male standard but accept her for what she was. In that case, he would realize that as a woman she had just as much to contribute to human progress as he: she was not "a mediocre masculine mind . . . possessed of some learning," she argued. "Separate but equal; equal but different," she had all the characteristics "anyone has to have to be a good female," and "unless one is a good member of one's own sex, one hasn't a very good chance to be a good member of [the] human race."[47] Margaret was not surrendering her goals to accept a helpmeet role. She argued for a model of gender parallelism that granted legitimacy to her needs and value to her particular talents and interests.

This letter was not the only instance in which Margaret theorized about gender. From other writings we can also see that, although she labeled certain personality traits as feminine, she was not a biological essentialist. In the diary entry in which she reflected on why she found it impossible to consent to intercourse, for example, she referred to "the inevitable result of my emotional make-up." The factors responsible for her "make-up," however, she did not see as merely biological but as the effects of experiences: Its "origins" were "many," including "remnants of religion," and the fact that she was brought up in an "inner-directed, conscience-ful [sic] New England family."[48] Gender in Margaret Hall's thought was not simply the product of biology but of the different existential experiences of the sexes. A diary entry she composed in the spring of 1955 further shows that she also did not see men and women as possessing mutually exclusive traits. "How does one ever effect a working relationship between one's hard, tough, sensible, practical, strength-loving masculine directness, and one's gentle, tender, loving & giving, helpful, self-less desires . . . ?"[49] As we can see, she assumed that either sex possessed certain traits that society conventionally attributed to the other. For her, a human being was only whole if he or she had achieved a balance between his or her masculine and feminine side. A fully developed human race, meanwhile, would not curtail the opportunities of either sex.

If we compare Margaret's writings to those of the scholars she encountered in college, it becomes clear that she was not just buying into the idealized portrayal of domestic mothers in popular culture. There are in fact striking parallels between Margaret's theory and the writings of, for instance, the anthropologist Margaret Mead. Mead, like Margaret, drew on a rhetoric of a right to be a self-realized member of the human race when she defined male and female. "A person without full sex membership is worse off than a man without a country," she had written in a 1935 *Fortune* article.[50] Sex membership in Mead's work referred to the male or female reproductive role. Because of this role, she saw women in a separate category than men. While she saw male and female as biological categories, she saw masculinity and femininity as cultural constructs that varied from one society to the next.[51]

A look at Mead's work shows the parallels between her definition of female distinctiveness and that of Margaret, who, in her insistence on the cultural importance of gender difference, was probably influenced by the anthropologist as well. As Mead had argued on a number of occasions, modern Western societies had so far failed to tap into women's true potential to contribute to human progress, and here she found feminists and gender conservatives equally at fault. While the former had tried to press women into a male mold, gender conservatives inflicted just as much damage by insisting on mutually exclusive sex traits. Being exposed to unrealistic demands regarding their sex-role performance, Mead argued, made men and women likely to suffer psychological damage. If a culture insisted that certain traits belonged only to women, then any man who detected traces of them in himself was likely to become neurotic. Alternatively, if women were asked to fit themselves into a male mold, they would have to deny parts of themselves.[52] Considering the overlap between the work of Mead and Margaret's diary, it seems unlikely that the young woman had only a domestic role in mind when she glorified "woman wisdom" and her own capacity to be the "bearer of children."[53]

Alice Gorton's diary provides evidence of a similarly complex definition of femininity. An entry she composed as a senior shows that college had not turned her into a biological essentialist. What were the limits to "human . . . freedom" she pondered? She identified distinct "limitations," some of which she labeled "absolute" and others "relative." Under the latter, she listed individual and clearly changeable factors such as "appearance" and "economic state." Under absolute limitations, she listed "sex" and "social conditioning." Yet although Alice here expressed a degree of determinism, she did not think that, just because they belonged to the same "sex," all women shared the same limitations. Even "absolute limitations," she wrote, were "different for each." She echoed in this entry a line of thinking about gender that was also developed by experts who clearly supported progressive gender roles for women.[54] Mirra Komarovsky in *Women in the Modern World* (1953), for example, addressed the essentialism of contemporary antifeminists. Drawing from a variety of studies, she offered evidence of greater variations in character and ability from one individual to the next than could be found between men and women as a group.

It becomes clear from the writings of Alice and Margaret that even after they put motherhood at the center of their identity, they did not turn into gender conservatives. Their particular version of femininity was sufficiently complex to accommodate gender progressive outlooks. Even more, their beliefs were not only reconcilable with nondomestic goals; the new way in which they defined their natures actually facilitated their academic successes. This was because the discovery of a moral yardstick in dating encounters eased tensions in their sexual lives and freed up psychic spaces to concentrate on class work and research. Moreover, the discovery of material that reflected their own subjective experiences enhanced the satisfaction these students gained from their studies. In Alice's diary in particular, we can see how her discovery of "the Great Subject" for her honors thesis positively affected her self-esteem. Once she started the research, she wrote: "I'm interested, I'm working on what I want. . . . I feel great." Finally, she felt she could talk on equal terms with some of the women whom she admired as particularly talented. Right after a diary entry in which she described her love for the "rich symbolism, the personal mythology, [and] the mystical dogma" in one of her readings for her thesis, she added that she had a "good talk with Poofy today. . . . I talk to her as an equal finally." That Alice was at this time at the height of self-confidence also shows in the fact that she was increasingly expressing her personal idiosyncrasies in front of Smith College peers. She decorated her study carrel with a "ghost + skull," and after the college painted over her art, she redecorated it with "an inverted black cross." Her peers also increasingly noticed her as a student who stood out positively as a "good kid," albeit one that was highly intelligent. As Poof told her, some of the younger students in particular "considered [her] as a god." The extent to which her satisfaction with college grew during this time also shows in another one of Alice's diary entries. Entering the English seminar room one day, Alice described paying tribute to her alma mater and the opportunities it offered her: "I went down on my knees to say 'thank you.' . . . I am very humble. How can a girl be so really lucky?"[55]

A surge in self-confidence was not the only positive change we can detect at this point in the journal of Alice Gorton. By the time she was a junior, she was also formulating for the first time a clear and realistic postgraduate goal. Alice had always had the ambition to combine a satisfying career and a fulfilling love life, but her ideas about her professional métier had tended to be rather vague. She was fond of picturing herself as a glamorous writer. In moments of low confidence, however, she doubted that her "dreams of glory" could ever become real.[56] With the discovery of her honors thesis subject, Alice's career plans became more realistic.

The writings of midcentury college women in general reflect the biases of a curriculum from which female authors, artists, or experts were virtually absent.[57] Women scholars historically lacked prestige in comparison to men, but Cold War changes in higher education heightened this marginalization. As one study put it, in the eyes of hiring committees, female applicants had not only low prestige, they were "outside the prestige system entirely."[58] Universities rarely recruited or admitted women to positions other than instructor. Women's colleges had traditionally been among the few spaces where female academics held high positions. Yet after World War II, opportunities were shrinking even there. By the late 1950s, male faculty members would outnumber female ones at Alice Gorton's alma mater. At the time when she was attending Smith College, this trend was already visible.

The invisibility of women as scholars, their clustering in low-status positions, and stereotypes of old maids and spinsters explain why female students rarely commented on older women in academia in ways that suggest that they saw them as role models. Female academics tended to lack the prestige of male colleagues. Women who were acknowledged experts and specialists in their fields, meanwhile, struck students as exceptions who must have had to deny themselves feminine fulfillment to get where they were. Alice Gorton's journal reflects these larger difficulties of her peers to imagine women as contributors to culture. The time when she homed in on a thesis subject, however, is an exception. Here the immediate inspiration was a book by a woman: Maud Bodkin, in whose work on British literary critique Gilbert Murray Alice found her topic: "the archetype from the collective unconscious in Bodkin's book which I must buy for my own. This is the great subject."[59]

We cannot underestimate how remarkable it was for a 1950s college woman to refer to a female academic and to express admiration for her work. Maud Bodkin stands out as a female author in a diary filled with quotations almost exclusively by men. Nevertheless, the example of this scholar had an impact. Prior to her reference to the literary critic, Alice did not comment on female teachers. This changed, however, for a short time during her junior year. When she started the work on her thesis, the first person she considered as an advisor was the T. S. Eliot expert and professor of literature Elizabeth Drew. In Alice's journal, this woman was the subject of a rare positive entry about an older female academic: "Miss Drew spoke in chapel today. Everyone was charmed and I was so proud of her. . . . Also in looking at her, I thought that it would be a fine life of hers. I wouldn't mind it. As long as you are good at what you are doing + don't get bored."[60]

It is no coincidence that this positive reference appeared at the same time that Alice had become intrigued with the work of Maud Bodkin. Alice had found in Bodkin a female scholar who discussed academic subjects in a way to which she could personally relate. Discovering an intellectual affinity with a learned woman of an older generation had the potential to contradict the pernicious stereotype of the repressed old maid teacher. It alerted Alice to the possibility that other female academics might have expertise to offer to her. Moreover, it enabled her to see these older women not as exceptional characters but as charming women who led a "fine" life. This meant for Alice that she was able (at least for a time) to consider college teaching as an appealing career option. For women trying to break into academia, gaining access to an instructor position was often no small feat. As a career plan, however, teaching was definitely more realistic than the "dreams of glory" that had dominated Alice's journal so far.

Margaret Hall's journal shows a similar dynamic of growing self-confidence combined with a more realistic adjustment of career plans. That the young woman believed in her ability to break into academia shows in her postgraduate actions. By 1956, she was enrolled in a master's program in education, and she applied for a Fulbright grant to go to Great Britain. This course of action also reflects that her ability to realistically assess her career options had grown. Originally, Margaret strove for a career in English. This highly competitive field offered women few opportunities, but it had the prestige of a male-dominated profession. With her growing comfort in a gender-separatist position, however, Margaret was beginning to consider more realistic and achievable options for herself. Having just started out at Harvard, she wrote a friend about her plans for the future. The letter shows that she had scaled down her ambitions, yet she remained committed to a life in which she was not the helpmeet/dependent of any man but a woman who had a sustaining career of her own. She wrote her friend about her new course of study: "And this won't be like English, with no openings for women unless one is a brilliantly original scholar. There's a place for the roundly, soundly intelligent person . . . and me for it! Not at the expense of a personal life, but in conjunction with a roundly, soundly interesting one. . . . To find my métier is still such a joyous thing. . . . And I won't have to worry about anyone's reaching clutching fingers towards The Little Woman . . . nor about becoming a hard person, either."[61]

The letter offers interesting insights into the growing sophistication of Margaret's social analysis. She had clearly come to understand that in order to break into a high-status field "like English" she would have to prove herself as exceptionally driven and talented. She also understood that these standards of super-performance applied only to women. In this letter to a male friend, she did not broach the topic of fairness of this double standard. Yet she also no longer wanted to accept that in order to take a professional position, she first needed to prove herself as an exception to her sex.

Were Alice and Margaret unusual? The papers of Stanford University student Susan Sperry Borman and the diary of Dori Schaffer, a Jewish

American woman who studied at the University of California at Los Angeles, show that they, too, were grappling with questions about the nature of femininity. In 1956 Susan's reflections in response to a writing assignment on "social techniques" show that she was beginning to understand femininity as at least in part a performance rather than a reflection of a biological essence. Pondering how she acted when she went on a date, she wrote: "I am confused about how I act with guys. Is it fake or isn't it? And more than that, is it wrong or isn't it to feel that way?" The college freshman was unable to formulate a conclusion. The assignment had clearly caused her to wonder, however, which aspects of femininity were based on nature and which were just a cultural convention. "Sometimes I think I'm just kidding myself along about feeling so feminine and protected," she mused, "because it couldn't be farther from me if it wanted to, and then, other times, it all seems almost natural."[62] Two years later, Dori Schaffer went to a "housewarming" with fellow students. "As I talked," wrote the young woman, "I came up with the thought that I should like to investigate the differential effects upon the personalities of children raised traditionally by family, and children raised in state nurseries." This reflection on the impact of environmental factors on the development of children then led her to reflect on the cultural basis of femininity: she believed that "almost all differences between men and women are culturally conditioned, not biological or innate."[63]

The evidence presented here adds another dimension to the growing body of revisionist works on women in the 1950s that show this generation as a bridge between the prewar progressive feminist movements and the sixties.[64] At the same time that women in labor and civil rights organizations continued to work for feminist goals, female undergraduates grappled with definitions of femininity and examined the relative importance of cultural and biological factors in shaping gender role expectations. Without finding and analyzing additional personal writings from the immediate post–World War II period, it is impossible to say with certainty how large a group we are dealing with. I can say, however, that none of these students had to dig up obscure pamphlets or tap secret resources. Among more than just a few isolated students, the question of what constitutes the basis of femininity was up for debate.

Nevertheless, a paradox remains. The college women discussed here had learned to identify and to articulate their self-interests. They became able to select from clashing messages those that best served their needs at a given moment. Faced with demands they clearly experienced as burdensome, they insisted that it was their right to reject them. Moreover, they learned to evaluate their options realistically. Still, in spite of clear evidence of personal and intellectual growth, many of these highly literate women married young and put their own career plans on the back burner. Margaret Hall and Alice Gorton followed in the footsteps of a majority. They also selected as their mates partners who did not share their progressive gender beliefs. It is still not clear exactly what happened here. Examining this question in more detail, the remainder of this chapter will look at the factors that ultimately undermined young women's self-confidence.

Examining the personal stories of a small number of college women soon makes clear that their intellectual resourcefulness was ultimately no match for the forces rallied against them. Against the background of a pervasive sense of male entitlement, any feminine "mystique," whichever way it was defined, was a weak counterdiscourse. Women never gained more than a temporary respite from doubts about their performance as sexual beings. In a sense, these conflicts are still common among adolescents. In the Cold War context, however, they loomed especially large. Because sex and gender roles were in a transitional stage, there literally was no longer one right way for women to perform. Yet, because matters of gender and sexuality carried such immense implications for social status, for notions of political reliability, and for intelligence, young women experienced psychological damage that they were badly equipped to deal with.

Anecdotal evidence about personal crises illustrate the limitations of the coping strategies available to young women who wanted careers but who also sought fulfillment as (hetero-)sexual and feminine beings. Alice and Margaret, as we have seen, tried to alleviate tensions in a very difficult social milieu by emphasizing their feminine distinctiveness. By doing so, however, they highlighted qualities about themselves that carried little prestige in the environment in which they moved where individualism and exceptionality were the values regarded most highly. We see vividly in the diary of Alice Gorton how this hierarchy of values opened up new sources of conflict. Alice's diary contains ample evidence for stimulating talks with other women in the honors program. Her journal also shows, however, that she and her friends had internalized a hierarchical ranking of gendered attributes that caused them to look down at desires for security, love, and community. Because these human needs in the Cold War discourse on civilization were marked as typically female and portrayed as obstacles to progress, young women's self-confidence suffered once they had to admit to themselves that these longings were impossible to exorcize.

That the hierarchical ranking of attributes deemed necessary for national progress had the potential to undermine young women's attempts to formulate realistic and achievable notions of self shows in

Alice's response to Poof, a woman whose intelligence and daring social behavior she admired. Both women had initially bonded over their beliefs in radical individualism and tried to live up to this ideal. Poof, however, flaunted a nonconformist persona much more openly than Alice did. Early on during her junior year, Alice wrote that Poof was "getting altogether too talked about." The exact nature of the activities that got Poof into trouble is not clear. From a reference about rumors circulating about her, including "negro kissing, making out, sexy dances" it seems that Poof frequented mixed-race bars and hangouts and dated African American men.[65] But it is equally possible that once Poof attracted attention for any kind of inappropriate behavior, rumors took on a life of their own. Alice's journal entries at a later point reveal that Poof had premarital intercourse. Yet, whether this was why she was already "getting . . . talked about" at the earlier occasion is impossible to say. Whatever Poof might have been doing, though, within her circle of friends her actions were not unusual. In her journal, Alice refused to condemn Poof because, as she wrote, she had "lived almost as she."[66]

The parallels in their experiences aside, Poof reacted to the growing strains in her personal life differently from Alice. While the latter, after her Brooklyn adventure, had redefined what she wanted from a relationship and why, Poof—at least in public—did not. Rather, she responded to an increase in peer criticism by fortifying her defense. In talks with Alice, Poof argued that she would be a writer, that she was seeking "unique experiences," and that the uproar among her peers just indicated their conformist mindset. Her motto, as Alice quoted her, was: "Sex—a terror to the coward, [a] treasure to the bold." Poof therefore continued to insist that her actions were not only legitimate but marked her as a superior, nonconforming, and self-aware woman. Considering her own recent experiences, Alice was skeptical. "Granted she is having unique experiences," she wrote, "but can she learn and evaluate them so they do her any good?" Face-to-face with the friend, however, she was not able to hold her own. "I don't know how to talk to her," she wrote and asked herself: "Why am I so inarticulate when it really matters?"[67]

The way in which Alice responded to her friend's arguments illustrates the extent to which, in her circle of friends, young women continued to hold themselves up to the exaggerated standards of radical individualism, and her responses show her difficulties in granting legitimacy to needs and desires gendered feminine. The question of how to evaluate Poof occupied Alice for months. She second-guessed what her own longing for comfort and security really said about her. In contrast to Poof's defiance of conventional norms, her fears and needs seemed to mark her as an inferior person. The question of the comparative worth of her own and Poof's outlook still occupied Alice the summer before her senior year. At home with her family in Ohio, she read Ayn Rand's *The Fountainhead*. Poof, who, according to Alice, considered this book her "'bible,'" had repeatedly referred to its main protagonist, the radically independent and nonconforming Howard Roark, as a model. At home and away from the student peer culture, Alice arrived at a perceptive and critical evaluation: "There is interdependence + no one is as strong as Roark." She described Poof as reading selectively in the volume, "accepting the freedom for individuality, missing or ignoring the stated need for discipline." But back at Smith, her insecurities soon got the better of her again. She soon reverted back to a dichotomy of people who lived in radical independence from the opinions of others, on the one hand, and those who had sacrificed their integrity for the sake of fitting in, on the other hand. "How can one steer a course between what one admires and would like to be—the integral man," she wondered, "and what gives one pleasure—being with people, . . . and being happy?" Poof, she pondered, was proving through her uncompromising stance that she was a superior person. Alice, by contrast, feared that she had "neither the talent as an excuse nor the courage necessary to be a [Howard] Roark."[68]

Alice's journal entries offer insights beyond the dynamics in her friendship with Poof. Her reading of *The Fountainhead* was critical and sophisticated. Her knowledge of alternative theories combined with her personal experiences had thrown in doubt the tenets of individualism. Alice understood clearly that in a complex modern world, an ethical human being would not and could not act like a Howard Roark. But as soon as she was back at Smith, she could no longer act on her insights. Using the same arguments Alice had routinely heard from her dating partners, Poof, echoing Ayn Rand, spoke with the authority of a male voice. Alice's inability to hold her own in confrontations with her peer reflects the extent to which female students privileged male arguments, male values, and male needs even in a homosocial setting. Because of this, the likelihood that a female student would internalize a drive to prove herself an individual devoid of stereotypically feminine needs first, before she could even aspire to a life or career not typical for her sex, was large.

By the end of Alice's junior year, the personal pressures created by high performance standards had taken a toll on her sense of self. Her belief in her own ability to actually make a contribution as a member of a profession or as a writer progressively declined. "I am pretty sure that I will never be a great critic or a great poet," she wrote. She also became less and less able to picture all but the most unusual women as amounting to anything in the public sphere. "No wonder nothing much great has come from a woman's college," she recorded. She now also changed her mind about Elizabeth Drew as her thesis adviser. Instead, she chose to ask a male faculty member who, although at the beginning of his academic career, still struck her as a better academic mentor by virtue of his sex alone. "Having a man" she wrote, would be "stimulating" especially as he was "a young one."[69]

Was Alice just a particularly insecure woman? A look at other women's writings suggests that we are faced with a larger dynamic. The way in which the friendship developed between Stanford University's Susan and her friend Holly illustrates that more than just a few Smith College students held in low esteem traits and interests culturally labeled as feminine. Holly and Susan befriended each other as freshmen in 1956 after they discovered an affinity in terms of their intellectual and social interests. Both wanted to write professionally, and neither was actively looking for a steady partner. Increasingly, however, Susan spent her free time in the company of one young man named Harry. Her journal offers only vague references to sexual activities, but it is clear that the longer she saw Harry, the more the question of how to interpret and define her relationship with him concerned her. Eventually Susan told Holly that she thought she was "falling in love" and that she might one day marry Harry.[70]

Considering the prevalence of conflicts over sexuality in the student dating culture, it is likely that Susan wanted to ease internal conflicts by redefining her relationship with Harry. Defending her actions as an expression of love would allow her to silence some of the turmoil that was so easily the consequence of premarital sexual experimentation for women. That she was indeed planning to settle for him is far from clear. In fact, although Harry was her most frequent dating partner, she kept going out with other men as well.[71] Yet, while Susan might have managed to alleviate some tensions in her life by justifying an increase in sexual intensity through love, this strategy put her friend Holly on the defensive. In response to Susan's declaration, Holly emphasized her own commitment to steer an individualistic course. Susan quotes her as saying: "'I am alone; I will never love a man completely.'" In her journal, Susan speculated that a personal neurosis might be at the root of the friend's attitude. "Is she denying everything but her mind so that she will be able to live only with it," she mused. Was this a rationalization in place of "the real reason" that she had been hurt by the "injustice done her" by judgmental others? In a letter to her parents, Susan also wrote that she thought Holly would benefit from psychological counseling.[72]

This notwithstanding, Susan could not help but feel inferior in comparison to her friend. "I think she is, in these things an unequitable [*sic*] person. I admire her individuality and her determination to be thus;

it reminds me of all the other great artists one hears of." In contrast to this idealized figure of the exceptional woman, her own desire for love and popularity now struck Susan as inferior. It seemed to show that she was simply destined for a helpmeet role. "I am wife material," she wrote. "This I am never sorry of and never could be, but it seems disconcerting and vaguely degrading that such should be the thing that I must admit will be my life. It seems to put Holly in a class somewhere above me."[73]

What we see in these journal entries are more than squabbles between competitive-minded friends. They illustrate how, as a consequence of growing normative pressures in the post–World War II collegiate setting, young women who all in their own way tried to find a balance between the demands of femininity and their nontraditional goals were pitted against each other. College women who wanted careers and who acted in socially idiosyncratic ways were united by the experience of strain and conflict. Poof and Holly in all likelihood experienced the same self-doubts as Alice and Susan. Susan and Alice, meanwhile, had not parted with professional goals. There was, however, no sympathetic public discussion of the conflicting and gender-specific pressures affecting them. Their main recourse in defense of personal idiosyncrasies was to the ideal of individualism. This ideology demanded of them, however, that they be able to sort through their doubts and difficulties all by themselves. Questions of gender performance thus became an issue even between female friends. Doubts about what their choices, wishes, and needs indicated about them distanced them from each other.

Parallels in the journals of other women suggest that they, too, interpreted their difficulties to make sense of clashing messages and normative pressures as personal weaknesses. Holding herself up to a standard of super-performance modeled after an unrealistic ideal, Margaret Hall was also incapable of granting legitimacy to her own need for security and comfort. "What do I want?" she asked herself in her journal during her senior year in 1955: "To marry, I suppose. . . ." She was still planning to go to graduate school and have a career. But she wanted a partner in her life with whom she could share the pleasures and pains of life, love, and work: "Someone who could come home with me at vacation time to the inlaws, someone who would be met by my friends as my husband, someone I'd come home to and be come home to by, all my life." The acknowledgment of having these interests in security and comfort, however, triggered a fear of failure. She called herself "a mediocre above-average" who might be "above average in brains" but who was "not brilliant enough to justify [her] idiosyncrasies."[74] In the diary of Dori Schaffer, meanwhile, the effects of Dori's investment into notions of exceptionality and individualism also show in the fact that, after she admitted to herself that she was "lonely" and wanted "a man to love," she also could not help but see it as a personal failure and defeat: "I have admitted that I am a woman. I have admitted that I am like 99% of the feminine sex: I want my own man. This is a horrible admission, to me. I have been denying and fighting this for three years. But had it not been true that I was deep inside, mostly woman, like every other, I would not have had to fight it so hard."[75]

This internalization of the notion that interests, traits, and concerns, stereotypically labeled feminine lacked value thus backfired once women tried to readjust their concept of self and their goals in more realistic ways. Fears of what their needs and desires might reveal about them taxed these women's female support networks. Trying to protect an increasingly embattled sense of self, women resorted to silence and defensiveness. These coping mechanisms, however, kept intact a gendered hierarchy in which men and exceptional women occupied the upper ranks. The nation's best-educated women thus contributed to an increasingly polarized concept of femininity with "brilliant" superachievers on the one side and placid, conformist "wife material" on the other.[76]

The standards of performance in the college setting disadvantaged all women. Career-oriented women who frequented the student dating culture, however, were particularly vulnerable. Against the background of unrealistic performance standards and the denigration of needs and interests associated with women, ordinary feelings of ambivalence so typical of adolescence and the perfectly human wish for community and acceptance appeared to be character flaws. In this situation in which self-doubts thrived easily, an increase of sexual conflicts could have devastating results. We have already seen how private conflicts over how to interpret their feelings and actions in sexual encounters preoccupied many women. The strains that grew out of these privately experienced doubts pale, however, in contrast to the damage caused once sexual issues became public.

That public exposure of sexual activities had such an extreme effect on the identity of ambitious young women once again needs to be seen in the context of the climate of national insecurity during the Cold War. Because sexual and gender performance was linked to notions of intelligence, status, political reliability, and mental health, sexual slander could gain the power to generate a toxic mix of guilt, shame, and fear that made it difficult for young women to follow through with postgraduate plans. By sexual slander, I mean public challenges of the way in which some women performed as sexual and gendered actors. Over the course of their studies, college women who personally became the object of gossip and public sanctions, or who witnessed the effects of these factors on others, realized their vulnerability and lack of support. Their heightened sense of isolation then negatively tainted their assessment of their society's ability to deal with dissent. As a result, they silenced their innermost feelings and retreated into outward conformity.

Examples of young women who were officially reprimanded by their colleges reveal the devastating effects of public exposure of their private acts. In early 1953 Smith College student Poof was called in front of the judicial board for a defense only vaguely defined as "disorderly conduct." It is not clear what the charges entailed. Because Poof did not leave any personal record of her own, we only have Alice Gorton's diary to rely on, and here we learn that Poof feared that she was pregnant. The nature of the sentence suggests, however, that a curfew violation was the official charge. Poof was "campused," which, as the term implies, prohibited her from leaving school grounds. This restriction, however, was not the only consequence of the public reprimand. Although Alice's diary does not describe the events that transpired, the style of the writing suggests that she was shocked by the intensity with which her peers conveyed their disapproval of Poof. "The stares," Alice wrote in reference to fellow students' reaction. She described them as lacking compassion and playing their role as hypocritical arbiters of morality: "Absolutely no feeling and acting a part." As a public violator of official morality, Poof had to run the gauntlet of her peers, and Alice now described her as a woman who "fell." She exclaimed: "There is so much horror and failure! What will happen to her now?"[77]

We should not attribute Alice's exclamations of "horror" and "failure" to hyperbole. The experience she describes was in all likelihood traumatizing for all parties involved. Although we have no way of assessing how Poof experienced her public exposure personally, it is unlikely that she was left unscathed. Current studies reveal the devastating and far-reaching effects of bullying on the budding identities of young female victims.[78] Yet Alice's diary also shows that the public exposure of moral offenders had consequences for more than the women who had the bad fortune of getting caught in the act of violating a rule. Seeing one woman "fall" also enhanced the sense of fear, self-doubt, and isolation among those who stood by. Alice was such a bystander. In her diary and in personal conversation, she refused to criticize Poof. But in public, she remained silent. She castigated herself for her failure to come out in defense of her friend. "I could perhaps have helped her," she wrote, "had I the strength of my convictions and enough self-confidence to speak my mind." She was, however, terrified that she would herself be implicated by Poof's actions. "When she fell, I fell," she wrote. As it turned out, Alice publicly maintained an image as a "good kid." Nonetheless, the strategy she used to protect her reputation backfired. Alice could not shake the sense that she had a duty to speak up in defense of actions that in theory she would not condemn. That in the end she did not speak out in Poof's defense, she interpreted as a severe character flaw. As a result, her self-confidence suffered another blow and she lost the sense of satisfaction in working on her honors thesis, satisfaction that she had only recently gained.[79]

Considering the increasingly sexualized dating culture and the diversity of views among students, we can assume that more women than Alice felt guilty for not coming out in defense of a friend. Guilt, however, was not the only negative feeling bystanders took away from watching another woman publicly reprimanded for actions many students practiced in private. Such public censures also brought to the fore fears about the meaning of their sexual and gender performance. When private acts were exposed, college women were forced to see themselves through the eyes of unsympathetic others. They now found confirmed what they had already suspected about themselves during times when their confidence was low: they were neither free lovers nor laudable nonconformists. They simply had no impulse control.

Private conflicts had the potential also to alter young women's views of their society's potential to tolerate dissent and diversity of views. The link between intimate experiences and the larger political context, however, is complicated. In 1953, parallel to the Judicial Board inquiry into Poof's conduct, for instance, the Smith College campus was also the site of a House Un-American Activities Committee (HUAC) investigation. That year, HUAC called English professor Robert Gorham Davis to testify about his affiliation with the Communist Party. In response, students called in a meeting, which Alice attended. The entry in her diary that she made after her return vividly conveys the chilling effect of the domestic Cold War. Emphasizing the value of discretion and privacy, she wrote: "Everyone's personal thoughts, opinions and actions should remain inviolate unless they choose to reveal them."[80]

It needs to be said, though, that prior to her Brooklyn affair, Alice had shared with her friends an irreverent attitude toward political events off campus. She and her friends had mocked McCarthy when he spoke on campus. They read literature that was considered controversial if not subversive in the nation at large, and they attended public talks by left-leaning individuals such as the Socialist Norman Thomas.[81] Like other college students, Alice had enjoyed the relative safe space of an academic setting in which controversial ideas were at least discussed. Her attitude was also possible because she shared with her friends an identity as members of an intellectual elite that stood above the prejudiced masses.

The threat of sexual slander combined with Alice's awareness of political dangers to unravel her self-confidence, and the increased attention she was paying to the question of control over her body illustrates her escalating personal crisis. Immediately after Poof was picked up by her parents, Alice recorded: "The first thing is to conquer the body to win respect. Let us please do so." In another journal entry, she wrote about the need to keep herself "clean" and "hide my badness." Repeatedly, she emphasized the need for "Discipline." This growing stress on self-control extended into various aspects of Alice's life. The thought that her roommate might have heard her snoring at one point, for instance, terrified her. At communal meals, she grew extremely self-conscious when she took a second helping of food. Her dieting, a common preoccupation of college women by mid century, at this time also took extreme forms. In at least one instance, she purged after a meal. These entries show a young woman under severe pressure and illustrate poignantly how easily issues of sexual and gender performance could lead to a profound crisis of identity.[82]

It was only after she realized her vulnerability to sexual slander that Alice's fear of scrutiny from the outside grew. Cold War political events were therefore not the only factors in the development of Alice's thoughts. Rather, her personal traumas heightened her awareness of the reality of political danger. Private experiences intersected with public events to shape Alice's perception of her situation, her options, and her abilities.

Sandra Iger's experiences a few years later offer additional insights into the effects of sexual slander on young women. Sandra attended college when the worst excesses of McCarthyism were over. Yet she was still affected by the atmosphere of ambivalence about female sexuality. Sometime between April and late May of 1959, the Mount Holyoke College student and her partner started having intercourse. In her letters to Richard, Sandra described their sexual relationship as a source of pleasure. For the couple to be able to meet in New York City, however, Sandra had to sign out under false pretenses, and her correspondence suggests that the need for secrecy imposed a heavy burden on the young woman. She referred in letters to feelings of "self disgust" and she started to dread going to sleep for fear of nightmares. She objected when Richard used frank language to describe their lovemaking and instead emphasized the spiritual aspects of sex in her letters. In the summer of 1959, Sandra had asked Richard to officially announce their intent to get married and he did so.[83]

While an engagement might have alleviated some of Sandra's internal conflicts, her sneaking suspicion that her history of clandestine sexual activities revealed something shameful about herself was confirmed by the way her peers' responded to an official reprimand for "false registration." In February of 1961, the college discovered that Sandra had signed out under false pretense to spend nights with her fiancé. By the time she returned to her dorm, the news of her rule violation had already spread among college officials and fellow students. Sandra was notified that she had to appear in front of the Judicial Board, an arm of the Student Government Association. Her letter to Richard vividly conveys how traumatizing she found the prospect of having to discuss her private affairs in front of a jury of her peers. "You don't know how hard it is for me to sit down and try to write to you," she wrote Richard. She could already tell from her peers' response that she would not be facing a sympathetic audience. The chairperson of the Judicial Board led the attacks against her. But in addition to this student leader, none of her peers came out publicly in Sandra's defense. In her letter to Richard, Sandra described the setting to which she returned as one where everyone seemed to engage in "dirty gossiping, talking about my clothes, my personality, etc." A faculty member suggested that "if I'd signed out wrong this past week, I'd probably been doing it all along." A more severe shock to Sandra was, however, that a member of her own generation, the student chairperson of the judicial board, called for maximum punishment. "Then came M.'s last remark about not knowing whether she wants me to graduate," Sandra wrote Richard. "Well, I found out all this hate that night . . . I couldn't take it all, and I felt so alone. . . . I have to go before Judicial Board Thursday night."[84]

As this snapshot of what was clearly a traumatizing experience for Sandra reveals, her peers felt that her sexual behavior justified a sweeping condemnation of her entire personality. Here, the comment about her "clothes" is revealing. In spite of its founder's original intent to reach women with modest financial resources, by the late 1950s Mount Holyoke College featured an overwhelmingly upper-middle-class student body.[85] Sandra, however, was a Jewish woman from Queens who attended college on a scholarship. Her letters show that she was very concerned when Mount Holyoke raised tuition in 1957. Considering her financial difficulties, we can assume that she did not dress in conformity with the genteel coed ideal. When fellow students thus disparaged her "clothes" and her "personality," they highlighted her minority and outsider status. The Judicial Board incident therefore touched Sandra's sense of self in complex and devastating ways. It fed her nagging sense that her acts and her sexual experiences revealed something shameful about her person. Moreover, it alerted her to her precarious position as a scholarship student and Jew in a collegiate setting that had not yet come to terms with the transition to mass higher education.

Clashes with the arbiters of official morality in Sandra's case, as in Alice's, fed misogynist stereotypes and disillusioned her with her education. Subsequent to her public reprimand, her opinion of her peers declined. While she had early on described her social circle as "a strong hold of the intelligentsia," she increasingly felt isolated among her fellow female students. Moreover, her sense of what she could gain from her education at Mount Holyoke was affected negatively. Her letters no longer show her enthusiasm for readings and ideas. Disillusioned with other members of her sex and reeling from blows to her self-confidence, she drew closer to Richard. Even though her correspondence does not allow us to trace the development of her thoughts about him in detail, a response she left in retrospect on an alumnae questionnaire suggests that by her graduation year she was won over to Richard's idea of complementary marriage: "In 1961 I thought I'd be the supportive, self-sacrificing wife of a great poet," she wrote here. What she had to relearn over time was "to be a poet myself, to be an equal partner in a marriage [and] to be far more selfish than I thought I would be, was, should be."[86]

Because her marriage ended in divorce, Sandra's hindsight view of might her decision might have differed from her 1961 evaluation. But considering her experiences at the end of her stay at Mount Holyoke, it does not seem incredible that self-sacrifice would play a part of her motivation to marry Richard Kohler. By the time she was ready to graduate, her own internal conflicts about her sexuality combined with the effects of sexual slander to erode her confidence and enhance her sense of isolation from her peers. The act of marrying a gifted young poet with the intent to further his career might very well have struck her as a way to prove to self and others that she was a virtuous person after all.

The sentiments expressed in the journals of Margaret Hall and Alice Gorton suggest that Sandra's desire to redeem herself through a selfless act was part of a broader phenomenon. Margaret and Alice both met their future husbands during a time when they had suffered serious damage to their sense of self. Although they still felt ambivalent about marriage, they no longer trusted their own feelings. As a consequence, they interpreted their ambivalence as just another sign that their character was severely flawed. She could not "see far beyond [her] ego," wrote Alice in an entry in which she questioned whether she loved George. She felt she needed to learn "that unselfish love that wishes for the other's happiness above your own." She vowed to "keep myself clean" and to "force herself into the conventional marriage pattern." "I must learn to work with George," she wrote during a time when she had not made up her mind yet about becoming his wife.[87]

The strain of having to reconcile clashing messages about her gender performance also caught up with Margaret Hall. By 1956 she recorded in her diary that she wanted "years of faith and loyalty given to someone to reassure myself that I can, that I am not hopelessly egocentric and inbound and unsharing." Shortly after this, marriage with Blake became a real possibility. Still ambivalent, Margaret approached her mother. The latter's reaction, however, fed all the doubts that had accumulated over the last years. Mrs. Hall reminded her daughter of the pain she had caused her first fiancé when she ended the engagement three years earlier. Margaret turned away from the talk feeling selfish, guilty, and undeserving. Her mother's remarks were one of the final deciding factors that caused her to follow through with her marriage plans.[88]

It is clear from the evidence that Alice, Margaret, and Sandra decided on marriage at a time of low self-confidence enhanced by their sense of shame and guilt about their sexuality. Because of this, they might very well have agreed on compromises that they later regretted. It is important to note how they saw their decision at the time they made it, however. What we see in Margaret and Alice's journals is that the timing of their marriage proposals was also in some way fortuitous because it offered them an option to adjust their plans while holding on to their core values. By the time George Hart and Blake Reeves proposed, neither Margaret nor Alice could any longer see herself as an example of an exceptionally driven woman. At a time of low confidence, their partners now promoted a role which they, thanks to their high level of cultural literacy, were able to see as worthy of the sacrifice of professional ambition. Both were familiar with a literature arguing that success in the public sphere came at the price of inauthenticity and conformism. In the same genre, the private realm, by contrast, appeared as a space in which the individual is still free to express his or her authentic and creative self. Cultural criticism offered literate young women an option to portray their choices not as a selling out but as a responsible and mature acceptance of a culturally and politically relevant role.

That it was indeed important to Margaret and Alice to cast their marriages in line with their core principles is reflected in their journals. Prior to marrying George Hart, for instance, Alice Gorton recorded a catalogue of principles that were supposed to form the basis for her marriage. She dated and signed what she referred to as a "contract" and sent it to George who in turn agreed on the terms. The document begins with a declaration of "love" as "freely given" and "willing service" to the loved one; followed by the stipulation that, although important, love ought "not [to be] all absorbing." Then, under point nine, the document affirms a dominant role for George: "No single thing should be considered more important than the chosen life work of the man," it said. Considering that the couple would have to move depending on where George entered graduate studies and, later, where he found work, Alice here surrendered authority in many important decisions pertaining to her own life. She also declared herself willing to not compete with George on his turf. "Each member" of a "partnership . . . is assigned to specific jobs." This, however, would not just grant an authoritative role to George. It also secured an area of expertise for Alice. Each spouse, the "contract" stipulated, ought to carry out his or her respective job "as well as possible so that pride of accomplishment is duly felt and acknowledged." In all areas except work, the document thus defined Alice's role and responsibilities as equal in worth to those of George. Each spouse would have an area of expertise that would not be intruded on by the other. In such a "union for a manifold purpose," "the mystery of the separate selves" would be "inviolable." And in the context of such a collaborative unit, Alice and George saw a "much greater" potential for accomplishments than that which could ever be made by "single selves." Clearly, it was important to Alice to define her marriage in line with her core beliefs. Significantly, by asking George to sign the contract, she also tried to make sure that he granted her a role comparable in worth to his own.[89]

Even though Alice gave up her ambitions for public achievement in her own right by choosing to marry George, settling for the indirect social influence that the contract model seemed to offer was not unreasonable. Her recent experiences had challenged Alice's belief in her own capabilities. What she stood to gain by marrying George was a reprieve from the constant struggle for leverage and authority in her social milieu. Renouncing her ambitions for the time being and working in support of George's allowed her to withdraw into a sphere sheltered from the prejudices of the mass. This would have been especially appealing because George gave her a written promise that he would value her specific contributions on an equal plane with what he accomplished by virtue of his "chosen life work."

A marriage contract drafted in a personal journal is of course a lucky find. Other women's diaries and letters yield far less information on the ways they imagined their marriage. There are, however, striking parallels in Margaret Hall's diary. Even though she did not present her suitor, Blake, with a document to sign, she also pondered the pros and cons of a marriage to him in her journal. Like Alice, she cast her decision as a free choice made after careful deliberations of her options. And just like her peer, she saw in entering a collaborative union with a worthy man the best way to leave a positive imprint on society as a whole. This emerges in an entry she recorded shortly before accepting Blake's proposal for marriage. Considering what she could expect in a marriage to Blake, Margaret once again articulated her impression that they lacked common interests. However, she now no longer saw this as a handicap. True, she could not "identify with him," like with men who shared her passions, but she could "ally [herself] with him." That each partner would bring complementary attributes into the marriage would make it "qualitatively" better than a marriage of equals. For her, this meant "cooking for him. Bearing his babies," instead of furthering her career. But just like Alice, she saw her role as a noble compromise for the good of all: "Considering my feelings for Blake, there is no moment of question. . . . Blake, like heaven is a compromise; he is the compromise for the Greater Good. His good, my good, and the Good we might do and be together. . . . Oh, nothing can compare with this; there is nothing, and no one, to compare this feeling with. It is relatively close to absolute."[90]

Their familiarity with cultural criticism made it easy for Alice and Margaret to present their choices in line with their core principles. When they presented entering into a "conventional marriage" as a conscious and voluntary sacrifice for a greater good, they cast their choice as a deliberate act, not as a mindless and automatic response to conventional gender role expectations. Moreover, they portrayed marriage as a culturally significant institution that they agreed to enter because they had come to understand its true meaning. Yet, as we know not only from Betty Friedan's questionnaires but also from women who responded to her after reading *The Feminine Mystique* or who wrote their own memoirs, many college women who made the same decision experienced the way in which it played out as disappointing. They had successfully avoided becoming part of a "lonely crowd," but they found themselves as part of a lonely couple. They might continue to read, they might volunteer, they might even create art and literature within the walls of their marital homes. They frequently felt, though, that neither their society nor their husbands actually rewarded their efforts with the kind of recognition that, according to the way the "humble role of housewife" had been portrayed, ought to have been their due. Unfortunately for these women, their political and sexual coming-of-age had occurred at a time when it was exceedingly difficult for even the most culturally literate of them to formulate ideas of femininity they could not only embrace but also realistically live by. In a sense, they became victims of not one but three influential mystiques: the myth that a longing for community equaled weakness, the myth that being a part of a nuclear couple sufficed to give their life meaning, and the myth that only brilliance justified idiosyncrasy.

Conclusion

Student diaries and letters reflect the difficulties of college women with professional aspirations to develop a positive self-image. Undeniably, they acquired critical thinking skills, but in the late 1940s and 1950s, even single-sex colleges with a long history of encouraging achievement failed to meet the needs of many of their female charges. Although there certainly remained educators who supported talented female undergraduates' ambitions, the academic setting reproduced the notion that professional success was available only for particularly driven and exceptional women. These expectations of super-performance were realistic considering the extent to which sexism limited professional and academic opportunities. Yet in the absence of a sympathetic and public discussion of the gender-specific factors that shaped their lives and options, the mantra of individualism put too high a burden on the shoulders of very young women and led them to attribute their doubts, fears, and confusions to character flaws. Moreover, when institutions of higher education imposed strict moral rules and curfews on their female charges, they failed to take into account the actual performance pressures these women faced in an increasingly sexualized student dating culture. This mid-twentieth-century version of a just-say-no approach to sex did little to help young women in setting limits once they were alone with a man, but it greatly increased the likelihood that they would experience shame and self-doubt.

Without class and heterosexual privilege, of course, the option of a withdrawal into domesticity would not have been imaginable. Yet, the experience of receiving advice that was either out of touch with their own reality or judgmental and unsympathetic must also have caused many more educated women than just the ones I discussed to grow disillusioned with the arbiters of official morality, most notably with their teachers and female peers. It appears only logical that even academically talented and ambitious female students grew resentful of their regulated lives in academia, longed to leave, and in this context latched on to the concept of the private sphere as, under conditions of the "machine age," the only space where an individual could still express herself authentically and creatively.

Before we once again portray college women as "casualties" of antifeminism, however, we should look at how their lives turned out in the long run. Many young women suffered as a consequence of sexism, sexual slander, and the lack of understanding mentors. Fortunately for most, however, the damages were not irreversible. While they often might have married in haste, what female students took with them from their years in college was a toolbox to interpret the world, and frequently a formal degree. And at least for the women whose papers I studied, I can say that, in fits and starts, they tended to "have it all" after all. For example, although she stayed home for a number of years to raise children, Margaret Hall continued to write. During the 1950s, she wrote theater reviews for the *Concord Journal* and a parody for the *Harvard Lampoon*. Beginning in the mid 1960s she published short stories under various pen names. She divorced Blake Reeves in 1964. Sandra Iger, on her 1991 Mount Holyoke College reunion questionnaire, also listed "poet, teacher" as her profession. She possessed, by then, master's and doctoral degrees and was no longer married to Richard Kohler. Susan Sperry Borman married right after graduation and had two children with her husband. In the 1970s she earned a graduate degree in dance from the University of Tennessee. She, too, divorced her first husband. She was coauthor of two books: *The Woman Who Lost Her Heart: A Tale of Reawakening* (1992) and *The Woman Who Found Her Voice: A Tale of Transforming* (1997). Alice Gorton also continued to mature as a writer. After earning her master's degree from Utah State University in 1970, she taught writing and in 1982 published a first book of her own poetry, *Prints and Poems*. Sadly, she died at the age of fifty-five. Her husband George Hart, to whom she remained married until her death, in 1988 showed his esteem for Alice's creative work and published a second volume of her poetry under the title *To Fly Once More*. June Calender also married the man she met as an undergraduate. After her 1980 divorce, and after her children were grown, she began to write plays and work as a professional script reader. She eventually moved to New York City, where today she is still doing "way off Broadway" plays. She also travels widely and is presently working on a biography of a Tibetan traveler based on his diary.[1]

As this casual look at the biographies of some of the women I have followed through their young adult years shows, their lives did not follow a linear path. This said, they nonetheless had full and complex postgraduate careers. Many mid-twentieth-century college women might look back at some of their youthful choices with regret, embarrassment, or maybe even anger. At least for the women whose personal papers I read, however, I will say that they entered the compromises they ended up making only after a period of conscious deliberation and after trying out different options. Their lives illustrate poignantly the complex challenges still faced by modern young women even today. Their intellectual and personal resourcefulness, however, has been an inspiration and a source of optimism for me in what the future can hold for women who take advantage of the opportunities inherent in a higher education, even in one received during less than ideal times.

Student Diaries and Letters Consulted

Beck, Patricia, papers. Sophia Smith Collection, Smith College Archives, Northampton, Mass.

Brown, Janet, papers. Archives and Special Collections, Mount Holyoke College, South Hadley, Mass.

Calender, June, papers. Arthur and Elizabeth Schlesinger Library on the History of Women in America, Radcliffe Institute for Advanced Study, Harvard University, Cambridge, Mass.

Delattre, Susan, papers. Arthur and Elizabeth Schlesinger Library on the History of Women in America, Radcliffe Institute for Advanced Study, Harvard University, Cambridge, Mass.

Dushkin, Dorothy Smith, papers. Sophia Smith Collection, Smith College Archives, Northampton, Mass.

Erisman, Ruth, papers. Smith College Archives, Northampton, Mass.

Everett, Beverly George, papers. Iowa Women's Archives, University of Iowa Libraries, Iowa City, Iowa.

Goldman, Louise Hilfman, papers. Iowa Women's Archives, University of Iowa Libraries, Iowa City, Iowa.

Gray, Grace, papers. Archives and Special Collections, Mount Holyoke College, South Hadley, Mass.

Harris, Claudine Maroni, papers, Iowa Women's Archives, University of Iowa Libraries, Iowa City, Iowa.

Hart, Alice Gorton, papers. Sophia Smith Collection, Smith College Archives, Northampton, Mass.

Honaman, Ruth papers. Smith College Archives, Northampton, Mass.

Hughes, Doris Bender, papers. Iowa Women's Archives, University of Iowa Libraries, Iowa City, Iowa.

Kedney, Janet, papers. Smith College Archives, Northampton, Mass.

Kidwell, Janice Mary, papers. Archives and Special Collections, Mount Holyoke College, South Hadley, Mass.

Kennedy, Frank Hunter, papers. Southern Historical Collection, The Wilson Library, Library of the University of North Carolina at Chapel Hill.

Kohler, Sandra Iger, papers. Archives and Special Collections, Mount Holyoke College, South Hadley, Mass.

Lauterbach, Judith. Transcripts of her letters and diary entries, as selected and excerpted by her father, Leo Lauterbach, 1957. Smith College Archives, Northampton, Mass.

Marcus, Merle Judith, papers. Jacob Rader Marcus Center of the American Jewish Archives, Hebrew Union College, Cincinnati, Ohio.

McClumpha, Margaret, papers. Smith College Archives, Northampton, Mass.

McClung, Gale Stubbs, papers. Archives and Special Collections, Mount Holyoke College, South Hadley, Mass.

Monks, Sheila Owen, papers. In possession of Sheila Monks, Milton, Mass.

Nash, Martha Ann Furgerson, papers. Iowa Women's Archives, University of Iowa Libraries, Iowa City, Iowa.

Offill, Elinor, papers. In possession of Elinor Offill, Santa Rosa, Calif.

Poullada, Leila Dean Jackson, papers. In possession of Leila Poullada, St. Paul, Minn.

Raskin, Judith, papers. Sophia Smith Collection, Smith College Archives, Northampton, Mass.

Rigby, Alice, papers. Archives and Special Collections, Mount Holyoke College, South Hadley, Mass.

Silverman, Alice, papers. Smith College Archives, Northampton, Mass.

Weis, Helene Harmon, papers. Arthur and Elizabeth Schlesinger Library on the History of Women in America, Radcliffe Institute for Advanced Study, Harvard University, Cambridge, Mass.

Welker, Mickey (Maxine) Campbell, papers. Center for Archival Collections, Bowling Green State University, Bowling Green, Ohio.

Whitfield, Margaret Hall, papers. In possession of Margaret Hall Whitfield, Martinez, Calif.

Worcester, Laurie (Lucy Lawrence Chauncey), papers. Smith College Archives, Northampton, Mass.

Notes

INTRODUCTION

1. Betty Friedan, *The Feminine Mystique* (New York: W. W. Norton, 1963), 15–16, 18.

2. Ibid., 69–70, 187, 181, 283.

3. Lucille Moncrieff, "Manhattan Girl with a Job," *Mademoiselle* (November 1946): 180–183, 282–286.

4. On Friedan, see Daniel Horowitz, *Betty Friedan and the Making of "The Feminine Mystique": The American Left, the Cold War, and Modern Feminism* (Amherst: University of Massachusetts Press, 1998). On the range of expert discourse about gender, see Janet Walker, *Couching Resistance: Women, Film, and Psychoanalytic Psychiatry* (Minneapolis: University of Minnesota Press, 1993), 1–23. An excellent synthesis of the various revisionist approaches to women in the Cold War era is Joanne Meyerowitz, ed., *Not June Cleaver: Women and Gender in Postwar America, 1945–1960* (Philadelphia: Temple University Press, 1994).

5. Stephanie Coontz, *The Way We Never Were: American Families and the Nostalgia Trap* (New York: Basic Books, 1992).

6. Elaine Tyler May, *Homeward Bound: American Families in the Cold War Era* (New York: Basic Books, 1988), 136–137; and Linda Eisenmann, *Higher Education for Women in Postwar America, 1945–1965* (Baltimore: Johns Hopkins University Press, 2006), 28, 69–70.

7. Elaine Kendall, *"Peculiar Institutions": An Informal History of the Seven Sister Colleges*, 2nd ed. (New York: G. P. Putnam's Sons, 1976), 220, 218. A notable exception to the focus on conformity is the literature dealing with the student branches of the Young Women's Christian Association. See especially Susan Lynn, *Progressive Women in Conservative Times: Racial Justice, Peace, and Feminism, 1945 to the 1960s* (New Brunswick, N.J.: Rutgers University Press, 1992).

8. Margaret Hall diary, April 20, 1955, in possession of Margaret Whitfield, Martinez, Calif. For other examples, see Alice Gorton diary, n.d., 102 (back), 160–161, box 3, folder 19, Alice Gorton Hart papers, Sophia Smith Collection, Smith College Archives, Northampton, Mass.; Susan Sperry Borman diary, October 31, 1956, box 2, folder 16–21, Susan Delattre papers, Arthur and Elizabeth Schlesinger Library on the History of Women in America, Radcliffe Institute for Advanced Study, Harvard University, Cambridge, Mass.; and Anne Schaffer, ed., *Dear Deedee: From the Diaries of Dori Schaffer* (Secaucus, N.J.: Lyle Stuart, 1978), 92.

9. Jessica Weiss, *To Have and To Hold: Marriage, the Baby Boom, and Social Change* (Chicago: University of Chicago Press, 2000).

10. Jane Hunter, *How Young Ladies Became Girls: The Victorian Origins of American Girlhood* (New Haven, Conn.: Yale University Press, 2002).

11. John C. Spurlock and Cynthia A. Magistro, *New and Improved: The Transformation of American Women's Emotional Culture* (New York: New York University Press, 1998).

12. Wini Breines, *Young, White, and Miserable: Growing up Female in the 1950s* (Boston: Beacon Press, 1992).

13. Maurice Halbwachs, *On Collective Memory*, ed. and trans. Lewis A. Coser (Chicago: University of Chicago Press, 1992).

14. Karen V. Kukil, ed., *The Unabridged Journals of Sylvia Plath, 1950–1962* (New York: Anchor Books, 2000). The other two published journals are Schaffer, *Dear Deedee*, and Elouise M. Bell, ed., *"Will I Ever Forget This Day?": Excerpts from the Diaries of Carol Lynn Pearson* (Salt Lake City, Utah: Bookcraft, 1980).

15. For scholarship that addresses the experiences of black women in academia in detail, see, for example, Stephanie Y. Evans, *Black Women in the Ivory Tower, 1850–1954* (Gainesville: University Press of Florida, 2007). The situation of African American students in the "Seven Sisters" is discussed by Linda M. Perkins in "The African American Female Elite: The Early History of African American Women in the Seven Sister Colleges, 1880–1960," *Harvard Educational Review* 67, no. 4 (1997): 718–756. On differences between women's college experience in the North and South of the United States, see Amy T. McCandless, *The Past in the Present: Women's Higher Education in the Twentieth-Century South* (Tuscaloosa: University of Alabama Press, 1999).

16. For a historical survey of the development of the concept of identity from a psychologist's perspective, see Roy F. Baumeister, *Identity: Cultural Change and the Struggle for Self* (New York: Oxford University Press, 1986).

17. For an intriguing analysis of the way in which journaling functioned as a device through which the writer attempts to actively construct identity, see Jochen Hellbeck, *Revolution on My Mind: Writing a Diary under Stalin* (Cambridge, Mass.: Harvard University Press, 2006). For scholarship on women's diaries see, for instance, Margo Culley, ed., *A Day at a Time: The Diary Literature of American Women from 1764 to the Present* (New York: Feminist Press at City University of New York, 1985); and Suzanne L. Bunkers and Cynthia A. Huff, eds., *Inscribing the Daily: Critical Essays on Women's Diaries* (Amherst: University of Massachusetts Press, 1996).

CHAPTER I — CAMPUS LIFE IN TIMES OF CRISIS

1. Helene Harmon diary, September 6, 1940, Helene Harmon Weis papers, Arthur and Elizabeth Schlesinger Library on the History of Women in America, Radcliffe College for Advanced Study, Harvard University, Cambridge, Mass.

2. Ibid.

3. Historians have extensively documented the evolution of the companionate marriage ideal. See Paula S. Fass, *The Damned and the Beautiful: American Youth in the 1920s* (New York: Oxford University Press, 1977); Nancy Cott, *The Grounding of Modern Feminism* (New Haven, Conn.: Yale University Press, 1987); Christina Simmons, "Modern Sexuality and the Myth of Victorian Repression," in *Passion and Power: Sexuality in History*, ed. Christina Simmons and Kathy Peiss (Philadelphia: Temple University Press, 1989), 157–177; and Steven Mintz and Susan Kellogg, *Domestic Revolutions: A Social History of American Family Life* (New York: Free Press, 1989).

4. Cott, *Grounding of Modern Feminism*, 156; and Mintz and Kellogg, *Domestic Revolutions*, 107–131.

5. Rebecca L. Davis, "'Not Marriage at All, but Simple Harlotry': The Companionate Marriage Controversy." *Journal of American History* 94, no. 4 (March 2008): 1137–1163.

6. On the lack of acceptance of women as members of the labor force, especially during the Great Depression, see Lois Scharf, *To Work and To Wed: Female Employment, Feminism, and the Great Depression* (Westport, Conn.: Greenwood Press, 1980); and Alice Kessler-Harris, "Gender Ideology in Historical Reconstruction: A Case Study from the 1930s," *Gender and History* 1 (Spring 1989): 31–49.

7. Helene Harmon diary, February 19, 1940, and July 4, 1940.

8. The middle class experienced the full impact of the Depression with a time lag. By 1932, however, the middle class had begun to feel the repercussions of the recession. Even Americans lucky enough to keep their jobs suffered wage decreases and pay cuts between 40 and 60 percent. Mary C. McComb, *Great Depression and the Middle Class: Experts, Collegiate Youth, and Business Ideology, 1929–1941* (New York: Routledge, 2006), 2.

9. Helene Harmon diary, July 15, 1940, and March 29, 1943.

10. Helene Harmon diary, July 15, 1940.

11. Compared to the number of laid-off male workers, the proportion of women who lost their jobs was lower. This, of course, was also a result of the fact that most men, even after the Depression hit them hard, still did not want the jobs women typically held because they were low-status and underpaid. See McComb, *Great Depression*, 48.

12. See Patricia A. Palmieri, "From Republican Motherhood to Race Suicide: Arguments on the Higher Education of Women in the United States, 1820–1920," in *Educating Men and Women Together: Coeducation in a Changing World*, ed. Carol Lasser (Urbana: University of Illinois Press in conjunction with Oberlin College, 1987), 49–64; Lynn D. Gordon, "The Gibson Girl Goes to College: Popular Culture and Women's Higher Education in the Progressive Era, 1890–1920." *American Quarterly* 39, no. 2 (Summer 1987): 211–230; and Margaret A. Lowe, *Looking Good: College Women and Body Image, 1875–1930* (Baltimore: Johns Hopkins University Press, 2003). It needs to be said, however, that even after a backlash against female higher education, women's colleges especially continued to feature a faculty and a curriculum that could be considered on the cutting edge of academic trends. See Helen Horowitz, "In the Wake of Laurence

Veysey: Re-examining the Liberal Arts College," *History of Education Quarterly* 45, no. 3 (September 2005): 420–426, at 423.

13. David O. Levine, *The American College and the Culture of Aspiration, 1915–1940* (Ithaca, N.Y.: Cornell University Press, 1986), 185–209.

14. Federal aid for education enabled a number of students from economically burdened families to continue their studies and constituted a move in the direction of democratizing access to formal degrees. However, federal aid was conceived as temporary relief. Moreover, the 93 million dollars dispensed until the program ended in 1943 covered only the tip of an iceberg of much greater need. On higher education during the Depression, see Levine, *American College,* 185–209.

15. While the Ivies competed "fiercely for the children of the less than 5 percent of American families that had incomes of over $5,000, brighter youngsters from poorer families were forced to forgo college or to attend less prestigious public schools." At many public institutions in the 1930s, approximately two-thirds of all students worked to finance their education. By contrast, only 15 percent of undergraduates at a "typical eastern elite institution" had to do so. Levine, *American College,* 192. On Dixon Fox, see McComb, *Great Depression,* 54.

16. Letters from a number of Mount Holyoke College students show that they held jobs to help them defray expenses, Grace Gray (Class of 1945) waited tables; Alice Rigby (Class of 1945) waited tables and worked as a math tutor. See Grace Gray papers and Alice Rigby papers, Mount Holyoke College Archives, South Hadley, Mass. For Smith College recipients of scholarships and financial aid see Janet Kedney, Class of 1944, Individuals A–Z; and Judith Lauterbach, folder "Transcripts of Judith Lauterbach's letters and diary entries, as selected and excerpted by her father, Leo Lauterbach, 1957," Class of 1947, Individuals A–Z, Smith College Archives, Northampton, Mass. For the increase in student diversity at the "Seven Sisters" see Kendall, *"Peculiar Institutions."*

17. Alumnae of the Ivy League and the Seven Sisters especially lobbied for changes in admissions policies of their alma maters. Starting in the 1920s, admissions officers used newly developed and allegedly objective intelligence tests to weed out applicants from families deemed undesirable. Admissions questionnaires increasingly asked for information on the birthplace of parents or the maiden names of mothers. In institutions outside the Ivy League, such a focus on exclusion was rarely possible. The practices in prestigious schools, however, helped set standards in higher education in general, and especially in the realm of social clubs and athletics, Jewish students experienced discrimination even in less prestigious institutions. These practices, while they did not disappear entirely, became much harder to sustain in the 1940s. See Marcia Graham Synnott, *The Half-Opened Door: Discrimination and Admission at Harvard, Yale, and Princeton, 1900–1970* (Westport, Conn.: Greenwood Press, 1979). For a case study of Dartmouth College's shift in admissions policies see Levine, *American College,* ch. 7.

18. On the situation of African Americans in academia, see James D. Anderson, "Race, Meritocracy, and the American Academy during the Immediate Post–World War II

Era," *History of Education Quarterly* 33, no. 2 (1993): 150–175. On the use of Holocaust analogy in the fight for civil rights, see Michael E. Staub, "'Negroes Are Not Jews': Race, Holocaust Consciousness, and the Rise of Jewish Neoconservatism," *Radical History Review* 75 (Fall 1999): 3–27. Staub sees a decline of solidarity based on a shared identity as an oppressed group by the late 1960s. During the immediate post–World War II period, however, Jewish supporters of black civil rights still drew parallels between Nazi racial oppression and southern apartheid.

19. Will Herberg, *Protestant-Catholic-Jew: An Essay in American Religious Sociology*, rev. ed. (Garden City, N.Y.: Doubleday, 1960), esp. ch. 10. For a critique of the alleged siege mentality of Catholics, see "Catholicism in America: A Series of Articles from The Commonweal" (New York: Harcourt, Brace & Co., 1953).

20. For examples of students with an ethnic minority or refugee background, see Judith Lauterbach, folder "Transcripts of her letters and diary entries, as selected and excerpted by her father, Leo Lauterbach, 1957," Individuals A–Z, Smith College Archives, Northampton, Mass.; "Judith Raskin papers," and "Patricia Beck papers," Sophia Smith Collection, Smith College; and "Claudine Maroni Harris papers," Iowa Women's Archives, University of Iowa Libraries, Iowa City, Iowa.

21. We know that such a dynamic was at work, for instance, in the case of Betty Friedan, who studied during the war at Smith College. See Horowitz, *Betty Friedan and the Making of "The Feminine Mystique."*

22. On the student peace movement, see Robert Cohen, *When the Old Left Was Young: Student Radicals and America's First Mass Student Movement: 1929–1941* (New York: Oxford University Press, 1993); and Eileen Eagan, *Class, Culture, and the Classroom: The Student Peace Movement of the 1930s* (Philadelphia: Temple University Press, 1981).

23. Eagan, *Class, Culture, and the Classroom*, 59–61.

24. Reinhold Niebuhr, for instance, spoke at Smith College in 1943 and at Mount Holyoke in 1944. See Janet Kedney to family, n.d., postmarked October 5, 1943, folder 4, Janet Kedney papers, Smith College Archives; and Grace Gray to parents, October 10, 1943, box 1, folder 9, Grace Gray papers, Mount Holyoke College Archives. On Eleanor Roosevelt and her appearances in front of female students, see Allida M. Black, *Casting Her Own Shadow: Eleanor Roosevelt and the Shaping of Postwar Liberalism* (New York: Columbia University Press, 1996).

25. Margaret W. Rossiter, *Women Scientists in America: Before Affirmative Action, 1940–1972* (Baltimore: Johns Hopkins University Press, 1995); and Eisenmann, *Higher Education for Women*.

26. See Leila Rupp, *Mobilizing Women for War: German and American Propaganda, 1939–1945* (Princeton, N.J.: Princeton University Press, 1978); and Ellen Hartmann, *The Home Front and Beyond: American Women in the 1940s* (Boston: Twayne Publishers, 1982).

27. See, for instance, Mary E. Murphy, "War and the Woman's College," *Journal of Higher Education* 12, no. 3 (March 1941): 143–145; and American Association of University

Professors, "The Post-War Responsibilities of Liberal Education," *Bulletin of the American Association of University Professors* 29, no. 3 (June 1943): 412–431; esp. 427–429.

28. Editorial, *Smith College Associated News*, November 23, 1943.

29. For the text of the flyer of the Women's War Council, see Brian A. Williams, *Michigan on the March: The University of Michigan in World War II* (Ann Arbor: University of Michigan, Bentley Historical Library, December 1995), 14.

30. Margaret McClumpha to parents, letter dated December 13, 1941, folder 2, Margaret McClumpha papers, Smith College Archives.

31. Ruth Honamann to parents, December 9, 1941, folder "September 1941–February 1942," Ruth Honamann papers, Smith College Archives.

32. See D'Ann Campbell, *Women at War with America: Private Lives in a Patriotic Era* (Cambridge, Mass.: Harvard University Press, 1984), 19–22; Kendall, *Peculiar Institutions*, 196–202; and Ruth Bordin, *Women at Michigan: The "Dangerous Experiment," 1870s to the Present* (Ann Arbor: University of Michigan Press, 1999), 57–58.

33. See, for instance, Mary E. Murphy, "War and the Woman's College," *Journal of Higher Education* 12, no. 3 (March 1941): 143–145; and Isabel K. Wallace, "Women's Use of Leisure," *Journal of Higher Education* 14, no. 6 (June 1943): 301–342.

34. Helene Harmon diary, February 16, 1941; June 4, 1941; December 7, 1941; and November 8, 1942.

35. On the Dalton and Walden schools, see Douglas Martin, "Walden School, at 73, Files for Bankruptcy," *New York Times*, June 23, 1987, B1. Leo Lauterbach's visit to Austria to assess Nazi racial policies is mentioned in David Cesarani and Sarah Kavanaugh, *Holocaust: Critical Concepts in Historical Studies* (London: Routledge, 2004), 37–38.

36. Judith Lauterbach to father, September 22, 1943.

37. Judith Lauterbach to father, October 13, 1943. Judith's impression of Jewish campus organizations as social in outlook conforms to what Harold Wechsler has argued about developments nationwide. While Jewish clubs and societies in the early twentieth century had often been literary and political in their orientation, by the 1920s they largely matched their Protestant counterparts in their emphasis on social activities. Harold D. Wechsler, "An Academic Gresham's Law: Group Repulsion as a Theme in American Higher Education," *Teachers College Record* 82 (Summer 1981): 567–588.

38. Judith Lauterbach to father, October 13, 1943; August 2, 1944; February 20, 1946.

39. Beth Bailey, *From Front Porch to Back Seat: Courtship in Twentieth-Century America* (Baltimore: Johns Hopkins University Press, 1988).

40. Paul Popenoe, *Modern Marriage: A Handbook* (New York: Macmillan, 1925); and Popenoe, *Marriage: Before and After* (New York: Wilfred Func, 1943), esp. vii and 16. The increase of expert concern also shows in the fact that the field of marriage counseling came into its own after World War II. Molly Ladd-Taylor, "Eugenics, Sterilization and

Modern Marriage in the USA: The Strange Career of Paul Popenoe." *Gender & History* 13, no. 2 (August 2001): 298–327. For early examples of the marital advice genre, see Ernest R. Groves and William F. Ogburn, *American Marriage and Family Relationships* (New York: Henry Holt, 1928).

41. The notion that women and girls, more so than men and boys, were susceptible to mass media images about relationships, dating, and marriage, was so deeply entrenched in American culture that it still shaped the teachings in high schools in the late 1950s. In curriculum guides published by the American Social Hygiene Association, high schools were explicitly advised to better prepare girls (but not boys) to be critical of representations of heterosexual encounters in popular culture. See Susan K. Freeman, *Sex Goes to School: Girls and Sex Education before the 1960s* (Urbana: University of Illinois Press, 2008), 40.

42. Elaine Tyler May, *Great Expectations: Marriage and Divorce in Post-Victorian America* (Chicago: University of Chicago Press, 1980), 2–7, 91.

43. Popenoe, *Marriage*, 26.

44. On the history of progressive education, see Diane Ravitch, *The Troubled Crusade: American Education, 1945–1980* (New York: Basic Books, 1983), esp. 43–80; and David B. Tyack, *Seeking Common Ground: Public Schools in a Diverse Society* (Cambridge, Mass.: Harvard University Press, 2003).

45. Helene Harmon diary, September 6, 1940; and July 4, 1940.

46. Ibid., September 6, 1940.

47. At a time when most Protestant denominations had come to accept divorce as a social reality, Pope Pius XI in his 1930 encyclical still condemned the practice forcefully. See Kristin Celello, *Making Marriage Work: A History of Marriage and Divorce in the Twentieth-Century United States* (Chapel Hill: University of North Carolina Press, 2009), 25. It would take until the late 1960s before attitudes of Catholics and Protestants converged. See John D'Emilio and Estelle B. Freedman, *Intimate Matters: A History of Sexuality in America* (New York: Harper & Row, 1988), 252.

48. Helene Harmon diary, September 6, 1940.

49. Ibid., October 13, 1940.

50. J. E. Janney, "Fad and Fashion Leadership among Undergraduate Women," *Journal of Abnormal and Social Psychology* 36 (April 1941): 275–278.

51. Ibid., 276–277.

52. On Bettye Goldstein at Smith, see Horowitz, *Making of "The Feminine Mystique."* The "agitator" quote is from Alice Rigby to family, February 2, 1944, folder 5, Alice Rigby papers, Mount Holyoke College Archives.

53. Alice Rigby to family, October 25, 1943, folder 3.

54. Gale Stubbs McClung to parents, February 16, 1942, box 1, folder 3, Gale Stubbs McClung papers, Mount Holyoke College Archives. Also see Margaret McClumpha to

mother, February 11, 1941; and May 21, 1941; Class of 1944, Individuals, Margaret McClumpha, folder 1, Smith College Archives.

55. See Henry L. Minton, "Femininity in Men and Masculinity in Women: American Psychiatry and Psychology Portray Homosexuality in the 1930s," *Journal of Homosexuality* 13, no. 1 (Fall 1986): 1–21.

56. On the negative stereotype of the "greasy grind," see Helen L. Horowitz, *Campus Life: Undergraduate Cultures from the End of the Eighteenth Century to the Present* (New York: Knopf, 1987), 142, 197.

57. Helene Harmon diary, December 22, 1941.

58. Helene Harmon diary, January 5, 1943; January 20, 1941; May 12, 1941; and January 22, 1943.

59. Ibid., July 4, 1941.

60. For biographical details, see Patricia Beck papers, esp. box 1, folder 2, Patricia Beck papers, Sophia Smith Collection, Smith College Archives.

61. Patricia Beck, typewritten notes in response to an in-class assignment, box 1, folder 2; and Patricia Beck, diary, see esp. the 1945 volume.

62. Judith Lauterbach to father, February 20, 1946.

63. On women's gains during the war, see Campbell, *Women at War with America*; and Hartmann, *Home Front and Beyond*. On the Austin-Wadsworth Bill, see Rebecca Jo Plant, "The Repeal of Mother Love: Momism and the Reconstruction of Motherhood in Philip Wylie's America," (Ph.D. diss., Johns Hopkins University, 2001), 94–95.

64. Eisenmann, *Higher Education for Women*, 66–68.

65. Campbell, *Women at War with America*, 19–22.

66. On the persistent marginalization of female scientists in wartime coverage of the field, see, for example, Marcel C. LaFollette, "Eyes on the Stars: Images of Women Scientists in Popular Magazines," *Science, Technology, & Human Values* 13, no. 3–4 (Summer–Fall 1988): 262–275; at 263.

67. *The Mount Holyoke News*, April 9, 1943, 2. Also see Eisenmann, *Higher Education for Women*, 5.

68. John Erskine, "The World Will Belong to the Women," *New York Times*, March 14, 1943, SM 15.

69. See, for instance, Rupp, *Mobilizing Women for War*.

70. "Parties Unlimited," *Women's Home Companion*, March 1942, 33–35.

71. "Spell 'IT' to the Marine." Advertisement, *Woman's Home Companion*, August 1943, 55; "Be His Pin-Up Girl!" Advertisement, *True Story*, June 1944, 87. For the advertisement by the American Labor Party, see *Daily Worker*, January 29, 1942.

72. Marilyn E. Hegarty, *Victory Girls, Khaki-Wackies, and Patriotutes: The Regulation of Female Sexuality during World War II* (New York: New York University Press, 2008), 126.

On the same topic, see Rupp, *Mobilizing Women for War*, 138, 147; and Robert B. Westbrook, "'I Want a Girl, Just Like the Girl That Married Harry James': American Women and the Problem of Political Obligation in World War II," *American Quarterly* 42, no. 4 (December 1990): 587–614; at 595.

73. Mickey Campbell Welker, "College Scrapbook, September 1943–May 1945," box 1, volume 2, Mickey (Maxine) Campbell Welker papers, Bowling Green State University College Archives, Bowling Green, Ohio.

74. Grace Gray to parents, April 17, 1943, box 1, folder 9, Grace Gray papers; and Alice Rigby to parents, September 23, 1943, folder 3, Alice Rigby papers; both Mount Holyoke College Archives.

75. See, for example, Nancy Shoemaker, ed., *Negotiators of Change: Historical Perspectives on Native-American Women* (New York: Routledge, 1995).

76. See, for instance, Alexander W. Astin, *Achieving Educational Excellence* (San Francisco: Jossey-Bass, 1985).

CHAPTER 2 — "BUT DAD!"

1. On the relationship between Great Britain and the United States under the Labour Administration, see Peter Weiler, "British Labour and the Cold War: The Foreign Policy of the Labour Governments, 1945–1951," *Journal of British Studies* 26 (January 1987): 54–82.

2. Janet Brown to father, March 25, 1949, box 1, folder 6, Janet Brown papers, Mount Holyoke College Archives, South Hadley, Mass.

3. Examples for literature that stresses the conservative elements of female student culture include Dorothy C. Holland, *Educated in Romance: Women, Achievement, and College Culture* (Chicago: University of Chicago Press, 1990); Wini Breines, *Young, White, and Miserable: Growing up Female in the Fifties* (Boston: Beacon Press, 1992). Betty Friedan's *The Feminine Mystique* (New York: Norton, 1963) and Sylvia Plath's *The Bell Jar* (London: Heinemann, 1963) have also been influential in shaping the image of female college culture as conformist and lending itself to the reproduction of traditional norms of femininity.

4. Ellen Schrecker, *No Ivory Tower: McCarthyism and the Universities* (New York: Oxford University Press, 1986). For further analyses of anti-Stalinism in postwar America, see Steven Gillon, *Politics and Vision: The ADA and American Liberalism, 1947–1985* (New York: Oxford University Press, 1987); and Michael Heale, *McCarthy's Americans: Red Scare Politics in State and Nation, 1930–1965* (London: Macmillan, 1998).

5. Jessica Wang, *American Science in an Age of Anxiety: Scientists, Anticommunism, and the Cold War* (Chapel Hill: University of North Carolina Press, 1999); and Diane Ravitch, *The Troubled Crusade: American Education, 1945–1980* (New York: Basic Books, 1983).

6. Janet Kedney to family, n.d., postmarked October 5, 1943, folder 4, Janet Kedney papers, Smith College Archives, Northampton, Mass.

7. Grace Gray to parents, October 10, 1944, box 2, folder 6, Grace Gray papers, Mount Holyoke College Archives.

8. Alice Rigby to family, September 23, 1943; and September 27, 1943; folder 3, Alice Rigby papers, Mount Holyoke College Archives; and Beverly George to parents, January 18, 1944, box 1, folder "Personal correspondence, 1944," Beverly George Everett papers, Iowa Women's Archives, University of Iowa, Iowa City, Iowa.

9. Janet Brown to parents, October 17, 1946, box 1, folder 1.

10. Judith Raskin to parents, April 19, 1947, box 2, folder 2–2, Judith Raskin papers, Sophia Smith Collection, Smith College.

11. See, for example, Judith Lauterbach to father, January 28, 1945; February 1, 1944; March 12, 1944, folder "Transcripts of Judith Lauterbach's letters and diary entries, as selected and excerpted by her father, Leo Lauterbach, 1957," Class of 1947, Individuals A–Z, Smith College Archives.

12. Whether Alice actually went is not clear, but she made plans to do so. See Alice Gorton diary, n.d., 103 (back) and 145, folder 19, "September 1952–February 1953" Alice Gorton Hart papers, Sophia Smith Collection, Smith College.

13. Susan Sperry Borman to parents, January 23, 1958; May 3, 1958, box 3, folder 25, Susan Delattre papers, Arthur and Elizabeth Schlesinger Library on the History of Women in America, Radcliffe Institute for Advanced Study, Harvard University, Cambridge, Mass.

14. Barbara Solomon, *In the Company of Educated Women: A History of Women and Higher Education in America* (New Haven, Conn.: Yale University Press, 1985), 189; and Linda Eisenmann, *Higher Education for Women in Postwar America, 1945–1965* (Baltimore: Johns Hopkins University Press, 2006), 28–29, 47–49.

15. Although conclusive figures do not exist, historians have estimated that only about 20 percent of veterans would not have been able to afford college or university without government subsidies. Daniel A. Clark, "The Two Joes Meet. Joe College, Joe Veteran: The G.I. Bill, College Education, and Postwar American Culture," *History of Education Quarterly* 38, no. 2 (Summer 1998): 165–189.

16. See ibid.; and Eisenmann, *Higher Education for Women*.

17. Clark, "The Two Joes Meet," 176.

18. Ellen Herman, *The Romance of American Psychology: Political Culture in the Age of Experts* (Berkeley: University of California Press, 1995). See also John R. Thelin, *A History of American Higher Education* (Baltimore: Johns Hopkins University Press, 2004), 260–284; and Richard M. Freeland, *Academia's Golden Age: Universities in Massachusetts, 1945–1970* (New York: Oxford University Press, 1992).

19. Walter A. Jackson, *Gunnar Myrdal and America's Conscience: Social Engineering and Racial Liberalism, 1938–1987* (Chapel Hill: University of North Carolina Press, 1990), 274; and Karen Brodkin, *How Jews Became White Folks* (New Brunswick, N.J.: Rutgers University Press, 1998), 38–44. See also Susan Lynn, *Progressive Women in Conservative*

Times: Racial Justice, Peace and Feminism, 1945 to the 1960s (New Brunswick, N.J.: Rutgers University Press, 1992); and Allida M. Black, *Casting Her Own Shadow: Eleanor Roosevelt and the Shaping of Postwar Liberalism* (New York: Columbia University Press, 1996).

20. On the impact of the SAT on the system of higher education, see Nicholas Lemann, *The Big Test: The Secret History of the American Meritocracy* (New York: Farrar, Straus and Giroux, 1999).

21. Female veterans were no less entitled to G.I. Bill benefits than men were, but their numbers were small. They also did not figure as prominently in public thinking than their male peers. Agencies administering G.I. Bill benefits did not always include women in their promotional material, and female veterans themselves often did not see their services in the same vein as those of men. Consequently, many eligible women did not benefit from the democratization of higher education. See Eisenmann, *Higher Education for Women*, 54–55.

22. The proportion of women as part of the student population fell below 30 percent in the peak years of the G.I. Bill. For figures, see Solomon, *Company of Educated Women*, 63, table 2; and Eisenmann, *Higher Education for Women*, 54–57.

23. Ernest Havemann and Patricia Salter West, *They Went to College: The College Graduate in America Today* (New York: Harcourt, Brace, & Co, 1952), 19.

24. The six-volume report of the Truman Administration's Presidential Commission on Higher Education, a landmark study published in 1947, addressed the situation of women in three short paragraphs. For a detailed discussion of this first-of-its-kind study, see Eisenmann, *Higher Education for Women*, 51–54.

25. Reacting to the expansion of the apparatus of higher education, the National Education Association (NEA), for instance, warned of impending faculty shortages. They also argued that the academic record of women had demonstrated their abilities as scholars and teachers. Using the term "womanpower" already familiar to Americans from World War II, the NEA called for concerted efforts to draw women into academia. See Eisenmann, *Higher Education for Women*, 58–59.

26. On the G.I. Bill's effect on women, see ibid., 47–50; and Ellen Hartmann, *The Home Front and Beyond: American Women in the 1940s* (Boston: Twayne Publishers, 1982), 106.

27. Eisenmann, *Higher Education for Women*, 103.

28. The best-known representative of what Linda Eisenmann called the "cultural conformist" camp of policy makers was probably Mills College President Lynn White. See Eisenmann, *Higher Education of Women*, 69–77; and Deborah M. Olsen, "Remaking the Image: Promotional Literature of Mount Holyoke, Smith, and Wellesley Colleges in the Mid-to-Late 1940s," *History of Education Quarterly* 40, no. 4 (Winter 2000): 418–459, esp. 429.

29. Louise Goldman papers, folder "State University of Iowa; Code for Coeds, 1944–1945," Iowa Women's Archives; and Doris Bender Hughes, letter to family, postmarked October 22, 1945, Doris Bender Hughes papers, box 1, folder: Correspondence; Sept. 1945–Dec. 1945, Iowa Women's Archives.

30. Kristin Celello, *Making Marriage Work: A History of Marriage and Divorce in the Twentieth-Century United States* (Chapel Hill: University of North Carolina Press, 2009), 88–89.

31. Ibid., 72–85.

32. Olsen, "Remaking the Image," 418–459, 426.

33. Ibid., 435.

34. The possibility that wives and mothers might also become scientists and professionals was always left open. Promotional brochures clearly downplayed the achievement and career-oriented purpose of higher education for women, however. Ibid., 430–443.

35. Mabel Newcomer, *A Century of Higher Education for American Women* (New York: Harper & Row, 1959), 145.

36. Freeland, *Academia's Golden Age.* 78.

37. James B. Gilbert, *Redeeming Culture: American Religion in an Age of Science* (Chicago: University of Chicago Press, 1997); and Neil Jumonville, *Critical Crossings: The New York Intellectuals in Postwar America* (Berkeley: University of California Press, 1991).

38. Adlai Stevenson, "A Purpose for Modern Woman," *Women's Home Companion*, September 1955, 30–31. Also see "Stevenson Stresses Individual Freedom," *Sophian*, June 6, 1955, 1, 3.

39. *Bee Gee News*, December 12, 1952, 2, Center for Archival Collections, Bowling Green State University, Bowling Green, Ohio.

40. See Mickey Campbell Welker diary, May 1, 1947; and May 17, 1947, folder "Post High School and College Diary, December 5, 1941–June 8, 1946," box 1, volume 4, Mickey (Maxine) Campbell Welker papers, Center for Archival Collections, Bowling Green State University.

41. State University of Iowa, "Code for Coeds, 1944–1945," Louise Hilfman Goldman Papers, Iowa Women's Archive.

42. Charles W. Hobart, "Freshman Disorientation," *Improving College and University Teaching* 9, no. 2 (Spring 1961): 77–78.

43. Alice Silverman, "Ever Appropriate Weekend," Scrapbook, 9, folder "Alice Silverman, 1951," Class of 1951, Individuals Q–Z, Smith College Archives.

44. Eugenia Kaledin, *Mothers and More: American Women in the 1950s* (Boston: Twayne Publishers, 1984), 44.

45. Newcomer, *Century of Higher Education*, 31.

46. Alice Gorton diary, n.d., 13, box 1, folder 2, "March 1, 1950–June 19, 1950," Alice Gorton Hart papers, Sophia Smith Collection.

47. Ibid., n.d., especially 5–8, box 1, folder 6, "December 1950–May 1951."

48. Ibid., n.d., 36 (back), box 1, folder 7, "December 1950–May 1951."

49. The greasy grind quote in this case is from Laurie Worcester to family, October 17, 1948, Laurie Worcester (Lucy Lawrence Chauncey) papers, box 1, folder 1, Smith College Archives, Northampton, Mass. For other students criticizing peers for lack of sociability, see also Lelah Dushkin to mother, November 25, 1949, box 1a, folder 1, Dorothy Smith Dushkin papers, Sophia Smith Collection, Smith College Archives.

50. June Calender diary, October 17, 1956, Arthur and Elizabeth Schlesinger Library on the History of Women in America.

51. Ibid.

52. Ibid., November 3, 1956.

53. Helene Harmon diary, September 16, 1940, Helene Harmon Weis papers, Arthur and Elizabeth Schlesinger Library on the History of Women in America.

54. Ibid., December 23, 1940.

55. Merle Judith Marcus papers, American Jewish Archives, Hebrew Union College, Cincinnati, Ohio.

56. Merle Judith Marcus to Barnard, August 6, 1947 (draft); father to Merle, n.d.; and mother to Merle, September 8, 1946, box 1, folder 1.

57. Merle Judith Marcus to anonymous, November 12, 48, box 1, folder 1.

58. On the "politics of respectability" in the black middle class, see, for instance, E. Frances White, *Dark Continent of Our Bodies: Black Feminism and the Politics of Respectability* (Philadelphia: Temple University Press, 2001).

59. Carol Kaminsky (Barnard College, Class of 1956), October 26, 2008, personal e-mail message to author.

60. While prejudices against Jews were increasingly seen as anti-American after the war, African Americans did not benefit to the same extent from the spread of new attitudes. See David Roediger, *Working toward Whiteness: How America's Immigrants Became White: The Strange Journey from Ellis Island to the Suburbs* (New York: Basic Books, 2006).

61. Tasha to Merle, April 15, 1955, folder 2, "personal correspondence 1950–1962," Merle Judith Marcus papers.

62. Helene Harmon diary, February 8, 1941.

63. Ibid., April 22, 1941.

64. John D'Emilio and Estelle B. Freedman, *Intimate Matters: A History of Sexuality in America* (New York: Harper & Row, 1988), 252.

65. See Schrecker, *No Ivory Tower.*

66. Paul F. Lazarsfeld and Wagner Thielens Jr., *The Academic Mind: Social Scientists in a Time of Crisis* (Glencoe, Ill.: Free Press, 1958). Although this work was published at the end of the decade, the researchers began to gather their data almost immediately after the worst excesses of McCarthyism had abated.

67. Ibid., 105, 111, 114.

68. Intellectual influences include Wilhelm Reich and Theodore P. Wolfe, *The Mass Psychology of Fascism* (1933; First English ed., New York: Orgone Institute Press, 1946); and Erich Fromm's *Escape from Freedom* (New York: Holt, Rinehart Winston, 1941).

69. For biographical detail on Harlow Shapley, see Wang, *American Science*, 118–130. On the Waldorf Conference controversy, see Jumonville, *Critical Crossings*, ch. 1.

70. Sidney Hook, a professor of philosophy and public intellectual who on occasion wrote articles for the *New York Times Magazine* and the *Saturday Review*, for instance, condemned the action. See Jumonville, *Critical Crossings*, 2–3.

71. Janet Brown to father, March 25, 1949, box 1, folder 6.

72. This information is from box 1, folder "Nash: biographical information: diary, 1947–1948, Martha Ann Furgerson Nash papers, Iowa Women's Archives, Iowa City.

73. Amy T. McCandless, *The Past in the Present: Women's Higher Education in the Twentieth-Century American South* (Tuscaloosa: University of Alabama Press, 1999). For a comparative study of two private women's colleges in the North and the historically black Spellman College, see Margaret A. Lowe, *Looking Good: College Women and Body Image, 1875–1930* (Baltimore: Johns Hopkins University Press, 2003).

74. After graduating from college with a major in history and working for a year for the Congress of Industrial Organizations, Martha Ann Furgerson married Warren Nash and moved to Omaha, Nebraska. While her husband was finishing his medical degree and after he began working as a physician, Martha Ann raised seven children and became an active community organizer. Starting in 1962, she served on the board of directors of the Black Hawk County Chapter of the National Association for the Advancement of Colored People (NAACP) and remained active in the Catholic Church and the international peace movement. Martha Ann Furgerson Nash papers, box 1, folder "Nash: biographical information: diary, 1947–1948."

75. Martha Ann Furgerson diary, September 14, 1947; September 19, 1947; and September 26, 1947.

76. Ibid., November 11, 1947.

77. Ibid., October 29, 1947.

78. Ibid.

79. Ibid., November 5, 1947.

80. See, for instance, Lynn, *Progressive Women in Conservative Times*; Stephanie Renee Landrum, "'More Firmly Based Today': Anti-Communism, Academic Freedom, and Smith College, 1947–1956" (Senior thesis, Smith College, 1998); and Sara M. Evans, *Journeys that Opened up the World: Women, Student Christian Movements, and Social Justice, 1955–1975* (New Brunswick, N.J.: Rutgers University Press, 2003).

81. See Lisle Abbott Rose, *The Cold Comes to Main Street: America in 1950* (Lawrence: University Press of Kansas, 1999).

82. "A Circus Comes to Town," April 11, 1952, *Smith College Associated News*, 2.

83. See Alice Gorton Hart diary, unidentified clippings, n.d., 36 (back), box 2, folder 14, "June 1951–August 1952"; and anonymous to Alice Gorton, letter pasted into diary, dated March 28, 1953, 21 (back), box 3, folder 20, "February–September 1953."

84. Alice Gorton, diary, n.d., 103 (back), folder 19, "September 1952–February 1953."

85. June Calender diary, folder "Removed from 1956 diary," typed report of senior year trip to Washington, D.C., and New York City in May 1956.

86. Ibid., February 24, 1958.

87. Ibid., December 24, 1958; December 25, 1958.

88. For similar sentiments, see also Sandra Iger to Richard Kohler, November 12, 1957, box 1, folder 4, October 24–November 19, 1957, Sandra Iger Kohler papers, Mount Holyoke College Archives.

CHAPTER 3 — NOT PART OF THE CROWD

1. Susan Sperry Borman diary, n.d., box 2, folder 16, Susan Delattre papers, Arthur and Elizabeth Schlesinger Library on the history of Women in America, Radcliffe Institute for Advanced Study, Harvard University, Cambridge, Mass.

2. Susan Sperry Borman diary, October 2, 1956, box 2, folder 16.

3. See, for instance, Kristin Celello, *Making Marriage Work: A History of Marriage and Divorce in the Twentieth-Century United States* (Chapel Hill: University of North Carolina Press, 2009), 72–75.

4. Up to the 1970s, most psychologists agreed that successful personality development hinged on acceptance of conventional sex roles. Highly influential in this regard was Erik Erikson, *Childhood and Society* (New York: Norton, 1950). Also see Jerome Kagan, "Acquisition and Significance of Sex Typing and Sex-Role Identity," in *Review of Child Development Research*, vol. 1, ed. M. L. Hoffman and L. W. Hoffman (New York: Russell Sage Foundation, 1964). For historical perspectives on the subject see: Mari Jo Buhle, *Feminism and Its Discontents: A Century of Struggle with Psychoanalysis* (Cambridge, Mass.: Harvard University Press, 1998), chs. 4 and 5; and Janet Walker, *Couching Resistance: Women, Film, and Psychoanalytic Psychiatry* (Minneapolis: University of Minnesota Press, 1993), 1–23.

5. Susan Sperry Borman diary, October 12, 1956, box 2, folder 16.

6. Erik Erikson's *Identity, Youth and Crisis* (New York: W. W. Norton, 1968) was one of the first works in the literature on adolescent identity development. For newer scholarship, see Jeffrey J. Arnett, "Emerging Adulthood: A Theory of Development from the Late Teens through the Twenties," *American Psychologist* 55 (May 2000): 469–480; and David Moshman, *Adolescent Psychological Development: Rationality, Morality, and Identity* (Mahwah, N.J.: Lawrence Erlbaum, 1999).

7. "Man in the machine age" is taken from the 1941 article by Frankfurt School philosopher Herbert Marcuse, "Some Social Implications of Modern Technology." Reprinted

in: Andrew Arato and Eike Gebhardt, eds., *The Essential Frankfurt School Reader* (New York: Continuum, 1982): 138–162, 141. Also see Erich Fromm, *Escape from Freedom* (New York: Holt Rinehart and Winston, 1941); Margaret Mead, *And Keep Your Powder Dry: An Anthropologist Looks at America* (New York: William Morrow and Company, 1942); Philip Wylie, *Generation of Vipers* (New York: Farrar and Rhinehart, 1942); David Riesman with Nathan Glazer and Reuel Denney, *The Lonely Crowd: A Study of the Changing American Character* (New Haven: Yale University Press, 1950); and C. Wright Mills, *White Collar: The American Middle Classes* (New York: Oxford University Press, 1951). The influence of the debate about national character also shows in the revival of the work of Alexis de Tocqueville. In the course of the 1950s, his *Democracy in America*, first published in 1835, went through multiple reprints, and by the early 1960s virtually every major publishing house had brought out its version of the book. By that time, most colleges and universities had specific "American Studies" departments and the *American Quarterly* served as the official professional publication for scholars in the field. See James Gilbert, *Men in the Middle: Searching for Masculinity in the 1950s* (Chicago: University of Chicago Press, 2006): 39–40.

8. Fromm, *Escape*, 185–186; and Riesman et al., *Lonely Crowd*, 8–9.

9. On the contrast with prewar life styles and the build up of the postwar military industrial complex, see Daniel Horowitz, *The Anxieties of Affluence: Critiques of American Consumer Culture, 1939–1979* (Amherst: University of Massachusetts Press, 2004), 8–9, 36–37. On the "magnitude" of postwar economic changes, see Wini Breines, *Young, White, and Miserable: Growing up Female in the 1950s* (Boston: Beacon Press, 1992), 2–7.

10. These concerns had already shaped the popular discourse during World War II. A first warning of the way in which cultural trends had emasculated the American male came from Edward Strecker, one of the psychiatrists employed to screen military recruits during the war. Once wartime censorship rules were relaxed, Strecker revealed in a lecture covered by the *New York Times* that he had had to reject an alarmingly large number of men for psychological reasons. These men, Strecker argued, had difficulties making a psychological break with the parental home. They remained unduly attached to their mothers and failed to develop in an autonomous fashion. The argument reached an even greater audience after Strecker published his thesis in 1946. See Edward A. Strecker, *Their Mothers' Sons: The Psychiatrist Examines an American Problem* (Philadelphia: Lippincott, 1946).

11. On the perception of female matriarchy in the suburbs, see Jennifer Kalish, "Spouse Devouring Black Widows and their Neutered Mates: Postwar Suburbanization. A Battle over Domestic Space," *UCLA Historical Journal*, 14, special issue (1994), 128–154. For a discussion of perceived gender convergence, see K. A. Cuordileone, "'Politics in an Age of Anxiety': Cold War Political Culture and the Crisis in American Masculinity, 1949–1960," *Journal of American History* 87, no. 2 (September 2000): 515–545, at 527. For mass media discussions of housewives, see Eva Moskowitz, "'It's Good to Blow Your Top': Women's Magazines and a Discourse of Discontent, 1945–1965," *Journal of Women's History* 8 (Fall 1996), 66–98.

12. See, for example, Philip Wylie, *An Essay on Morals* (New York: Rinehart, 1947); Theodore W. Adorno, Else Frenkel-Brunswik, and Daniel J. Levinson, *The Authoritarian Personality* (New York: Harper, 1950); and Vance Packard, *The Hidden Persuaders* (New York: Mckay, 1957).

13. An early voice pointing to the tendency to make generalizations about American history "mostly in masculine terms" came from historian David Potter in 1962. In his case, he commented on David Riesman's *The Lonely Crowd* (1950), a book that counted among its intellectual influences, among others, the work of Margaret Mead. See Gilbert, *Men in the Middle*, 50–51.

14. The phrase "upper-middle-class myopia" is from Roland Marchand, "Visions of Classlessness, Quests for Dominions: American Popular Culture," in *Reshaping America: Society and Institutions, 1945–1960*, ed. Robert H. Bremner and Gary W. Reichard (Columbus: Ohio State University Press, 1982), 163–190.

15. For examples of this debate, see Fred M. Hechinger, "Has Training Been Good? Now That Women Have Survived Education"; n.d.; and Hechinger, "Beyond Pots and Pans," n.d. (ca. 1950), unidentified clippings, box 4, folder 6, Education Collection, Sophia Smith Collection, Smith College, Northampton, Mass.

16. See, for instance, Steven E. Kagle and Lorenza Gramegna, "Rewriting Her Life: Fictionalization and the Use of Fictional Models in Early American Women's Diaries," in *Inscribing the Daily: Critical Essays on Women's Diaries*, ed. Suzanne L. Bunkers and Cynthia A. Huff (Amherst: University of Massachusetts Press, 1996), 38–55, at 39, 51.

17. Paula Fass, *The Damned and the Beautiful: American Youth in the 1920s* (New York: Oxford University Press, 1977); Kathy L. Peiss, *Cheap Amusements: Working Women and Leisure in Turn-of-the-Century New York* (Philadelphia: Temple University Press, 1986); and Beth L. Bailey, *From Front Porch to Back Seat: Courtship in Twentieth-Century America* (Baltimore: Johns Hopkins University Press, 1988).

18. Willard Waller, "The Rating and Dating Complex," *American Sociological Review* 2 (October 1937): 727–734. Also see Mary C. McComb, "Rate Your Date: Young Women and the Commodification of Depression Era Courtship," in *Delinquents and Debutantes: Twentieth Century American Girls' Cultures*, ed. Sherrie A. Inness (New York: New York University Press, 1998), 40–60.

19. *Michigander*, April 26, 1951, 3, in Twitchell family papers, box 2, folder: "University—Triangle Fraternity, at U-M (Ed Rich) 1942–51," Michigan Historical Collections, Bentley Historical Library, University of Michigan, Ann Arbor.

20. Alice Silverman, Scrapbook, "Sophomore Slump," 45, folder "Alice Silverman, 1951," Individuals Q–Z, Class of 1951, Smith College Archives, Northampton, Mass.

21. Celello, *Making Marriage Work*, 75.

22. Ferdinand Lundberg and Marynia F. Farnham, *Modern Woman: The Lost Sex* (New York: Harper & Brothers, 1947), 126–134, 140–149, 363–377.

23. Psychoanalysis was a relatively young field, but its influence grew rapidly after some of the field's most important theorists entered the United States as émigrés in the 1930s and 1940s. Buhle, *Feminism and Its Discontents*; and Beth L. Bailey, "Scientific Truth . . . and Love: The Marriage Education Movement in the United States," *Journal of Social History* 20, no. 4 (Summer 1987): 711–732.

24. Margaret Mead, *Male and Female: A Study of the Sexes in Changing World* (New York: William Morrow & Company, 1949), 382. Also see Ashley Montagu, *The Natural Superiority of Women* (New York: Macmillan, 1952); Karl Menninger, *Love against Hate* (New York: Harcourt, Brace & World, 1942); and Mirra Komarovsky, *Women in the Modern World* (Boston: Little, Brown, 1953).

25. Laurie Worcester to family, n.d., November 1950, box 1, folder 7, Laurie Worcester (Lucy Lawrence Chauncey) papers, Smith College Archives, Northampton, Mass.; Alice Silverman, Scrapbook, "Sophomore Slump," 45; Lelah Dushkin to mother, January 6, 1950, box 1a, folder 1, Dorothy Smith Dushkin papers, Sophia Smith Collection, Smith College Archives; and Janice Mary Kidwell to parents, February 24, 1952, box 1, folder 2, Janice Mary Kidwell papers, Archives and Special Collections, Mount Holyoke College, South Hadley, Mass.

26. Susan Sperry Borman to Roland Delattre, September 22, 1958, box 5, folder 47.

27. Judith Raskin to parents, October 8, 1945, box 2, folder 1–2, Judith Raskin papers, Sophia Smith Collection, Smith College Archives.

28. Ibid., October 15, 1946; and November 7, 1946, box 2, folder 1–2.

29. Alice Gorton diary, n.d., 65 (back), 32, 35 (back), box 2, folder 14, "January–August 1952," Alice Gorton Hart papers, Sophia Smith Collection, Smith College.

30. Ibid., n.d., 84 (back), box 2, folder 15, "January–August 1952."

31. Ibid., n.d., 132, box 2, folder 15, "January–August 1952."

32. Ibid., n.d., 121, box 2, folder 15, "January–August 1952."

33. Ibid., n.d., 65 (back), box 2, folder 15, "January–August 1952."

34. Margaret Hall diary, April 26, 1953, vol. 7, "Miscellaneous, 1949–1953," her emphasis. In possession of Margaret Hall Whitfield, Martinez, CA.

35. Margaret Hall to "Aunt Julia," February 21, 1955, postcard in possession of Margaret Hall Whitfield.

36. Sandra Iger to Richard Kohler, September 21, 1957; October 21, 1957, box 1, folder 3, Sandra Iger Kohler papers, Mount Holyoke College Archives.

37. June Calender diary, April 10, 1958; May 12, 1958, June Calender papers, Arthur and Elizabeth Schlesinger Library on the History of Women in America.

38. Sandra Iger to Richard Kohler, November 14, 1957, box 1, folder 4.

39. Ibid.

40. June Calender diary, November 25, 1956.

41. Especially when it came to the higher education of women, this argument was at least in part in defense of proposals to feminize the curriculum by adding more classes that specifically prepared female undergraduates for their role as wives and mothers. See Barbara Solomon, *In the Company of Educated Women: A History of Women and Higher Education in America* (New Haven: Yale University Press, 1985), 192–194.

42. Perusing class notes and schedules of college women, I found that the following works were showing up with particular frequency: Philip Wylie, *Generation of Vipers* (1942), Margaret Mead, *And Keep Your Powder Dry* (1943), the fiction of D. H. Lawrence and the poetry of T. S. Eliot, the work of philosophers associated with the Frankfurt School, Freud's *Civilization and Its Discontents* (1930), and David Riesman, *The Lonely Crowd* (1950).

43. Fromm, *Escape from Freedom*, 200–201.

44. Sigmund Freud, *Civilization and Its Discontents* (New York: W. W. Norton, 1961), 50.

45. Wylie, *Generation of Vipers*, 194–217.

46. For an analysis of Wylie's *Generation of Vipers*, including readers' reactions and the sociodemographic composition of his fan base, see Rebecca Jo Plant, "The Repeal of Mother Love: Momism and the Reconstruction of Motherhood in Philip Wylie's America" (Ph.D. diss., Johns Hopkins University, 2001).

47. Komarovsky, *Women in the Modern World*, 92–99.

48. Ibid., 93.

49. Because heterosocial activities tend to dominate women's descriptions of campus life, a reader easily gets the impression that female peers did not matter a lot to women. The relative absence of female friends as topics in women's writings is not necessarily a reflection of their absence in real life, however. A close reading of Margaret Hall's journal shows that she had at least one peer whom she considered like-minded and with whom she exchanged views and opinions. Margaret Hall diary, April 17, 1955, vol. 13, "Bryn Mawr Senior 1955." Another student, Dori Schaffer, who attended the University of California at Los Angeles and whose mother published her journal after Dori's untimely death, is also largely silent on other women. From her mother's annotations, however, the reader learns that Dori had a close friend named Rose to whom she turned for support and who joined her in many events and activities. Anne Schaffer, ed., *Dear Deedee: From the Diaries of Dori Schaffer* (Secaucus, N.J.: Lyle Stuart, 1978), 157.

50. Alice Gorton diary, n.d., 12 (back), box 3, folder 17, "September 1952–February 1953"; and 65, 71 (back), box 3, folder 18, "September 1952–February 1953." For Alice's reflections on Poof's philosophy, see diary, n.d., 82 (back), box 3, folder 21, "February–September 1953."

51. Ibid., n.d., 7 (back), box 3, folder 20, "February–September 1953."

52. Ibid., n.d. 21 (back), box 3, folder 20, "February–September 1953."

53. Susan Sperry Borman diary, October 19, 1956; November 4, 1956, box 2, folder 16.

54. See, for instance, Linda W. Rosenzweig, *Another Self: Middle-Class American Women and Their Friends in the Twentieth Century* (New York: New York University Press, 1999); and McComb, *Great Depression*, 72–73.

55. Susan Sperry Borman diary, November 9, 1956, box 2, folder 16.

56. Judy Robinson to Alice Gorton, March 30, 1953; and Alice Gorton diary, n.d., 21 (back), box 3, folder 20, "February–September 1953."

57. Alice Gorton diary, n.d., 123 (back), box 3, folder 20, "February–September 1953."

58. Susan Sperry Borman diary, October 2, 1956, box 2, folder 16.

59. See ibid., October 12, 1956, box 2, folder 16.

60. Alice Gorton diary, n.d., 7 (back), box 3, folder 20, "February–September 1953."

61. For examples of the plea for tolerance, see for instance Wylie, *Generation of Vipers*; and Robert Mitchell Lindner, *Must You Conform?* (New York: Rinehart, 1956).

62. Janet Brown papers, box 1, folder Y2.

63. Patricia Beck diary, July 24, 1945, folder: "diary 1945–1946," Patricia Beck papers, Sophia Smith Collection, Smith College Archive.

64. Alice Gorton diary, n.d., 28 (back), 9–10 (back), box 1, folder 6, "December 1950–May 1951."

65. Ibid., n.d., 40 (back), box 1, folder 7, "December 1950–May 1951."

66. Ibid., n.d., 8, 41, box 1, folder 6, "December 1950–May 1951"; and 28, box 2, folder 14, "January–August 1952."

67. Ibid., n.d., 107 (back), box 3, folder 21, February–September 1953.

68. Richard H. to Alice Gorton, February 11, 1952, letter pasted between pages 6 and 7 of diary; Marc H. to Alice Gorton, March 20, 1952, letter pasted into diary, 20 (back); and Al P. to Alice Gorton, February 17, 1952, letter pasted into diary, 8; box 2, folder 13, January 1952–August 1952.

69. Margaret Hall to Bill R., not sent, October 4, 1951, diary vol. 7, "Miscellaneous, 1949–1953."

70. My account of the meeting between Margaret and Frank is based on Margaret's diary and her as of yet unpublished essay: "Address Unknown," 12th revision, 1–2, in possession of author. Although Margaret wrote this essay many years after the initial encounter, she offers extensive quotes from the letters she received from Frank over the years, which she has since donated to the Bryn Mawr College Archives.

71. Margaret Hall diary, April 4, 1953; April 25, 1953; May 22, 1953; and April 7, 1955; and Margaret Hall, "Address Unknown."

72. Margaret Hall diary, April 28, 1953.

73. Susan Sperry Borman to parents, October 2, 1956; and November 27, 1956, box 2, folder 23.

74. Susan Sperry Borman diary, November 3, 1956, box 2, folder 16.

75. Susan Sperry Borman to parents, January 11, 1957; June 1, 1957; and November 27, 1957, box 3, folder 24.

76. Alice Gorton diary, n.d., 27–28, 65 (back), box 1, folder 14, "January–August 1952."

77. Komarovsky, *Women in the Modern World*, 94–99.

CHAPTER 4 — INDIVIDUALISM AND SEXUALITY

1. Philip Kennedy diary, n.d., 72, box 5, folder 197, Frank Hunter Kennedy papers, Southern Historical Collection, The Wilson Library, University of North Carolina at Chapel Hill.

2. Ibid., 43.

3. Ibid., 44–45.

4. Ibid., 75.

5. Ibid., 75, 179.

6. Ibid., 75, 128, 183.

7. Under "vernacular" sexuality, I understand attitudes conveyed orally that coexisted with the official morality of the middle class as articulated in print and that have been explored for the nineteenth century in particular by Helen Lefkowitz Horowitz in her *Rereading Sex: Battles over Sexual Knowledge and Suppression in Nineteenth-Century America* (New York: Knopf, 2002), and by Christine Stansell in her *City of Women: Sex and Class in New York, 1789–1860* (Urbana: University of Illinois Press, 1987).

8. William Graebner discusses the fictional characters of Stanley Kowalski in Tennessee Williams's *A Streetcar Named Desire* (1947) and Mike Hammer in Mickey Spillane's *I, the Jury* (1947) in this context. See Graebner, *The Age of Doubt: American Thought and Culture in the 1940s* (Boston: Twayne Publishers, 1991), 36.

9. Allan Bérubé, *Coming Out under Fire: The History of Gay Men and Women in World War II* (New York: Free Press, 1990).

10. On the anxieties surrounding male gender performance and the link to national security issues, see K. A. Cuordileone, "'Politics in an Age of Anxiety': Cold War Political Culture and the Crisis in American Masculinity, 1949–1960," *Journal of American History* 87, no. 2 (September 2000): 515–545; Robert Dean, *Imperial Brotherhood: Gender and the Making of Cold War Foreign Policy* (Amherst: University of Massachusetts Press, 2001); and David Johnson, *The Lavender Scare: The Cold War Persecution of Gays and Lesbians in the Federal Government* (Chicago: University of Chicago Press, 2004).

11. Quoted in Cuordileone, "'Politics in an Age of Anxiety,'" 521, 520.

12. For a general account of women's roles during the war, see, for instance, Sara M. Evans, *Born for Liberty: A History of Women in America* (New York: Free Press, 1989), 221–222. On the extent of and limits to women's economic gains, see Ruth Milkman,

Gender at Work: The Dynamics of Job Segregation by Sex during World War II (Urbana: University of Illinois Press, 1987). For a discussion of sexual and gender politics within the military, see Leisa D. Meyer, *Creating G.I. Jane: Sexuality and Power in the Women's Army Corps during World War II* (New York: Columbia University Press, 1996).

13. John D'Emilio and Estelle B. Freedman, *Intimate Matters: A History of Sexuality in America* (New York: Harper & Row, 1988), 260–261.

14. U.S. Children's Bureau figures for the 1930s through the early 1940s show a ratio of the rate of male to female delinquency of six to one. This margin, however, began to shrink in the course of the war and in its aftermath. By 1946 girls constituted one out of every four juvenile delinquents in court cases. See Rachel Devlin, *Relative Intimacy: Fathers, Adolescent Daughters, and Postwar American Culture* (Chapel Hill: University of North Carolina Press, 2005), 53.

15. Mr. Rigby to Mount Holyoke College, February 7, 1944, folder 6, Alice Rigby papers, Mount Holyoke College Archives, South Hadley, Mass.

16. Alice Rigby to family, March 4, 1944, folder 6.

17. Dean of Residence Catherine P. Robinson to Mr. and Mrs. Rigby, March 11, 1944, folder 6, Alice Rigby papers.

18. On attitudes in reaction to young women's service as USO hostesses, see Marilyn Hegarty, *Victory Girls, Khaki-Wackies, and Patriotutes: The Regulation of Female Sexuality during World War II* (New York: New York University Press, 2008), 53–55.

19. Grace Gray to family, April 17, 1943, box 1, folder 9, Grace Gray papers, Mount Holyoke College Archives.

20. Ibid., April 21, 1943, box 1, folder 9.

21. Ibid., April 17, 1943, box 1, folder 9.

22. Ibid., April 21, 1943, box 1, folder 9.

23. Alice Rigby to parents, April 2, 1944, box 1, folder 5.

24. For a description of Mount Holyoke College at the eve of World War II, see McComb, *Great Depression*, 11.

25. D'Emilio and Freedman, *Intimate Matters*, 258.

26. Smith College and Cornell University, for instance, in the early 1950s in their official publications still referred to men visiting on campus as "callers." For Smith College, see "Rules and Regulations, 1951–1952," Smith College Archives. For Cornell, see "Women's Self Government Association By-Laws," in Charlotte Williams Conable, *Women at Cornell: The Myth of Equal Education* (Ithaca: Cornell University Press, 1977), appendix 2, 176.

27. On the spread of more permissive sexual mores on college campuses, see Barbara Solomon, *In the Company of Educated Women: A History of Women and Higher Education in America* (New Haven, Conn.: Yale University Press, 1985), 161–162. Also see Paula S. Fass,

The Damned and the Beautiful: American Youth in the 1920s (New York: Oxford University Press, 1977), 262–270; and Helen L. Horowitz, *Campus Life: Undergraduate Cultures from the End of the Eighteenth Century to the Present* (New York: Knopf, 1987), 208–211.

28. Daniel A. Clark, "The Two Joes Meet. Joe College, Joe Veteran: The G. I. Bill, College Education, and Postwar American Culture," *History of Education Quarterly* 38, no. 2 (1998): 165–189.

29. Mary Browning Nelson papers, Mount Holyoke College Archives.

30. Mary Browning to mother, September 26, 1947; and October 5, 1947, box 1, folder 3.

31. Ronald Story, "The Ordeal of the Public Sector: The University of Massachusetts," in *Five Colleges: Five Histories*, ed. Ronald Story, 51–78 (Amherst, Mass.: Five Colleges, Inc. and Historic Deerfield, 1992), 52, 60.

32. Louise Browning to Mary Browning, October 14, 1947, box 1, folder 3.

33. On official and tacit policies toward service members' sexual activities, see Hegarty, *Victory Girls, Khaki-Wackies, and Patriotutes*, 100–103. On changing attitudes toward male sexuality during World War II, also see Joanne Meyerowitz, "Women, Cheesecake, and Borderline Material: Responses to Girlie Pictures in the Mid-Twentieth-Century U.S.," *Journal of Women's History* 8, no. 3 (Fall 1996): 9–35.

34. "The Rites of Spring," *Time*, May 11, 1953, 82, quoted in Beth Bailey, "From Panty Raids to Revolution: Youth and Authority, 1950–1970," in *Generations of Youth: Youth Cultures and History in Twentieth-Century America*, ed. Joe Austin and Michael Nevin Willard (New York: New York University Press, 1998): 187–204.

35. Mary Browning to mother, n.d., ca. January 29, 1950.

36. Ibid.

37. Unidentified newspaper clipping, Maxine Joyce Campbell, College Scrapbook, box 1, 3, Mickey (Maxine) Campbell Welker papers, Center for Archival Collections, Bowling Green State University, Bowling Green, Ohio.

38. Alfred C. Kinsey, Wardell B. Pomeroy, Clyde E. Martin, and Paul H. Gebhard, *Sexual Behavior in the Human Female* (Philadelphia: W. B. Saunders, 1953), 282–345.

39. This was found, for instance, by Clifford Kirkpatrick, Sheldon Stryker, and Philip Buell in "An Experimental Study of Attitudes towards Male Sex Behavior with Reference to Kinsey Findings," *American Sociological Review* 17, no. 5 (October 1952): 580–587.

40. Ira Reiss, *Premarital Sexual Standards in America: A Sociological Investigation of the Relative Social and Cultural Integration of American Sexual Standards* (Glencoe, Ill.: Free Press, 1960), 91; and Reiss, "Sexual Codes in Teen-Age Culture," *Annals of the American Academy of Political and Social Science* 338 (November 1961): 58, 62.

41. D'Emilio and Freedman, *Intimate Matters*, 264–265.

42. Anonymous to Richard Kohler, September 23, 1957, box 1, folder 3, Sandra Iger Kohler papers, Mount Holyoke College Archives.

43. Fulton John Sheen, *Three to Get Married* (New York: Appleton-Century-Crofts, 1951), 16.

44. Citations are from R. Marie Griffith, "The Religious Encounters of Alfred C. Kinsey," *Journal of American History* 95, no. 2 (September 2008): 349–377, at 363, 368–369. Griffith argues in the article that the response of "Christian authorities" to the Kinsey report was actually more complex and less hostile than it has been portrayed in the historiography. For the most part, however, a positive reception of and active engagement with Kinsey's ideas took the form of private exchanges between mainline Protestants and Kinsey and vice versa. The tenor of the public discussion of the second volume especially was overwhelmingly negative if not alarmist.

45. Janet Brown to parents, January 30, 1949, folder 6, Janet Brown papers, Mount Holyoke College Archives.

46. Evelyn Millis Duvall, *Facts of Life and Love for Teenagers* (New York: Association Press, 1950). For biographical information on Evelyn Duvall, see Suzanne K. Steinmetz and Gary W. Peterson, *Pioneering Paths in the Study of Families: The Lives and Careers of Family Scholars* (New York: Haworth Press, 2002), 703–707. On the popularity of *Facts of Life and Love*, see Freedman and D'Emilio, *Intimate Matters*, 264.

47. Duvall, *Facts of Life and Love for Teenagers*, 78.

48. Ibid., 81.

49. Ibid., 247–248, 82.

50. An early example is John Dollard, *Caste and Class in a Southern Town* (New Haven, Conn.: Yale University Press, 1937); also see August B. Hollingshead, *Elmtown's Youth* (New York: John Wiley, 1949).

51. Duvall, *Facts of Life and Love for Teenagers*, 80, 95.

52. Smith College, "Rules and Regulations, 1954–1955," 1, Smith College Archives.

53. Women's League/Women's Self-Government Association/Association of Women Students Records, Center for Archival Collections, Bowling Green State University, Bowling Green, Ohio. Also see Bailey, "From Panty Raids to Revolution."

54. Betty Robinson to Noel Phyllis Birkby, February 21, 1953, box 8, folder 117, Noel Phyllis Birkby papers, Sophia Smith Collection, Women's History Archive, Smith College.

55. See for instance Mary Browning to mother, n.d., ca. January 29, 1950.

56. Alice Gorton diary, n.d., 6–7, box 2, folder 13, "January 1952–August 1952."

57. Ibid.

58. D'Emilio and Freedman, *Intimate Matters*, 262–263.

59. Mary Browning to mother, January 15, 1950.

60. Anonymous to Richard Kohler, July 21, 1959, box 3, folder 1, Sandra Iger Kohler papers.

61. D'Emilio and Freedman, *Intimate Matters*, 262–263.

62. Ibid., *Intimate Matters*, 334.

63. Lelah Dushkin to mother, October 31, 1949, box 1a, folder 1, Dorothy Smith Dushkin papers, Sophia Smith Collection, Smith College Archives. For another example for mother–daughter exchanges about dating, see the papers of Mary Browning Nelson. Mary's mother had also gone to college. In this case, she was a Wellesley alumna. Mary Browning Nelson papers, Mount Holyoke College Archives.

64. My contention based on anecdotal evidence is confirmed by Otto Butz, *The Unsilent Generation: An Anonymous Symposium in which Eleven College Seniors Look at Themselves and Their World* (New York: Rinehart, 1958).

65. Both had their own copy: Sandra Iger to Richard Kohler, August 13, 1957, box 1, folder 2.

66. Richard Kohler to Sandra Iger, September 26, 1957, box 1, folder 3.

67. Sandra Iger to Richard Kohler, November 8, 1957, box 1, folder 4.

68. Ibid., January 10, 1958, box 1, folder 6.

69. Richard Kohler to Sandra Iger, January 6, 1958, box 1, folder 6.

70. Ibid., November 18, 1957, box 1, folder 4.

71. Ibid., January 6, 1958, box 1, folder 6.

72. Ibid., January 13, 1958, box 1, folder 6.

73. Sandra Iger to Richard Kohler, January 10, 1958, box 1, folder 6.

74. Alice Gorton diary, n.d., 27, box 2, folder 14, "January–August 1952."

75. Ibid., n.d., 54, box 1, folder 7, "December 1950–May 1951."

76. Ibid.

77. For examples of discussions of Lawrence's concepts of love and sexuality that Sandra would have encountered in college, see Mark Spilka, *The Love Ethic of D. H. Lawrence* (Bloomington: Indiana University Press, 1955); Peter Nazareth, "D. H. Lawrence and Sex," *Transitions* 6/7 (October 1962): 54–57; and Nazareth, "D. H. Lawrence and Sex," *Transitions* 8 (March 1963): 38–43.

78. An example for this harmful female influence is the character of "Hermione Roddice" in Lawrence's *Women in Love* (1920).

79. Alice Gorton diary, n.d., 40, box 1, folder 7, "December 1950–May 1951."

80. Ibid.

81. Ibid., n.d., 119, box 2, folder 15, "January 1952–August 1952."

82. Sandra Iger to Richard Kohler, May 8, 1961, box 7, folder 1.

83. Alice Gorton diary, n.d., 77, box 3, folder 18, "September 1952–February 1953."

84. Margaret Hall diary, September 30, 1956, vol. 19, June 1956 to June 1957, diary in possession of Margaret Whitfield, Martinez, Calif.

85. Susan Sperry Borman diary, October 10, 1956, box 2, folder 16–21, Susan Delattre papers, Arthur and Elizabeth Schlesinger Library on the History of Women in America, Radcliffe Institute for Advanced Study, Harvard University, Cambridge, Mass.

CHAPTER 5 — COLLEGE WOMEN AND THE CLASH OF MYSTIQUES

1. Margaret Kennedy to Andy A., August 12, 1951, box 4, folder 140, Frank Hunter Kennedy papers, Southern Historical Collection, Library of the University of North Carolina at Chapel Hill.

2. Anonymous to Philip Kennedy, n.d., box 5, folder 179.

3. Ken to Margaret Kennedy, n.d., postmarked November 15, 1949, box 4, folder 132.

4. Ibid.

5. Ibid., n.d., postmarked September 18, 1949, box 4, folder 132.

6. Ibid., n.d., postmarked September 21, 1949; October 18, 1949; and November 15, 1949, box 4, folder 132.

7. Richard Kohler to Sandra Iger, January 8, 1961, box 6, folder 2, Sandra Iger Kohler papers, Mount Holyoke College Archives, South Hadley, Mass.

8. Ibid., May 8, 1961, box 7, folder 1.

9. Ibid., January 16, 1961, box 6, folder 2.

10. Alice Gorton diary, n.d., 91, 104, box 3, folder 21, "February–September 1953, Alice Gorton Hart papers, Sophia Smith Collection, Smith College, Northampton, MA.

11. Ibid., n.d., 94–95 (back), box 3, folder 24, "February–September 1953."

12. Wini Breines, *Young, White, and Miserable: Growing up Female in the Fifties* (Boston: Beacon Press, 1992), 127–166.

13. Alice Gorton diary, n.d., 108, box 3, folder 24, "February–September 1953."

14. Ibid., n.d., 108 (back)–113, box 3, folder 24, "February–September 1953."

15. Ibid., n.d., 107 (back), folder 24, "February–September 1953."

16. Ibid., n.d., 131, box 3, folder 21, "February–September 1953."

17. For evidence of ambivalence, see ibid., n.d., 38, 49, 78 (back), 88, 90, 109 (back), box 3, folders 21–24, "February–September 1953."

18. Margaret Hall diary, October 14, 1956, vol. 19, "June 1956 to June 1957," diary in possession of Margaret Whitfield, Martinez, Calif.

19. Margaret Hall diary, September 30, 1956; December 17, 1956, vol. 19, "June 1956 to June 1957."

20. Alice Gorton diary, n.d., 152, box 3, folder 19, "September 1952–February 1953."

21. For example, Alice read Maud Bodkin, *Archetypal Patterns in Poetry* (1934), which combined the theories of Murray and Jung. For contemporary discussions, see

Lauriat Lane Jr., "The Literary Archetype: Some Reconsiderations," *Journal of Aesthetics and Art Criticism* 13, no. 2 (December 1954): 226–232.

22. Alice Gorton diary, n.d., 156, box 3, folder 19, "September 1952–February 1953."

23. Ibid., n.d., 132, box 2, folder 15, "January 1952–August 1952."

24. Ibid., n.d., 22 (back), folder 20, "February–September 1953."

25. Margaret Hall diary, May 21, 1953, vol. 7, "Miscellaneous, 1949–1953"; and April 20, 1955, vol. 13, "Bryn Mawr Senior 1955."

26. Alice Gorton diary, n.d., 156, box 3, folder 20, "February–September 1953."

27. Ibid., n.d., 40, box 1, folder 7, "December 1950–May 1951"; and 27, box 1 folder 14, "January–August 1952."

28. Jim M. to Alice Gorton, n.d., Alice Gorton diary, 38, box 3, folder 17, "September 1952–February 1953."

29. Alice Gorton diary, n.d., 38–40, box 3, folder 17, "September 1952– February 1953."

30. Ibid., n.d., 54, box 3, folder 17, "September 1952–February 1953."

31. Ibid., n.d., 82 (back), box 3, folder 18, "September 1952–February 1953."

32. Ibid.

33. Ibid., n.d., 85, box 3, folder 18, "September 1952–February 1953."

34. Ibid., n.d., 65, box 3, folder 18, "September 1952–February 1953."

35. Ibid., n.d., 109, 115, box 3, folder 18, "September 1952–February 1953."

36. Margaret Hall to Peter, April 20, 1955, vol. 13, "Bryn Mawr Senior 1955."

37. Margaret (Hall) Whitfield to author, April 6, 2003, letter in possession of author.

38. Margaret Hall to Peter, April 20, 1955, vol. 13, "Bryn Mawr Senior 1955."

39. One other woman is Janet Brown, whose reaction I discussed in the previous chapter. See Janet Brown to parents, January 30, 1949, box 1, folder 6, Janet Brown papers, Mount Holyoke College Archives, South Hadley, Mass.

40. Margaret Hall diary, loose sheets inserted in vol. 13, "Bryn Mawr Senior 1955."

41. Ibid.

42. Alice Gorton diary, n.d., 108 back; 84 (back)–86, box 3, folder 21, "February–September 1953."

43. Margaret Hall diary, April 20, 1955, vol. 13, "Bryn Mawr Senior 1955."

44. Ibid., September 30, 1956, vol. 19, "June 1956 to June 1957."

45. Alice Gorton diary, n.d., 152–153, box 3, folder 19, "September 1952–February 1953"; and n.d., 16, folder 24, "September 1953–September 1954."

46. Christine Stansell and Nancy Cott have illustrated a historical precedent for the dynamic we can see at work here for women in the early republic. At a time when economic changes left an increasing number of women vulnerable, advice writers countered the stereotype of women as carnal and cunning by idealizing "passionless"

women as paragons of virtue. Eventually, this notion became codified in a new norm of true womanhood and as essential traits of all women. Initially, however, women participated in the creation of the ideal because it seemed to offer them a way to exercise agency and to establish their own sphere of authority. Nancy F. Cott, "Passionlessness: An Interpretation of Victorian Sexual Ideology, 1790–1850," *Signs: Journal of Women in Culture & Society* 4, no. 2 (1978): 219–236; and Christine Stansell, *City of Women: Sex and Class in New York, 1789–1860* (New York: Knopf, 1986).

47. Margaret Hall to anonymous, April 20, 1955, vol. 13, "Bryn Mawr Senior 1955."

48. Margaret Hall diary, September 30, 1956; and Margaret Hall to anonymous, October 15, 1956, vol. 19, "June 1956 to June 1957."

49. Ibid., April 7, 1955, vol. 13, "Bryn Mawr Senior 1955."

50. Margaret Mead, "Sex and Achievement," *Forum* 5 (November 1935): 301–303.

51. For an excellent discussion of Margaret Mead's work, see Lois Banner, "Mannish Women, Passive Men, and Constitutional Types: Margaret Mead's Sex and Temperament in Three Primitive Societies as a Response to Ruth Benedict's Patterns of Culture," *Signs: Journal of Women in Culture & Society* 28, no. 3 (Spring 2003): 833–858.

52. Ibid., 834, 843, 844.

53. Margaret Hall diary, May 21, 1953, vol. 7, "Miscellaneous, 1949–1953."

54. Alice Gorton diary, n.d., 50, 52, box 3, folder 21, "February–September 1953."

55. Ibid., n.d., 143, 145, box 3, folder 19, "September 1952–February 1953."

56. Ibid., n.d., 123 (back), box 3, folder 19, "September 1952–February 1953."

57. Carolyn G. Heilbrun describes her own education in an academic environment almost entirely dominated by men in *When Men Were the Only Models We Had: My Teachers Barzun, Fadiman, and Trilling* (Philadelphia: University of Pennsylvania Press, 2002).

58. Theodore Caplow and Reece J. McGee, *The Academic Marketplace* (New York: Science editions, 1961), 111; quoted in Geraldine J. Clifford, *Lone Voyagers: Academic Women in Coeducational Universities, 1870–1937* (New York: Feminist Press, 1989), 7.

59. Alice Gorton diary, n.d., 152; also see 159, box 3, folder 19, "September 1952–February 1953."

60. Ibid., n.d., 148, box 3, folder 19, "September 1952–February 1953."

61. Margaret Hall to anonymous, October 15, 1956, diary, vol. 19, "June 1956 to June 1957."

62. Susan Sperry Borman diary, October 21, 1956, box 2, folder 16–21, Susan Delattre papers, Arthur and Elizabeth Schlesinger Library on the History of Women in America, Radcliffe Institute for Advanced Study, Harvard University, Cambridge, Mass.

63. Anne Schaffer, ed., *Dear Deedee: From the Diaries of Dori Schaffer* (Secaucus, N.J.: Lyle Stuart, 1978), 135; 137.

64. See Joanne J. Meyerowitz, ed., *Not June Cleaver: Women and Gender in Postwar America, 1945–1960* (Philadelphia: Temple University Press, 1994); Jessica Weiss: *To Have and To Hold: Marriage, the Baby Boom, and Social Change* (Chicago: University of Chicago Press, 2000); Daniel Horowitz, *Betty Friedan and the Making of "The Feminine Mystique": The American Left, the Cold War, and Modern Feminism* (Amherst: University of Massachusetts Press, 1998); and Kate Weigand, *Red Feminism: American Communism and the Making of Women's Liberation* (Baltimore: Johns Hopkins University Press, 2001).

65. Alice Gorton diary, n.d., 105, box 3, folder 19, "September 1952–February 1953."

66. Ibid., n.d., 105 (back), box 3, folder 19, "September 1952–February 1953."

67. Ibid., n.d., 123 (back), 131, box 3, folder 19, "September 1952–February 1953."

68. Ibid., n.d., 17 (back), 9–10, 29 (back), box 3, folder 20; 68, 83 (back), folder 21, "February–September 1953."

69. Ibid., n.d., 9–10, 29 (back), box 3, folder 20; 68, folder 21, "February–September 1953."

70. Susan Sperry Borman diary, November 1, 1956, box 2, folder 16–21.

71. Susan Sperry Borman to parents, April 12, 1957, box 3, folder 24.

72. Susan Sperry Borman diary, May 12, 1956, folder 16–21; and Susan to parents, May 20, 1956, box 2, folder 23.

73. Susan Sperry Borman diary, May 12, 1956; and November 5, 1956, box 2, folder 16–21.

74. Margaret Hall diary, January 10, 1955, journal vol. 13, "Bryn Mawr Senior 1955."

75. Schaffer, ed., *Dear Deedee*, 106, 92.

76. Margaret Hall diary, January 10, 1955, vol. 13, "Bryn Mawr Senior 1955"; and Susan Sperry Borman diary, May 12, 1956; and November 5, 1956, box 2, folder 16–21.

77. Alice Gorton diary, n.d., 7 (back)–8, box 3, folder 20, "February–September 1953."

78. See, for instance, Leora Tanenbaum, *Slut!: Growing Up Female with a Bad Reputation* (New York: Seven Stories Press, 1999); and Emily White, *Fast Girls: Teenage Tribes and the Myth of the Slut* (New York: Scribner, 2002).

79. Alice Gorton diary, n.d., 7–8, box 3, folder 20, "February 1953–September 1953"; and 143, folder 19, "September 1952–February 1953."

80. Ibid., n.d., 6 (back), folder 20, "February–September 1953."

81. Ibid., n.d., 103 (back); and 145, folder 19, "September 1952–February 1953."

82. Ibid., n.d., 130 (back)–131; and 84, folder 24, "February–September 1953."

83. In one of her letters she wrote that "one of the most wonderful things" she had witnessed "in this past year" was that she had "seen [Richard] change from a boy to a man." He was now "stronger, more purposeful, mature, inspiring" and she was "proud to have caused some of the change." Sandra Iger to Richard Kohler, September 25, 1959,

box 3, folder 2. In an earlier letter, by contrast, she had objected to Richard's use of the phrase "lay you." She wrote that it made her feel like "a whore." Ibid., January 15, 1958, box 1, folder 6. For Sandra's fear of nightmares, see Richard Kohler to Sandra Iger, January 16, 1961, box 6, folder 2. On the topic of their engagement, see the letters in box 2, folder 8.

84. Sandra to Richard, February 27, 1961, box 6, folder 4, "February 6–28, 1961." Also see Student Government Association Records, S. S. 3 Meetings: Minutes and Agenda, Judicial Board 1959/60 + 1960/61, box 1, folder 14, Mount Holyoke College Archives.

85. See Mabel Newcomer, *A Century of Higher Education for American Women* (New York: Harper & Row, 1959), 131.

86. For her initial impression of being part of an intelligent minority, see Sandra Iger to Richard Kohler, November 12, 1957, box 1, folder 4. For 1991 reunion questionnaire, see folder "biographical material" box 7, folder 8.

87. Alice Gorton diary, n.d., 94, 131 (back), box 3, folder 24, "February–September 1953."

88. Margaret Hall diary, October 28, 1956; and Margaret Whitfield, "Proposals: The 'Revolving Door Period' of my Life," unpublished typescript, in possession of author.

89. Alice Gorton diary, n.d., 121–122 (back), box 3, folder 24, "February–September 1953."

90. Margaret Hall diary, December 17, 1956, vol. 19, "June 1956 to June 1957."

CONCLUSION

1. The biographical information on Alice Gorton Hart, Susan Sperry Borman Delattre, and Sandra Iger Kohler can be found in their papers. Margaret Hall Whitfield kindly shared her vita with me. My information about June Calender is from an e-mail exchange: June Calender, correspondence with author, e-mail dated July 11, 2008 and July 12, 2008.

Selected Bibliography

PRIMARY SOURCES

Adorno, Theodore W., Else Frenkel-Brunswik, and Daniel J. Levinson. *The Authoritarian Personality*. New York: Harper, 1950.

American Association of University Professors. "The Post-War Responsibilities of Liberal Education." *Bulletin of the American Association of University Professors* 29, no. 3 (June 1943): 412–431.

Bell, Elouise M., ed. *"Will I Ever Forget this Day?" Excerpts from the Diaries of Carol Lynn Pearson*. Salt Lake City, Utah: Bookcraft, 1980.

Bodkin, Maud. *Archetypal Patterns in Poetry*. London: Oxford University Press, 1934.

Butz, Otto. *The Unsilent Generation: An Anonymous Symposium in which Eleven College Seniors Look at Themselves and Their World*. New York: Rinehart, 1958.

"Catholicism in America: A Series of Articles from *The Commonweal*." New York: Harcourt, Brace & Co., 1953.

Duvall, Evelyn Millis. *Facts of Life and Love for Teenagers*. New York: Association Press, 1950.

Erikson, Erik. *Childhood and Society*. New York: Norton, 1950.

Erskine, John. "The World Will Belong to the Women." *New York Times*, March 14, 1943: SM 15.

Freud, Sigmund. *Civilization and Its Discontents*. New York: Norton, 1961.

Friedan, Betty. *The Feminine Mystique*. New York: Norton, 1963.

Fromm, Erich. *Escape from Freedom*. New York: Holt, Rinehart Winston, 1941.

Hartshorne, Edward Y. "Undergraduate Society and the College Culture." *American Sociological Review* 8, no. 3 (1943): 321–332.

Havemann, Ernest, and Patricia Salter West. *They Went to College: The College Graduate in America Today*. New York: Harcourt, Brace, 1952.

Herberg, Will. *Protestant-Catholic-Jew: An Essay in American Religious Sociology*. Rev. ed. Garden City, N.Y.: Doubleday, 1960.

Hobart, Charles W. "Freshman Disorientation." *Improving College and University Teaching* 9, no. 2 (Spring 1961): 77–78.

Hollingshead, August B. *Elmtown's Youth*. New York: John Wiley, 1949.

Janney, J. E. "Fad and Fashion Leadership among Undergraduate Women." *Journal of Abnormal and Social Psychology* 36 (April 1941): 275–278.

Kinsey, Alfred C., Wardell B. Pomeroy, and Clyde E. Martin. *Sexual Behavior in the Human Male*. Philadelphia: W. B. Saunders, 1948.

Kinsey, Alfred C., Wardell B. Pomeroy, Clyde E. Martin, and Paul H. Gebhard. *Sexual Behavior in the Human Female*. Philadelphia: W. B. Saunders, 1953.

Kirkpatrick, Clifford, Sheldon Stryker, and Philip Buell. "An Experimental Study of Attitudes towards Male Sex Behavior with Reference to Kinsey Findings." *American Sociological Review* 17, no. 5 (October 1952): 580–587.

Komarovsky, Mirra. *Women in the Modern World: Their Education and Their Dilemmas*. Boston: Little, Brown, 1953.

Lane, Lauriat, Jr. "The Literary Archetype: Some Reconsiderations," *Journal of Aesthetics and Art Criticism* 13, no. 2 (1954): 226–232.

Lazarsfeld, Paul F., and Wagner Thielens Jr. *The Academic Mind: Social Scientists in a Time of Crisis*. Glencoe, Ill.: Free Press, 1958.

Lindner, Robert Mitchell. *Must You Conform?* New York: Rinehart, 1956.

Lundberg, Ferdinand, and Marynia F. Farnham. *Modern Woman: The Lost Sex*. New York: Harper, 1947.

Mead, Margaret. *And Keep Your Powder Dry: An Anthropologist Looks at America*. New York: William Morrow, 1942.

McComb, Mary C. *Great Depression and the Middle Class: Experts, Collegiate Youth, and Business Ideology, 1929–1941*. New York: Routledge, 2006.

———. *Male and Female: A Study of the Sexes in a Changing World*. New York: William Morrow, 1949.

———. "Sex and Achievement." *Forum* 5 (November 1935): 301–303.

Menninger, Karl A. *Love against Hate*. New York: Harcourt, Brace & World, 1942.

Mills, C. Wright. *White Collar: The American Middle Classes*. New York: Oxford University Press, 1951.

Moncrieff, Lucille. "Manhattan Girl with a Job." *Mademoiselle* (November 1946): 180–183, 282–286.

Montagu, Ashley. *The Natural Superiority of Women*. New York: Macmillan, 1952.

Nazareth, Peter. "D. H. Lawrence and Sex." *Transitions* 6/7 (October 1962): 54–57.

———. "D. H. Lawrence and Sex." *Transitions* 8 (March 1963): 38–43.

Newcomer, Mabel. *A Century of Higher Education for American Women*. New York: Harper & Row, 1959.

Packard, Vance. *The Hidden Persuaders*. New York: Mckay, 1957.

Patterson, Margaret E. "Shortage of Scientists." *The Science News-Letter* 50, no. 14 (October 5, 1946): 218–220.

Popenoe, Paul. *Marriage: Before and After*. New York: Wilfred Func, 1943.

————. *Modern Marriage: A Handbook.* New York: Macmillan, 1925.

Reich, Wilhelm, and Theodore P. Wolfe. *The Mass Psychology of Fascism.* 1933; First English ed., New York: Orgone Institute Press, 1946.

Reiss, Ira. *Premarital Sexual Standards in America: A Sociological Investigation of the Relative Social and Cultural Integration of American Sexual Standards.* Glencoe, Ill.: Free Press, 1960.

Riesman, David, with Nathan Glazer and Reuel Denney. *The Lonely Crowd: A Study of the Changing American Character.* New Haven: Yale University Press, 1950.

Schaffer, Anne, ed. *Dear Deedee: From the Diaries of Dori Schaffer.* Secaucus, N.J.: Lyle Stuart, 1978.

Sheen, Fulton John. *Three to Get Married.* New York: Appleton-Century-Crofts, 1951.

Smith College. "Rules and Regulations." Northampton, Mass.: Smith College Archives, n.d.

Spilka, Mark. *The Love Ethic of D. H. Lawrence.* Bloomington: Indiana University Press, 1955.

State University of Iowa. "Code for Coeds, 1944–1945."

Stevenson, Adlai. "A Purpose for Modern Woman." *Women's Home Companion.* September 1955, 30–31.

Strecker, Edward. *Their Mothers' Sons: The Psychiatrist Examines an American Problem.* Philadelphia: Lippincott, 1946.

Wallace, Isabel K. "Women's Use of Leisure." *Journal of Higher Education* 14, no. 6 (1943): 301–342.

Waller, Willard. "The Rating and Dating Complex." *American Sociological Review* 2 (1937): 727–734.

Women's League/Women's Self-Government Association/Association of Women Students Records. Center for Archival Collections, Bowling Green State University, Bowling Green, Ohio.

Whicher, George F. "Education for Democracy." *Bulletin of the American Association of University Professors* 31, no. 1 (Spring 1945): 60–71.

Wylie, Philip. *An Essay on Morals.* New York: Rinehart, 1947.

————. *Generation of Vipers.* New York: Farrar and Rinehart, 1942.

SECONDARY SOURCES

Anderson, James D. "Race, Meritocracy, and the American Academy during the Immediate Post–World War II Era." *History of Education Quarterly* 33, no. 2 (1993): 150–175.

Arnett, Jeffrey J. "Emerging Adulthood: A Theory of Development from the Late Teens through the Twenties." *American Psychologist* 55 (May 2000): 469–480.

Bailey, Beth L. *From Front Porch to Back Seat: Courtship in Twentieth-Century America.* Baltimore: Johns Hopkins University Press, 1988.

———. "From Panty Raids to Revolution: Youth and Authority, 1950–1970." In *Generations of Youth: Youth Cultures and History in Twentieth-Century America,* ed. Joe Austin and Michael Nevin Willard, 187–204. New York: New York University Press, 1998.

———. "Scientific Truth . . . and Love: The Marriage Education Movement in the United States." *Journal of Social History* 20, no. 4 (Summer 1987): 711–732.

Banner, Lois. "Mannish Women, Passive Men, and Constitutional Types: Margaret Mead's Sex and Temperament in Three Primitive Societies as a Response to Ruth Benedict's Patterns of Culture." *Signs: Journal of Women in Culture & Society* 28, no. 3 (Spring 2003): 833–858.

Baumeister, Roy F. *Identity: Cultural Change and the Struggle for Self.* New York: Oxford University Press, 1986.

Bérubé, Allan. *Coming Out under Fire: The History of Gay Men and Women in World War Two.* New York: Free Press, 1990.

Black, Allida M. *Casting Her Own Shadow: Eleanor Roosevelt and the Shaping of Postwar Liberalism.* New York: Columbia University Press, 1996.

Bordin, Ruth. *Women at Michigan: The "Dangerous Experiment," 1870s to the Present.* Ann Arbor: University of Michigan Press, 1999.

Breines, Wini. *Young, White, and Miserable: Growing up Female in the 1950s.* Boston: Beacon Press, 1992.

Brodkin, Karen. *How Jews Became White Folks.* New Brunswick, N.J.: Rutgers University Press, 1998.

Buhle, Mari Jo. *Feminism and Its Discontents: A Century of Struggle with Psychoanalysis.* Cambridge, Mass.: Harvard University Press, 1998.

Bunkers, Suzanne L., and Cynthia A. Huff, eds. *Inscribing the Daily: Critical Essays on Women's Diaries.* Amherst: University of Massachusetts Press, 1996.

Campbell, D'Ann. *Women at War with America: Private Lives in a Patriotic Era.* Cambridge, Mass.: Harvard University Press, 1984.

Celello, Kristin. *Making Marriage Work: A History of Marriage and Divorce in the Twentieth-Century United States.* Chapel Hill: University of North Carolina Press, 2009.

Clark, Daniel A. "The Two Joes Meet. Joe College, Joe Veteran: The G.I. Bill, College Education, and Postwar American Culture." *History of Education Quarterly* 38, no. 2 (Summer 1998): 165–189.

Cohen, Robert. *When the Old Left Was Young: Student Radicals and America's First Mass Student Movement: 1929–1941.* New York: Oxford University Press, 1993.

Conable, Charlotte Williams. *Women at Cornell: The Myth of Equal Education.* Ithaca, N.Y.: Cornell University Press, 1977.

Coontz, Stephanie. *The Way We Never Were: American Families and the Nostalgia Trap.* New York: Basic Books, 1992.

Cott, Nancy F. *The Grounding of Modern Feminism.* New Haven, Conn.: Yale University Press, 1987.

———. "Passionlessness: An Interpretation of Victorian Sexual Ideology, 1790–1850." *Signs: Journal of Women in Culture & Society* 4 (1978): 219–236.

Culley, Margo, ed. *A Day at a Time: The Diary Literature of American Women from 1764 to the Present.* New York: Feminist Press at City University of New York, 1985.

Cuordileone, K. A. *Manhood and American Political Culture in the Cold War.* New York: Routledge, 2005.

———. "'Politics in an Age of Anxiety': Cold War Political Culture and the Crisis in American Masculinity, 1949–1960." *Journal of American History* 87, no. 2 (September 2000): 515–545.

Davis, Rebecca L. "'Not Marriage at All, but Simple Harlotry': The Companionate Marriage Controversy." *Journal of American History* 94, no. 4 (March 2008): 1137–1163.

Dean, Robert. *Imperial Brotherhood: Gender and the Making of Cold War Foreign Policy.* Amherst: University of Massachusetts Press, 2001.

D'Emilio, John, and Estelle B. Freedman. *Intimate Matters: A History of Sexuality in America.* New York: Harper & Row, 1988.

Devlin, Rachel. *Relative Intimacy: Fathers, Daughters, and Postwar American Culture.* Chapel Hill: University of North Carolina Press, 2005.

Eagan, Eileen. *Class, Culture, and the Classroom: The Student Peace Movement of the 1930s.* Philadelphia: Temple University Press, 1981.

Eisenmann, Linda. *Higher Education for Women in Postwar America, 1945–1965.* Baltimore: Johns Hopkins University Press, 2006.

Erikson, Erik. *Identity, Youth, and Crisis.* New York: Norton, 1968.

Evans, Sara. *Born for Liberty: A History of Women in America.* New York: Free Press, 1989.

———. *Journeys that Opened up the World: Women, Student Christian Movements, and Social Justice, 1955–1975.* New Brunswick, N.J.: Rutgers University Press, 2003.

Evans, Stephanie Y. *Black Women in the Ivory Tower, 1850–1954.* Gainesville: University Press of Florida, 2007.

Fass, Paula. *The Damned and the Beautiful: American Youth in the 1920s.* New York: Oxford University Press, 1977.

Freeland, Richard M. *Academia's Golden Age: Universities in Massachusetts, 1945–1970.* New York: Oxford University Press, 1992.

Gilbert, James B. *Men in the Middle: Searching for Masculinity in the 1950s.* Chicago: University of Chicago Press, 2005.

Gillon, Steven. *Politics and Vision: The ADA and American Liberalism, 1947–1985.* New York: Oxford University Press, 1987.

Gordon, Lynn D. "The Gibson Girl Goes to College: Popular Culture and Women's Higher Education in the Progressive Era, 1880–1920." *American Quarterly* 39, no. 2 (Summer 1987): 211–230.

Graebner, William. *The Age of Doubt: American Thought and Culture in the 1940s.* Boston: Twayne Publishers, 1991.

———. "Coming of Age in Buffalo: The Ideology of Maturity in Postwar America." *Radical History Review* 34 (1986): 53–74.

Graham, Patricia A. "Expansion and Exclusion: A History of Women in American Higher Education." *Signs: Journal of Women in Culture & Society* 3, no. 4 (Summer 1978): 759–773.

Griffith, R. Marie. "The Religious Encounters of Alfred C. Kinsey." *Journal of American History* 95, no. 2 (September 2008): 349–377.

Halbwachs, Maurice. *On Collective Memory.* Edited and translated by Lewis A. Coser. Chicago: University of Chicago Press, 1992.

Hartmann, Ellen. *The Home Front and Beyond: American Women in the 1940s.* Boston: Twayne Publishers, 1982.

Heale, Michael. *McCarthy's Americans: Red Scare Politics in State and Nation, 1930–1965.* London: Macmillan, 1998.

Hegarty, Marilyn E. *Victory Girls, Khaki-Wackies, and Patriotutes: The Regulation of Female Sexuality during World War II.* New York: New York University Press, 2008.

Heilbrun, Carolyn G. *When Men Were the Only Models We Had: My Teachers Barzun, Fadiman, and Trilling.* Philadelphia: University of Pennsylvania Press, 2002.

Hellbeck, Jochen. *Revolution on My Mind: Writing a Diary under Stalin.* Cambridge, Mass.: Harvard University Press, 2006.

Herman, Ellen. *The Romance of American Psychology: Political Culture in the Age of Experts.* Berkeley: University of California Press, 1995.

Holland, Dorothy C. *Educated in Romance: Women, Achievement, and College Culture.* Chicago: University of Chicago Press, 1990.

Horowitz, Daniel. *The Anxieties of Affluence: Critiques of American Consumer Culture, 1939–1979.* Amherst: University of Massachusetts Press, 2004.

———. *Betty Friedan and the Making of "The Feminine Mystique": The American Left, the Cold War, and Modern Feminism.* Amherst: University of Massachusetts Press, 1998.

Horowitz, Helen L. *Alma Mater: Design and Experience in the Women's Colleges from Their Nineteenth Century Beginnings to the 1930s.* New York: Knopf, 1984.

———. *Campus Life: Undergraduate Cultures from the End of the Eighteenth Century to the Present.* New York: Knopf, 1987.

————. "In the Wake of Laurence Veysey: Re-examining the Liberal Arts College." *History of Education Quarterly* 45, no. 3 (September 2005): 420–426.

————. *Rereading Sex: Battles over Sexual Knowledge and Suppression in Nineteenth-Century America.* New York: Knopf, 2002.

Hunter, Jane. *How Young Ladies Became Girls: The Victorian Origins of American Girlhood.* New Haven, Conn.: Yale University Press, 2002.

Johnson, David. *The Lavender Scare: The Cold War Persecution of Gays and Lesbians in the Federal Government.* Chicago: University of Chicago Press, 2004.

Jumonville, Neil. *Critical Crossings: The New York Intellectuals in Postwar America.* Berkeley: University of California Press, 1991.

Kagle, Steven E., and Lorenza Gramegna. "Rewriting Her Life: Fictionalization and the Use of Fictional Models in Early American Women's Diaries." In *Inscribing the Daily: Critical Essays on Women's Diaries,* ed. Suzanne L. Bunkers and Cynthia A. Huff, 38–55. Amherst: University of Massachusetts Press, 1996.

Kaledin, Eugenia. *Mothers and More: American Women in the 1950s.* Boston: Twayne Publishers, 1984.

Kalish, Jennifer. "Spouse Devouring Black Widows and their Neutered Mates: Postwar Suburbanization. A Battle over Domestic Space." *UCLA Historical Journal* 14 (special issue, 1994): 128–154.

Kendall, Elaine. *"Peculiar Institutions": An Informal History of the Seven Sister Colleges.* New York: G. P. Putnam's Sons, 1976.

Kessler-Harris, Alice. "Gender Ideology in Historical Reconstruction: A Case Study from the 1930s." *Gender and History* 1 (Spring 1989): 31–49.

Ladd-Taylor, Molly. "Eugenics, Sterilization, and Modern Marriage in the USA: The Strange Career of Paul Popenoe." *Gender & History* 13, no. 2 (August 2001): 298–327.

LaFollette, Marcel C. "Eyes on the Stars: Images of Women Scientists in Popular Magazines." *Science, Technology, & Human Values* 13, no. 3–4 (Summer–Fall 1988): 262–275.

Landrum, Stephanie Renee. "'More Firmly Based Today': Anti-Communism, Academic Freedom, and Smith College, 1947–1956." Senior thesis, Smith College, 1998.

Lemann, Nicholas. *The Big Test: The Secret History of the American Meritocracy.* New York: Farrar, Straus and Giroux, 1999.

Levine, David O. *The American College and the Culture of Aspiration, 1915–1940.* Ithaca, N.Y.: Cornell University Press, 1986.

Lowe, Margaret A. *Looking Good: College Women and Body Image, 1875–1930.* Baltimore: Johns Hopkins University Press, 2003.

Lynn, Susan. *Progressive Women in Conservative Times: Racial Justice, Peace, and Feminism, 1945 to the 1960s.* New Brunswick, N.J.: Rutgers University Press, 1992.

Marchand, Roland. "Visions of Classlessness, Quests for Dominions: American Popular Culture." In *Reshaping America: Society and Institutions, 1945–1960*, ed. Robert H. Bremner and Gary W. Reichard, 163–190. Columbus, Ohio University Press, 1982.

May, Elaine Tyler. *Homeward Bound: American Families in the Cold War Era*. New York: Basic Books, 1988.

McCandless, Amy T. *The Past in the Present: Women's Higher Education in the Twentieth-Century American South*. Tuscaloosa: University of Alabama Press, 1999.

McComb, Mary C. "Rate Your Date: Young Women and the Commodification of Depression Era Courtship." In *Delinquents and Debutantes: Twentieth Century American Girls' Cultures*, ed. Sherrie A. Inness, 40–60. New York: New York University Press, 1998.

Meyer, Leisa D. *Creating G.I. Jane: Sexuality and Power in the Women's Army Corps during World War II*. New York: Columbia University Press, 1996.

Meyerowitz, Joanne J. "Beyond the Feminine Mystique: A Reassessment of Postwar Mass Culture, 1946–1948." *Journal of American History* 79, no. 4 (March 1993): 1455–1482.

———, ed. *Not June Cleaver: Women and Gender in Postwar America, 1945–1960*. Philadelphia: Temple University Press, 1994.

———. "Women, Cheesecake, and Borderline Material: Responses to Girlie Pictures in the Mid-Twentieth-Century U.S." *Journal of Women's History* 8, no. 3 (Fall 1996): 9–35.

Milkman, Ruth. *Gender at Work: The Dynamics of Job Segregation by Sex during World War II*. Urbana: University of Illinois Press, 1987.

Mintz, Steven, and Susan Kellogg. *Domestic Revolutions: A Social History of American Family Life*. New York: Free Press, 1989.

Olsen, Deborah M. "Remaking the Image: Promotional Literature of Mount Holyoke, Smith, and Wellesley Colleges in the Mid-to-Late 1940s." *History of Education Quarterly* 40, no. 4 (Winter 2000): 418–459.

Palmieri, Patricia A. "From Republican Motherhood to Race Suicide: Arguments on the Higher Education of Women in the United States, 1820–1920." In *Educating Men and Women Together: Coeducation in a Changing World*, ed. Carol Lasser, 49–64. Urbana: University of Illinois Press in conjunction with Oberlin College, 1987.

Perkins, Linda M. "The African American Female Elite: The Early History of African American Women in the Seven Sister Colleges, 1880–1960." *Harvard Educational Review* 67, no. 4 (Winter 1997): 718–756.

Plant, Rebecca Jo. "The Repeal of Mother Love: Momism and the Reconstruction of Motherhood in Philip Wylie's America." Ph.D. diss., Johns Hopkins University, 2001.

Ravitch, Diane. *The Troubled Crusade: American Education, 1945–1980*. New York: Basic Books, 1983.

Roediger, David. *Working toward Whiteness. How America's Immigrants Became White: The Strange Journey from Ellis Island to the Suburbs*. New York: Basic Books, 2006.

Rose, Lisle Abbott. *The Cold War Comes to Main Street: America in 1950*. Lawrence: University Press of Kansas, 1999.

Rosenzweig, Linda W. *Another Self: Middle-Class American Women and Their Friends in the Twentieth Century*. New York: New York University Press, 1999.

Rossiter, Margaret W. *Women Scientists in America: Before Affirmative Action, 1940–1972*. Baltimore: Johns Hopkins University Press, 1995.

Rupp, Leila. *Mobilizing Women for War: German and American Propaganda, 1939–1945*. Princeton, N.J.: Princeton University Press, 1978.

Scharf, Lois. *To Work and To Wed: Female Employment, Feminism, and the Great Depression*. Westport, Conn.: Greenwood Press, 1980.

Schrecker, Ellen. *Many Are the Crimes: McCarthyism in America*. Boston: Little, Brown, 1998.

———. *No Ivory Tower: McCarthyism and the Universities*. New York: Oxford University Press, 1986.

Shoemaker, Nancy, ed. *Negotiators of Change: Historical Perspectives on Native-American Women*. New York: Routledge, 1995.

Simmons, Christina. "Modern Sexuality and the Myth of Victorian Repression." In *Passion and Power: Sexuality in History*, ed. Christina Simmons and Kathy Peiss, 157–177. Philadelphia: Temple University Press, 1989.

Solomon, Barbara. *In the Company of Educated Women: A History of Women and Higher Education in America*. New Haven, Conn.: Yale University Press, 1985.

Spurlock, John C., and Cynthia A. Magistro. *New and Improved: The Transformation of American Women's Emotional Culture*. New York: New York University Press, 1998.

Stansell, Christine. *City of Women: Sex and Class in New York, 1789–1860*. Urbana: University of Illinois Press, 1987.

Staub, Michael E. "'Negroes Are Not Jews': Race, Holocaust Consciousness, and the Rise of Jewish Neoconservatism." *Radical History Review* 75 (Fall 1999): 3–27.

Steinmetz, Suzanne K., and Gary W. Peterson. *Pioneering Paths in the Study of Families: The Lives and Careers of Family Scholars*. New York: Haworth Press, 2002.

Story, Ronald. "The Ordeal of the Public Sector: The University of Massachusetts." In *Five Colleges: Five Histories*, ed. Ronald Story, 51–78. Amherst: Five Colleges, Inc. and Historic Deerfield, 1992.

Synnott, Marcia Graham. *The Half-Opened Door: Discrimination and Admission at Harvard, Yale, and Princeton, 1900–1970*. Westport, Conn.: Greenwood Press, 1979.

Tanenbaum, Leora. *Slut! Growing Up Female with a Bad Reputation*. New York: Seven Stories Press, 1999.

Thelin, John R. *A History of American Higher Education*. Baltimore: Johns Hopkins University Press, 2004.

Ulrich, Laurel Thatcher, ed. *Yards and Gates: Gender in Harvard and Radcliffe History.* New York: Palgrave Macmillan, 2004.

Walker, Janet. *Couching Resistance: Women, Film, and Psychoanalytic Psychiatry.* Minneapolis: University of Minnesota Press, 1993.

Wang, Jessica. *American Science in an Age of Anxiety: Scientists, Anticommunism, and the Cold War.* Chapel Hill: University of North Carolina Press, 1999.

Wechsler, Harold D. "An Academic Gresham's Law: Group Repulsion as a Theme in American Higher Education." *Teachers College Record* 82 (Summer 1981): 567–588.

Weiler, Peter. "British Labour and the Cold War: The Foreign Policy of the Labour Governments, 1945–1951." *Journal of British Studies* 26 (January 1987): 54–82.

Weiss, Jessica. *To Have and To Hold: Marriage, the Baby Boom, and Social Change.* Chicago: University of Chicago Press, 2000.

Westbrook, Robert B. "'I Want a Girl, Just Like the Girl That Married Harry James': American Women and the Problem of Political Obligation in World War II." *American Quarterly* 42, no. 4 (December 1990): 587–614.

White, Emily. *Fast Girls: Teenage Tribes and the Myth of the Slut.* New York: Scribner, 2002.

White, E. Frances. *Dark Continent of Our Bodies: Black Feminism and the Politics of Respectability.* Philadelphia: Temple University Press, 2001.

Williams, Brian A. *Michigan on the March: The University of Michigan in World War II.* Ann Arbor: University of Michigan, Bentley Historical Library, December 1995.

Index

abortions, 120

academia, *see* colleges and universities; higher education

"Address Unknown" (Hall), 203n.41

adjustment, in advice literature, 27, 77–78

admissions, colleges and universities: quotas, 50; and standardized tests, 50, 188n.17

adolescence, as time of introspection, 79

Adorno, Theodor, 72

advertising: and political fanaticism, 81; and the promotion of single-sex women's colleges, 54–55

advice literature: bolsters Alice Gorton's arguments against early sex, 128; conservative, 6–7; etiquette, 115; informed by mental health experts, 77–78; marital, 65; on the mature individual, 27; and the passionless woman, 211–212n.46; as purveyor of middle-class morality, 108

affluence, 79, 80; and ability to "score" dates, 85; of Ivy League families, 188n.15; new, of Catholic and Jewish families, 44. *See also* prosperity

African Americans: middle-class, 63, 69; postwar discrimination against, in academia, 50; prejudice against, 197n.60; scarcity of diaries and letters, 19; women's labor and politicization, 9

agency: insistence on feminine distinctiveness as, 7; and passionlessness, 212n.46

alibi function of dating, 100

American Labor Party, 39

American Quarterly (academic journal), 200n.7

American Social Hygiene Association, 191n.41

American Student Union, 20

American Studies, as academic discipline, 80, 200n.7

And Keep Your Powder Dry (Mead), 203n.42

anticommunism, 46, 66–67; parental and priestly, 70, 71. *See also* communism

antifeminism, 54, 55

anti-Semitism: American, 35; European, 23, 24; in higher education, 62; open expression of, loses favor after war, 50

anxiety, societal, Cold War–era, 79; about masculinity, 81, 108–109, 130–131; spike in homophobia, 99–100, 109

apartheid, in southern U.S., 189n.18

appeasement, prewar failure of, 20

Archetypal Patterns in Poetry (Bodkin), 210n.21

archetype: and femininity, 148–150, 151; and sexuality, Alice Gorton on, 159

"The Artistic Use of Myth in Certain Poems of William Blake and T. S. Eliot" (Gorton), 148

assault and battery, and sexual "roguishness," 106

assimilation, 40, 63

athletic teams, exclusivity of, 48

Attlee, Clement, 42

Austin, Warren, 37

authenticity, 79

The Authoritarian Personality (Adorno et al.), 72

authority: cultural, of mental health experts, 85; through gender difference, 158

autonomy, sexual and social, of young women in wartime, 111–112

baby boom, postwar, 52, 80–81

Bailey, Beth, 25, 126

bar culture, homosexual, 109

Barnard College: accessibility to Jewish students, 61; Komarovsky's study, 93–94, 104

Beat subculture, 145–146. *See also* bohemianism

Beck, Margaret, 34

Beck, Patricia: as Bennington misfit, 34–35; friendship with faculty wife, 99

The Bell Jar (Plath), 193n.3

Bennington College, 34, 35

conformity, 88, 138; and advice literature, 27; Cold War, 46; discourse on pitfalls of, 94; and elevated social status, 40; in female student culture, 44, 193n.3; to group mores, *vs.* absolute right, 123; as intelligent comprehension of one's own best interests, 125; student ambivalence about, 78; and YWCA student-branch literature, 185n.7. *See also* nonconformity
conscription, *see* draft
consumer culture, 79, 80, 81, 138
contraceptives, 120, 127
Coontz, Stephanie, 3
Cosmopolitan Club, Iowa State University, 57
Cott, Nancy, 211n.46
courtship culture: postwar, 84–85; wartime shifts in, 112, 114–115. *See also* dating culture
crisis of masculinity, alleged, 108–109
critical thinking, women students' acquisition of, 41, 45, 60, 180
"cruiser" servicemen, 112, 116
Cultural and Scientific Conference for World Peace, 67. *See also* Waldorf Conference
"cultural conformist" policy makers, 195n.28
cultural critics, 79–80, 81, 139, 177, 179
culture brokers, women students as, 21, 56–57, 65–66, 75
culture lag, 27
curfews, 121, 172, 180
curricula: cutting-edge, at women's colleges, 187n.12; gender-specific, 53, 55–57; postwar, national narrative underlying, 81–82; preparing women to be wives and mothers, 53, 203n.41; women authorities virtually absent from, 162

Dalton (prep school), 23
dances, USO, 39–40, 113–114
date rape, male fantasy of, 106
dating, 26; media images of, 191n.41; as preparation for marriage, 29; sexualization of, 7–8, 106; utility of, 136; as youth norm, 28
dating culture, 115; implicit gendered conflicts in, 110; postwar, 84–85, 100–104, 117–118; smart women as role models within, 96
Davis, Herbert, 22
Davis, Rebecca, 14

Davis, Robert Gorham, 173
day students, marginalization of, 63
debutantes, upper-class, as norm, 36
decision making, within marriage, 14
defense industry, wartime, women in, 36, 111
Delattre, Susan, *see* Borman, Susan Sperry
delayed gratification, 108
delinquency, male to female ratio, 206n.14
Democracy in America (Tocqueville), 200n.7
Depression, *see* Great Depression
desires: lack of language to discuss, 127; unconscious, danger of, 81
Deutsch, Helene, 85–86, 108
deviancy, sexual, and homosocial spaces, 54
diaries, 8; and the construction of female identity, 6; as exploration of identities, 11; mythmaking and the production of ideology in, 83–84; as source texts, 4–5
dieting, 174
"difference" feminism, Margaret Hall's formulation of, 159–160
diversity: on campus, and the G.I. Bill, 118–119; government public relations campaign to promote, 19; of identity, and ideology of individualism, 93–94; socioeconomic, spread of, on Depression-era college campuses, 17–18
divorce: condemned by Pius XI, 191n.47; and lack of dating experience, 26; rising rates of, in 1920s, 13, 25; U.S. postwar rate highest in world, 54
domination: female, through sexual limit-setting, 140; "mastering" woman within partnership, 144, 145
double standard, 121–122, 130, 136, 151, 152, 153, 158
draft: Wadsworth-Austin proposal, for women, 37; wartime, for men, 37–38
Drew, Elizabeth, 163, 169
drinking, public, by college women, 111
"drips": female, 32; male, 118. *See also* "grinds"
Du Bois, W.E.B., 70
Dushkin, Lelah, discusses sexuality with mother, 131–132
Duvall, Evelyn Millis, 123–126

education: financed by student employment, 188nn.15–16 (*see also* financial aid); and power relations in family, 60–61
egalitarianism, economic and intellectual, 104

exclusions of, lose favor after war, 49;
experience discrimination, 188n.17;
female students, 175; parent-student
perspective gap, 62–63; in postwar
diversification, 51
Jews: as civil rights supporters, 189n.18;
newly affluent, 44; prejudice against, 30,
118, 197n.60 (*see also* anti-Semitism); and
youth culture, 29
jobs, student, financing education,
188nn.15–16
Judy, friend of Alice Gorton, 95, 97
Jung, C. G., 148, 151, 210n.21
junior colleges, 10

Kaledin, Eugenia, 58
Kedney, Janet, on Reinhold Niebuhr, 46
Kendall, Eileen, 4
Kennedy, Frank Hunter, 141
Kennedy, Margaret, 107; boyfriend's
marriage ideas, 141–143
Kennedy, Philip, 105–107, 141
"khaki wackies," 111, 113
Kinsey, Alfred C., 122; research team
raises awareness of male homosexuality,
109
Kinsey reports, 122, 156; public discussion
of, 208n.44. *See also Sexual Behavior in the
Human Female; Sexual Behavior in the
Human Male*
Koestler, Arthur, 72
Kohler, Richard, 90, 132–135, 143–144, 181
Komarovsky, Mirra, 93–94, 104, 161

labor shortages, wartime, 37
language, lack of, to discuss desires, 127
Lauterbach, Judith: and campus social life,
35; discusses politics with father, 23–24,
46; on Jewish campus organizations,
190n.37
Lauterbach, Leo, 23
Lawrence, D. H., 137, 139, 203n.42
layoffs, Depression-era, male *vs.* female,
187n.11
League of Nations, failure of U.S. to join,
20–21
lesbianism: and displays of female intellect,
32; as prolonged immaturity, 54
letters, as source documents, 9
Levine, Lawrence, 18
Lindner, Robert, 128–129
Lodge, Henry Cabot, Jr., 42
The Lonely Crowd (Riesman), 80, 132,
201n.13, 203n.42

love, "true" *vs.* "Hollywood," 28
"love making," 127
love object, want of, 4
Lundberg, Ferdinand, 85

Mademoiselle magazine, 2
Mad Men cable TV series, 3–4
Magistro, Cynthia, 6
"Manhattan Girl with a Job" (Moncrieff),
2–3
Marcus, Antoinette Brody, 61–62, 63
Marcus, Jacob Rader, 61–62, 63
Marcus, Merle Judith: parental
expectations of respectability, 61–62,
63; study and career plans, 74
marginalization: of day students, 29–30; of
female academics, 162–163; of "grinds,"
31–32; of least popular students, 30–31; of
political nonconformists, 31; by religion,
class, or ethnic origin, 29–30
marriage: companionate, 13–14, 26;
as flight into security, 88, 89; media
images of, 191n.41; postwar boom,
52, 80–81; privileging of, 5 (*see also*
heteronormativity); as questionably
fulfilling, 87–88; as ultimate prize, 86
marriage counseling, 190n.40
Mary Charlotte, friend of Susan Sperry
Borman, 95
masculinity: Cold War–era anxieties about,
81, 108–109, 130–131; fear of emasculation,
130, 200n.10
masculinization of middle-class culture, 108
Massachusetts State, 117–118. *See also*
University of Massachusetts
"mass man" discourse, 80
mass media: concepts of femininity
internalized from, 77; coverage of
women in wartime work, 37; images of
relationships, dating, and marriage in,
190n.40; midcentury expansion of, 81;
print, as purveyors of middle-class
morality, 108; unrealistic portrayal of
relationships in, 26
The Mass Psychology of Fascism (Reich and
Wolfe), 198n.68
"mastering" woman within partnership,
144, 145. *See also* domination
masturbation, female, 121
material culture, and postwar prosperity,
80–81
May, Elaine Tyler, 4
McCarthy, Joseph, 46, 68, 72, 173
McCarthyism, 46

studiousness, wartime, praised by Smith
campus newspaper, 31. *See also* "grinds"
supervised courtship, 115
Swiderski, Paul, 35

"talented tenth," 70
"Tasha," friend of Merle Marcus, 63–64
teacher's colleges, 10
technocrats, fear of, 56
Thomas, Norman, 47, 173, 194n.12
Tocqueville, Alexis de, 200n.7
To Fly Once More (Hart), 181
To Have and To Hold (Weiss), 5
totalitarianism, and defense of free
speech, 67
"trouble," getting into, 124
"true love" *vs.* "Hollywood love," 28
trueness to self, 78–79. *See also* authenticity

unconscious, collective, 148–149, 159
unconscious desires, dangerous, 81
United States Armed Forces Institute
Marriage and the Family courses, 124
United States Children's Bureau, on male-
to-female delinquency ratio, 206n.14
University of Massachusetts: looked down
on by Smith students, 103; postwar
enrollment surge, 117–118
University of North Carolina, challenge to
moral regulations at Women's College
(1953), 126
urban Northeast, students from outside, 44.
See also WASP elite
USO (United Service Organizations), 38–39,
112–113; dances, 39–40

vaginal penetration, penile, as "real" sex, 110
value judgments, class- and ethnicity-
based, 33. *See also* prejudice
vernacular sexuality, *vs.* middle-class
morality, 108, 205n.7
veterans: female, and G.I. Bill eligibility,
195n.21; as postwar students, 116, 119,
194n.15
Victory Ball, Mount Holyoke (1943), 113–114
The Vital Center (Schlesinger), 72, 109–10

Wadsworth, James W., 37
wage labor, women's: ambivalence
toward, during Depression, 14;
marriage/wage-labor choice, 9;
wartime, 36
Walden School, 23–24
Waldorf Conference, 67–68

Wallace, Henry, 68
Waller, Willard, 85, 104
WASP (White Anglo-Saxon Protestant)
elite, 18, 31, 44, 51
Wechsler, Harold, 190n.37
weekends, in student culture, 87; and
exodus from single-sex women's
colleges, 58; football, 58; off-campus,
first intercourse during, 153
Weiss, Jessica, 5
Wellesley College, resists feminized
curriculum, 53
White, Lynn, 195n.28
Wolfe, Theodore P., 198n.68
"womanpower": discourse of, and NEA
call for increased female faculty, 195n.25;
U.S. government promotional campaign,
21, 38
*The Woman Who Found Her Voice:
A Tale of Transforming* (O'Halloran
and Delattre), 181
*The Woman Who Lost Her Heart:
A Tale of Reawakening* (O'Halloran
and Delattre), 181
"woman wisdom," 150, 159, 161
women: alleged values and interests
devalued, 82, 83, 97, 166, 171 (*see also*
individualism: modeled on maleness);
changing expectations of, and family
crisis, 26–27; at colleges and universities
(*see* women students); in defense work,
36, 111; in medicine, 37; as moral arbiters,
107; parasitic, 13; retarding influence of,
92–93 (*see also* "momism"); Wadsworth-
Austin draft proposal, 37; in wartime
military, 111
Women in the Modern World (Komarovsky),
161
Women's College of the University of
North Carolina, challenge to moral
regulations at (1953), 126
women's liberation movement, 6
Women's Self-Government Association,
Bowling Green State University, 57
women students: considering postgraduate
careers, 86–87; and critical thinking, 41,
45, 60, 180; as culture brokers, 21, 56–57,
75; ethnic and religious diversification of,
51; falling proportion of total postwar
enrollment, 195n.22; friendships among,
94–97, 154; least popular, campus
marginalization of, 30–31; postwar trends
in enrollments and concentrations, 51–52;
works commonly read by, 203n.42

Women's War Council, Michigan State
University, 22, 36
Worcester Polytechnic Institute, 119
working class: male heroes in movies, 108;
prejudices against, 30; students from, and
youth culture, 29
World War II: college social environment,
36; effects of, on student culture, 19–20;
homosexual coming-out during, 109;
wartime appeals to women, 20–21, 22;
women students' sexuality during, 111–116

Wright, Frank Lloyd, 94
Wylie, Philip, 72, 93, 94, 138, 139, 203n.42

Young, White, and Miserable (Breines), 6
Young Women's Christian Association
(YWCA), 39, 53, 54, 76, 185n.7
youth culture: college (*see* student culture,
college); high school, 25, 28; less active
participants in, 29

Zionism, 35

About the Author

Babette Faehmel grew up in Germany. She first became interested in women's history while pursuing a degree in American Studies at Hamburg University. After moving to the United States, she earned a master's degree in history from the University of Cincinnati, Ohio, and a doctorate degree from the University of Massachusetts at Amherst. She held a Sexuality Research Dissertation Fellowship with the Social Science Research Council from September 2003 to August 2004, and a Leonard Richards Dissertation Writing Fellowship from the University of Massachusetts from September to December 2007. She was an associate at the Five College Women's Studies Research Center at Mount Holyoke College from September 2008 to May 2009. Dr. Faehmel has taught in Continuing Education and for the University without Walls at the University of Massachusetts, and as a visiting instructor at Smith College. She is currently an associate professor in the Humanities and Social Sciences Department at Schenectady County Community College in New York.

CPSIA information can be obtained at www.ICGtesting.com
Printed in the USA
242024LV00001B/4/P